Helping Students Learn to Write

Related Titles of Interest

Webbing with Literature: Creating Story Maps with Children's Books, Second Edition
Karen D'Angelo Bromley
ISBN: 0-205-16975-9; H6975-0

Developing Verbal Talent: Ideas and Strategies for Teachers of Elementary and Middle School Students
Joyce VanTassel-Baska, Dana T. Johnson, and Linda Neal Boyce
ISBN: 0-205-15945-1; H5945-4

Literature-Based Reading Activities, Second Edition
Hallie Kay Yopp and Ruth Helen Yopp
ISBN: 0-205-16387-4; H6387-8

An idea book for K–7 teachers

Helping Students Learn to Write

JOYCE C. BUMGARDNER

Allyn and Bacon
Boston   London   Toronto   Sydney   Tokyo   Singapore

Library of Congress Cataloging-in-Publication Data

Bumgardner, Joyce C.
    Helping students learn to write : an idea book for K-7 teachers /
by Joyce C. Bumgardner : illustrations by students Liesl VerSteeg
and Ryan Carney.
        p.   cm.
    ISBN 0-205-17571-6
    1. English language—Composition and exercises—Study and teaching
(Elementary)—Handbooks, manuals, etc.   I. Title.
LB1576.B888 1996
372.6'23--dc20   95-12816
                                                           CIP

Printed in the United States of America
10 9 8 7 6 5 4 3 2   99 98

This book is dedicated to those who read to me,
who gave me books, who nurtured my insatiable
love of words, of language;
To my parents, who first read to me;
To Teachers who encouraged my dreams of writing;
To students who share my joy in written language;
To Gaye, who proofread and helped to guide the beginning project;
To Karin, who edited and made everything as it should be;
And to my Cheerleaders—friends and family who patiently and
cheerfully encourage my efforts to help readers and
writers of all ages discover the beauty, the joy and the power to be
found in written language.

Thank you!

Teaching is meeting on a bridge,
wide enough for two or more
to walk abreast together.

If I don't think I've much to learn
from one whom I'm about to teach,
I will but maim and insult—
it's better not to try.

Respect involves one in response,
shared struggle and excitement
on a bridge and crossing over
side by side.

from **Kept Moments** *by Gerhard Frost*
with warmest thanks to Ivern Frost for allowing me
to use this wonderfully insightful piece

Contents

14   *Reproducible Handouts*   167

Preface: Notes from Author to Teacher

The term language refers to the means we use for communicating with others. Many programs have been created to assist children in reading. This book places its emphasis on written language. The two are related, for activity in one "feeds" the other. This book will assist you in helping children become competent users of language by beginning where the children are in their skills and moving on from there, by emphasizing ways in which reading and oral-language activities nurture writing. You will notice that throughout this book, the word Teacher is capitalized. That is to remind readers of the important role you as educators play in the lives of your students. It implies responsibility and privilege as well.

The acquisition of language skills seldom develops in predictable, orderly steps. It can grow slowly, or it may show itself in giant, exciting leaps. We also find many surprises in the teaching of written language, for the student considered to be bright and able is not necessarily a wonderful writer; and often the student for whom school is difficult may be the one who has beautiful, thoughtful, original things to say on paper.

For many reasons, most having to do with our own experiences in learning to write, some Teachers may consider the teaching of writing to be difficult, scary, unpleasant—or all of these. However, it can be exciting, surprising, fun, and wonderful! It is my hope that this book will help to make your teaching of written language an enjoyable experience for you and for your students. It is not a curriculum presentation; it is an idea book, a companion to your teaching of written language. I have written down here what I would say to you in person if I could talk with you.

Please read the entire book. You will find ideas at all levels—beginning writers, middle grades, and advanced writers—easily adaptable to your own grade level.

Acknowledgment
The illustrations that appear throughout were drawn by my former students Liesl VerSteeg and Ryan Carney.

Helping Students Learn to Write

1 *From Product to Process and Power*

When most of us were in grade school and high school, we knew nothing about a *process* for writing. Our Teachers usually told us when to write and what to write about and we began, knowing that we would get red marks all over our papers if we didn't please our Teacher and that if he or she liked what we wrote, we would get a good grade—the single most important goal to keep in mind as we wrote. We were writing according to what we now call the Product Method.

The Teacher was, in most cases, our only audience; rarely did we hear or see what our classmates were writing. We wrote in solitude, sitting at our desks like small islands placed neatly on a checkered linoleum sea. I wondered, but never knew, what Peggy was writing; whether Garth was writing about racing cars, his special interest; if Sally was putting on paper her dream of being a champion swimmer. Writing was a group activity only in that we all started and stopped at the same time. The scary fact was that none of us knew how a "good" piece of writing came to be; the way to write a high-quality piece seemed to be a secret known only by a few. The act of writing a "winner" seemed to be based mostly on luck. Sole responsibility for choosing the winners rested with the Teacher, and it seemed that the same people were successful each time.

When most of us were students in early grades, we actually did little writing. Most "writing" consisted of filling in blanks in workbooks, and when we discussed the subject of "writing," it meant printing or writing in cursive. It wasn't until about third or fourth grade that most of us had substantive practice in writing. Then, as you may recall, that practice usually began with a first-day-of-school piece called "What I Did During My Summer Vacation."

Except for assignments printed neatly on the chalkboards, we never saw a Teacher write, never saw a Teacher model the process of writing—finding an idea to write about, taking it from first draft through revisions to final form, showing us how to develop a good piece. We heard nothing of a process, a step-by-step recipe for producing a piece of quality.

Whenever I present workshops for educators I ask how many, as students, had a Teacher who modeled, who wrote with the class. Even in a group as large as 200 or 300, no more than two or three will say they had a role model. Interestingly, those role models were almost always high school or college instructors. Clearly, when it came to writing, our Teachers *told* us; they did not *show* us.

In recent years, the teaching of written language has shifted from the *product* method, where only the final product is considered, to the *process* method: We show children how to achieve a high-quality final product that pleases themselves and others. We teach and model steps they can take to write papers that are their best. And most Teachers write with their students, becoming important role models for these young writers.

Teachers, take out your pens and pencils!
Recently I was in a second-grade classroom where we were preparing to write about our specialties, things we do well. As I began to explain details of how we would write about this topic, the Teacher went to an empty desk and joined her students.

When I handed out the special writing papers we would use, she accepted one and immediately began to do what her students were doing in following my directions. She participated in the brainstorming of ideas, in the writing of first drafts, in the discussion that followed as we revised, in the give-and-take of the writing-workshop atmosphere we created, and in the class conferencing we did together in the process of coming to final copies ready for publishing. She was doing an important part of a Teacher's work—modeling the *process* for her students.

Things change in the classrooms where Teachers and students write together; a closeness, a unity develops in a special way when we share our writing.

Some time ago, I was working with a sixth-grade class. We were writing about special memories. The Teacher wrote too, and students frequently turned to watch him as he wrote, hesitated, thought, then wrote some more. During our sharing time, I asked him if he would read what he had written. He hesitated a moment, then began. There was total silence in the room as students quickly sensed how special this piece was, for he had written of the day when he was small, when his mother had come into his room to tell him and his brother that their father would not be coming home again; he had been killed that morning in a car accident. As their Teacher read, students understood that he was giving them something: a part of himself that they had not known before, a human part. They understood he had suffered hurt and loss and sadness, just as they did. There was a feeling of oneness in that classroom.

In a third-grade classroom, students, Teachers, and visiting administrators wrote in first person about being subjects they had drawn from a basket. They giggled when a male administrator drew the word *worm*. As students wrote, they watched him from the corners of their eyes; they could hardly wait to hear what he was writing. When sharing time started, they eagerly insisted, "Let's hear his!" He graciously shared his descriptive piece, telling how it felt to be a worm—what he heard, smelled, saw, and felt as he traveled underground, knowing that at any moment a bird's sharp beak might reach him or a shiny shovel might scoop him out for fish bait. When he finished reading, they responded with a loud burst of clapping. He was participating in the same activity they were doing; they were sharing this experience of writing and the students loved it.

Model; write with your students. As they write at their desks, let them see you writing on the board or at your own desk. Let them watch you gather ideas, then choose one to use (*getting ready to write*). Let them watch you put together a good beginning sentence, then develop it into a paragraph (*first draft, rough draft, sloppy copy*). Show them how to cross out, change, and maybe change again what you have written; make it the best it can be (*revising, editing*). Let them see you finish your piece, hear you read it aloud to see if it is the best you can do (*ready for publishing*). Show them that Teachers are writers too, that you understand the hard work that goes into a piece of writing, that you know the satisfaction of publishing a piece that reflects the hard work you have done.

Many students are lazy; they want things to be easy. A friend told me about her son who hopes this fall to get the sixth-grade Teacher who gives no homework. "This is a nice Teacher, a good person," says my friend, "but he doesn't teach students how to work. Each year, students leave his room unprepared for the next year, unprepared for the hard work real life will require." Many of us mourn students' lack of desire to excel, to achieve important things. Who will help to motivate students, show them how to do their best? Teach them the value of excellence? It can be learned by students who see it modeled by their Teachers.

Sometimes you may wish to do your writing in advance so you will be aware of difficulties students may encounter in their own writing. Other times, you may begin but not complete a piece of writing as you take time to help students with their own writing efforts. Just as a dance Teacher demonstrates the two-step; just as a coach demonstrates kicking a ball; just as a music Teacher demonstrates proper singing techniques, so children need to *see* how we do this incredibly complicated business of writing. Clean off your chalkboards and write on them. Star charts and posters, professionally printed sets of directions, yellowing lists of "Classroom Rules"—these are not nearly so useful for students' learning as is written communication that is alive, that changes, that invites students to watch and learn all day long.

It is often in written language that we recognize—and our students can discover—those unique and personal things inside of them that make them who they are. *If you want to get to know your students, let them write.* Watch for what they say, as well as for the way in which they say it.

Listen:

Each second we live is a new and unique moment of the universe, a moment that never was before and never will be again. And what do we teach our children in school? We teach them that two and two make four and that Paris is the capital of France. When will we also teach them what they *are*? We should say to each of them: Do you know what you are? You are a marvel. You are unique. In all of the world there is no other child exactly like you. In the millions of years that have passed, there has never been a child like you. And look at your body—what a wonder it is! Your legs, your arms, your cunning fingers, the way you move! You may become a Shakespeare, a Michelangelo, a Beethoven. You have the capacity for anything. Yes, you are a marvel. And when you grow up, can you then harm another who is, like you, a marvel? You must cherish one another. You must work—we all must work—to make this world worthy of its children.

Those marvelous words were written by world-famous cellist Pablo Casals. The Teacher who looks at his or her students as Pablo Casals looked at children will find teaching to be exciting, satisfying, rewarding—and students will respect, love, and remember this Teacher.

Being a writer is exciting. It means knowing we have a special way of speaking. It means we have an important kind of power—for what a sense of power, of voice, of satisfaction it gives us to be able to write letters, words on paper that make people smile, laugh, cry—words that say exactly what we want them to say—pieces that will be different from everyone else's, because, while we are alike in many ways, we also are unique.

The sense of power that comes with competency in written language is a lifelong strength, because decisions that affect us most often have to do with the written word. When we need, for example, to express our wishes and feelings, our outrage, our sadness, our pleasure to those in positions who make decisions that affect us, our families, our cities, our country, our world, we must be able to do so in written language. We use this power to write letters, position statements, petitions, newspaper responses, and more.

Writing can be exciting, fun, satisfying. It also can be scary, because, as a friend of mine says, "Once you have written it down on paper, it can never be hidden in your mind again."

That is why one of the most important ingredients in the process of acquiring skills in written language is a classroom atmosphere where students feel safe knowing that what they write will be accepted, encouraged, never put down—an atmosphere where children feel free to experiment, to make mistakes as they learn. We must give them permission to write, to make mistakes, and to enjoy writing—then they can learn.

I had been invited to teach several first-grade classes. While the Teachers and I were having early morning coffee in the lounge before the school day began, one of the Teachers approached me, an intense look on her face.

"I have to warn you about my class," she said. I waited, puzzled. "These kids can't do anything. They can't read, they can't write, they can't follow directions. They don't listen, and they can't even sit still!" She went on to say that they would sit on the floor as I wrote with them, because they "wiggled" in their seats. She could not tell by the look on my face, but what I was feeling inside could only be described as a challenge rising. She turned to the other first-grade Teachers. "Isn't that right?" she asked. Heads nodded in agreement. She had convinced them too.

I could hardly wait to get into her classroom. There I found a class of about 25 students sitting motionless on the floor, faces grim as they waited for their guest's arrival.

"Good morning!" I said. "I can tell by looking at you that you are one of the most fantastic classes in this school!" They began to smile. We talked a bit about good stories, and students eagerly contributed titles and authors of their favorites to discuss.

"I'll bet you're good writers too!" I whispered. They assured me that they certainly were. "Well, then, let's talk about what makes a good story, and maybe we can write some!" I said.

Together we brainstormed, then wrote first drafts (*sloppy copies*—they loved that term) and made revisions as we listened to and cheered their writing efforts. The "wiggles" that morning came from enthusiasm and incredibly delightful imaginations at work, and I left the room with many new friends that day. I hoped the Teacher could see how wonderful and bright her students truly were.

Some time ago I was invited to do some writing with another class of first-graders. I knew they had done little writing before, as their Teacher was new to first grade and seemed not convinced of their ability to write by themselves. I indicated to the Teacher that after I had introduced my big stuffed green frog, Romietta, and talked with the students about reading and writing, I would read them a frog story by Arnold Lobel. Then students would all write their own frog stories. "Oh, but they haven't had vowels yet," she said in a concerned voice.

"Don't worry," I assured her. "It will be all right." We talked about reading and writing. Romietta "watched" as we shared Lobel's *Frog and Toad* story. "Sometimes," I told them, "we get ideas for stories of our own as we read those written by other authors." We talked about some favorite story beginnings—*Once upon a time, A long time ago, One dark night*—and more. We agreed that something needed to happen in a good story, somthing exciting or funny or scary or surprising. I told the students not to worry about spelling, but to use *invented* or *temporary spelling* where they were uncertain about how to spell. The students were excited, pencils in their hands. "I think we're ready," I said. "Go ahead and start your stories." As the other students began writing, a girl in the front row looked up, on her face an expression of complete panic. "I can't read," she whispered, "and I can't write either!""Sure you can," I answered, getting down on my knees beside her desk. "Do you have a story idea?"

"Yes," she replied.

"Tell me about it," I said. I began writing the words for her. She watched, fascinated. After a few minutes, I handed her the pencil and told her to go on—her story was good. She looked at me, took the pencil, and hesitatingly began to print. I watched. She printed a few more letters and looked up at me as I moved away to circulate around the room. During the next ten minutes, I stopped by other students' desks, offering help and encouragement. Out of the corner of my eye, I saw her writing, slowly at first as she followed my movements around the room, then more quickly as she gathered confidence. Soon she was writing, totally involved in the excitement of her own story.

A short while later, she was one of the first to volunteer to share her story. Then, as I thanked the students for letting me write with them, she hurried out of her desk and followed me to the door. She looked up at me, her eyes shining, a big smile on her face, and exulted, "And do you know what? When I get home, I'm going to write some more!" She had been given permission to write.

Observing thousands of student writers has shown me clearly that from the beginning, someone must give them *permission* to write. When writing is presented as something wonderful to do, as something they *can do*, they are eager to try. And they will get better at it.

Let students share their writing

Students need access to other students, to share what they write, to hear others say, "That's good!" or, "I wish I'd written that!" They "feed" one another good things about what they have written; they come to value what other students write, and see examples of what they themselves might like to write. They offer suggestions to one another appropriate to their own writing abilities: In a small-group writing situation, a boy shared a piece he had written about a soccer game his team had won. The student, normally a good writer, observed correctly that his piece was "dull, boring." I asked the students in the group if anyone could help him out; one girl, her eyes bright with excitement, said, "Write it in first-person! Then it will be right!" He immediately realized she was correct, and headed back to his desk to change his piece to first-person. The Teacher didn't do this for him— a fellow student did.

Reading builds writing skills

Writing begins with speaking and listening. Teachers who read to students, talk with them, and listen to them will find that they too enjoy these activities.

When you read to your students, follow with discussion, asking questions that will involve thinking as students answer. Encourage them to talk about what they "saw" and heard as they listened. Ask specific questions: "What color was the horse?" It may be that each student sees and hears something different from the others. That is just fine—that is imagination at work!

Tell your students that writers are like artists who make pictures with paints, brushes, and canvas. But writers use words to make pictures; good writers use *sense* words that tell how something looked, felt, smelled, tasted, sounded. Tell them, "The better you paint your stories with words, the better your readers will be able to see them." Read them descriptive passages from library books without pictures and tell them to make the pictures in their heads, in their "mind's eyes," using descriptions written by the authors.

Even young children can understand the concept of the "mind's eye." Talk about our eyes through which we see things around us; then tell them you are going to "paint a picture" for their third eye, their mind's eye. Tell them to close their eyes, to listen, and to raise their hands when they can "see" what you are describing. Then begin to describe a cat or dog: Tell its color, size, shape, how its fur feels when you rub it, how it sounds when it makes noises, how it smells, how it moves about. As you talk, students will begin raising their hands. (Sometimes an especially imaginative student, listening to my description, will call out excitedly, "I see it! I see it!" before I get far into my description.) Now tell your students to open their eyes. Discuss what they "saw." Tell them that the place in which they "saw" the cat or dog is what we call our "mind's eye," and that this is an important, invisible part of every writer and reader. You might then ask a student to "paint a picture" of his or her own cat or dog as you and the others listen and "picture" it in your minds' eyes.

Reader-writers

Tell your students that to write well, they must read, for it is in reading that they will learn to recognize words, to spell, and to use their imaginations. Good writers are almost invariably readers. Talk with your students about the relationship between reading and writing. Ask them why you can guarantee that if they read and listen when others read to them they will improve both reading and writing skills. Students will quickly recognize the direction in which you are going with your questions and will be able to give you reasons why this is true. They will answer that they learn how to spell through seeing the same words over and over again, that they learn new words through seeing them in books, and that they use those words in their own writing. They will say they get writing ideas when they read. In many other ways, reading helps develop competency in written language: We often model our own writing on books written by other authors.

Ask them for the titles of some good books. After they name several, ask what it is that makes the books "good." They will tell you, as your discussion continues, that in a good book, they can see what is happening, hear it, feel like they are being drawn into the book: this happens when a writer is good at describing, at painting pictures we can see in our minds. Tell your young reader-writers to think about their first books: picture books. In them, we "read" the pictures, and everything we know about what is happening is in the pictures. As children grow, they move into books with pictures accompanied by one or several words. Now the words help tell the story. What happens when they get into kindergarten? First and second grade? The pictures are made a bit smaller, usually, to make room for more words. What happens in third or fourth grade? Students will triumphantly tell you, "We read chapter books!" "Now," you ask them, "do you still know what is happening? Can you still "see" the characters? The places? The happenings?" *Yes,* your students will say. "But there are almost no pictures in those books. How do you know what's happening? How can you 'see' it?" *Because the words tell us; they make the pictures.* Bingo!

Now we're talking about how writers make pictures with descriptive words! When we read books where professional authors do this, we learn to do it ourselves. We model our writing after that of good writers.

One young student, having immersed himself in Louis L'Amour's books for several years, was accused by a junior high school Teacher of "copying from a

book" a wonderful Western story he himself had written for a homework assignment. His punishment for this terrible, unproven crime? To stay after school and write another story in the Teacher's presence. The student did as he was told, writing for nearly an hour in a classroom occupied only by himself and the Teacher, then turning in another lively Western where the hero's boots "came stomping through the swinging doors," where his gun "jumped from his pocket" almost by itself. Appropriately, the Teacher's apology was made before the student left the room. Fortunately, this student's self-concept was strong enough to withstand the Teacher's accusation. A less confident student might have crumpled in the same situation. This young writer had modeled his own writing so completely after that of his favorite author that even the Teacher was convinced!

Developing an ear for language
Tell your students that in reading and in listening, they develop something special—an "ear for language"—that will help them know if their own writing sounds "right." That is why it is important they proofread aloud, listening to the sound of their own writing, to see if it pleases them and to be sure it will be understood by others.

Learning to write isn't easy
Learning to write is hard work. It is a lifetime skill that takes years to acquire. And just as your Teachers influenced your feelings about written language, you will influence your students' feelings about writing. These are attitudes they may take with them through their entire lives.

What really works
The best advice I can give you about teaching written language is to write with your students. Let them see you struggle with finding the right words, with getting the meanings clear; let them see your satisfaction in working to create something that pleases you. You are their model; if they see you writing, they will know it is not just something to be done in school. They will know they do not write to please a Teacher, but to please themselves first, just as you do. They are their own "first audience." Teachers who do this develop their own writing skills. Their pleasure in writing becomes contagious. Not only will their students feel it, but other Teachers too may see what is happening in your class and be motivated to write for themselves and with their students.

Share your own feelings about writing
Recently, I was in a third-grade classroom where students and Teacher wrote for some time, then stopped to share. After many students had read their pieces, I

asked the Teacher if she too would read. She hesitated, frowned, looked down at her paper. Then, looking at her class, she said, "I have to tell you students something. This is hard for me; when I was in school, writing was never fun. It was just plain hard work, and I didn't like it. Also, we never shared what we had written with our class, and I'm not used to doing that. We didn't even do much writing, and I've never been comfortable with it. I do like the things you have shared, though, and so I will share mine too. But I want you to know I'm a beginner and what I wrote will sound a lot like yours." The students listened intently, eyes wide, to this forthright confession. They understood how serious this was for their Teacher. Then she began to read. They listened. And when she finished, they not only clapped—they cheered! Something special had happened—and they responded as only children can.

Students who do not like to write most likely have had unpleasant, discouraging experiences with written language; so have many Teachers. If our own Teachers insisted on perfect spelling from us as beginning writers; if they demanded neat, perfect papers the first time around that met only the Teacher's requirements, and if they required us to write about subjects that did not interest us; if the classroom atmosphere was hard, strict, stifling of creative ideas and pleasure in written language, and if we were required to write according to rules learned by rote without understanding, what else could possibly be expected as a result?

Let them write
Students generally do not learn to write well by learning rules and then writing to meet those rules. They learn to write by writing often and by acquiring the rules as they can understand and use them. One way to help our students is to tell them that often, rather than relying on rules, they can rely on their "ear for language," which will tell them if what they have written sounds "right." It is thus important that they hear rich language used correctly.

It also is important that students understand the writing assignments; Teachers should encourage their students to ask questions if they do not understand and to know that it is not their fault when something is confusing. It is a Teacher's responsibility to explain clearly and patiently. Sometimes, even though we think we have given a clear explanation, we find we must approach an assignment from a different angle and explain it again in different words.

I visited a fifth-grade classroom one January and was horrified by the realization, as the Teacher introduced me, that the class had not done any writing the entire semester! "Students, this is the lady we've been waiting for—she will introduce you to your first writing for this school year," their teacher announced proudly. Writing should begin in preschool and should be done daily throughout every grade and year of school. It should not be saved for something special or presented as a treat to be earned!

2 *What Is Process Writing?*

Put simply, process writing is like a recipe writers follow to produce a high-quality piece of writing.

Prewriting
Drafting
Revising
Proofreading, editing
Publishing

It's 1949 and I'm in my sixth-grade class. "Class, it's writing time. Today we will write about what you want to be when you grow up. Take out your pencils and start...and no talking." We begin in silence, write in silence, occasionally raise a hand for help with spelling a word. At the end of writing time we hand in our papers to the Teacher who will read them, mark them in red, and then give them back to us. We throw away the ones covered with red marks, save only the best ones, and most likely share even those with no one except, perhaps, a proud parent who may think to put them away "for later."

What a contrast with the way we teach writing today! Now we set the stage for writing, take time to get ready to write. We may do it by talking, by listening to others as they contribute information or ideas to a group discussion. The Teacher may write these ideas on the board; students may jot them down in a writing notebook.

We can set the stage by sharing a common experience—reading and discussing a book together, taking a field trip, turning off the lights and looking out classroom windows at a lovely fall rain. We may discuss a classroom problem that becomes a writing assignment. Perhaps we watch a film, discuss it, then write. We may listen to music and write as it plays. Paul Winter's wonderful recordings, for example—*Callings, Wolf Eyes,* and others—become an invitation to write about whales, dolphins, wolves, eagles. In one school four sixth-grade Teachers told me they had been having a wonderful time playing the music of Mozart as their students wrote.

Children enjoy listening to music while they write and often will ask that the music continue to play as they create. Lively music may encourage the writing of peppy, happy pieces; calm, gentle music may nurture more contemplative writing. Music played on "Hearts of Space" on National Public Radio invites students into a world of unusual, intriguing, sometimes strange, hauntingly beautiful music that makes them feel, if they close their eyes, that they really are in outer space, perhaps on a peaceful planet with rainbow-colored waterfalls and beautiful ponds and mountains. This kind of music encourages its own special writing. (Encourage students to close their eyes and listen, think, *be* before they begin to write.)

This—"getting ready to write," "setting the stage"—is the *prewriting* part of writing that was missing when I was a student. Now we know it is important to help students and ourselves "get into the mood" to write. It should be an enjoyable time, a comfortable time as students prepare to write. Watch for varied ways of helping students prepare to write, and *when they are ready, let them begin.* Sometimes the eagerness to write is so strong that one can actually *feel* it in the room. Then it is time to stop getting ready and let them *do* it.

When students are creating first drafts, they will find it helpful to write on every other line. Paper with alternating colored lines (blue and white, green and white) comes both in looseleaf and in notebook form, making it easy for students to write first drafts on lines of one color, then to make revisions on lines of alternating color. This can eliminate students' reluctance to squeeze changes into already-filled lines of writing.

Revising is the act of reading carefully what has been written and making changes to improve a piece of writing. As students read and change their first drafts, they are *revising*. Drafting and revising are writing steps that go together; they are not separate. A first draft that is read and changed—becomes a revised first draft. Copied over with corrections made, it is called a *second draft*.

Beginning writers usually create only one draft. However, Teachers should seize opportunities to teach the language of writing, the terms used by writers. Even in writing a group story on a chalkboard with kindergartners, the term *revising* can be introduced. Explain that writers often make changes in pieces they write. Ask, for example, if the story is just the way they want it or if any changes should be made. Someone may express a wish to change the color of a character's sweater from red to blue. Make that change on the board and casually mention that when we do this it is called *revising*. Students will remember and use this term, this skill.

First- and second-grade writers may make few changes in their writing, but when a third- or fourth-grade student shows me a paper with no cross-outs or changes on it, I always ask, "Have you read this aloud to yourself?" Usually, the student will say "*Yes*." It may be that the student *thinks* he or she has done this, but we must insist that they actually do it. "Will you read it to me, please?" I ask. Almost always, as the student begins to read aloud, out comes the pencil to make changes. We must teach students that they need to read their writing aloud. This is the first step in conferencing—being an audience. Tell them they are their own first audience. They write their pieces, and they get to read them before anyone else. (Conferencing, though not a "step" in process writing, is an integral and important part of writing for students today. Conferencing is addressed in the next chapter.)

As writers grow in experience, often they will write a first draft, then a second, and on occasion more. They will learn that each of these revisions is part of a published piece of high quality, that there is real value in following the steps of the process. We do not follow this entire process for everything students write; if we did, few students would come to love writing, because it is hard work. But we can complete a writing the *process way* for perhaps one out of every four or five pieces assigned.

Proofreading/editing follows revising. (Note: *Proofreading* is the term generally used for reading/correcting one's own work; *editing* usually refers to that action performed by someone other than the writer.) Here we deal with *mechanics*— punctuation, spelling, capitalization, etc. Teachers can easily demonstrate proofreading as they put written work on the chalkboard. From the beginning of the school year, emphasize it. Go back over your own writing as students watch, and correct errors; look for improvements you can make. Make deliberate mistakes on occasion; encourage your students to watch for them, to suggest ideas that might help you say something in a better way. They will be more than happy to help! Proofreading is the step where even children who have great difficulty with spelling can be assured that, working with other students and/or with the Teacher, corrections will be made so their final product looks good. We do not ever want a student to be embarrassed by a published piece filled with errors.

With corrections made, the piece is ready for *publishing*. Students should learn that publishing can take many forms. Several years ago I shared with some students a compilation of family memories I had gathered from aunts, uncles, and cousins and put into a spiral bound book for each relative who attended our family reunion. One student looked at the book, and, in great delight said, "This is great! You ought to get it published!"

I answered that I had done just that: This book was indeed *published*. I had written it for my family, then made copies for everyone. They all read and enjoyed it: the book was *published*. I explained that he could publish his own books too and share them with his friends and family. With a wide smile, he said, "I can do that!"

Together, you and your class can create a long list of publishing options. Hang it on the wall and allow students to choose the publishing form they feel is appropriate for the things they write during the year. Your list may include: final copy in student's best handwriting; final copy done on computer; final copies pasted on construction paper and displayed on a classroom wall or in school halls where others can see them; writing a story (most likely) turned into a play; publishing in the form of a book; actually sending a completed letter to someone; having an evening of "readings" done by students; a celebration of students' writings, attended by parents and friends (this celebratory gathering should include punch and cookies and balloons!); sharing their reading with a special friend at school (a school secretary, a custodian, a well-loved Teacher, the principal, etc.); reading stories to a class of younger students, one-on-one; putting final copy on audiotape or videotape (ideally, each student should have his or her own audiotape on which to record final published stories, verse, etc. during the year and take it home at the end of the school year); and more!

The process works with all kinds of writing—stories, essays, reports, personal pieces: It is the new tool for success in writing for students of all ability levels. If producing a good piece of writing seemed mostly a mystery to us as students, now we can assure our own students that following the steps of the process will help them produce high-quality writing whether they are 5 or 95. Where the same top students usually got the good grades in our school days, now every student, working on his or her own writing ideas, can be successful. This knowledge gives them a sense of power, of competency that enhances self-esteem, and it motivates them to continue to learn and to succeed.

Walking down a school hallway early in the morning, a fourth-grade boy came rushing up to me. "Mrs. B! Guess what! I'm writing a book—what do you think about that?" I shared the delight of this special education student who, through learning and using the steps of the writing process, had acquired confidence in his ability to write whatever he wants. I was excited too: He had just given me my "million-dollar paycheck" for the day!

3 Conferencing: How We Do It

The purpose of a writing conference

The purpose of conferencing is to meet with students for consultation or discussion, for asking questions, for sharing advice or information with students so that each will have the best final piece of writing possible. Conferencing allows Teachers to see where students need help. It often leads us into minilessons of perhaps five or 10 minutes where we address a specific problem being experienced by students who come to conference with us. For example, if students are having difficulty knowing where to end a sentence and using run-ons (connecting short sentences with and...and...and), we might demonstrate that a sentence of four or five lines is probably too long. Demonstrate on the board. Ask, "Can we end this sentence here and start a new one?"

If students are having difficulty using dialogue, the Teacher can present a minilesson demonstrating use of effective dialogue. (See "All Dialogue Piece" in the reproducible section of this book.) Use the chalkboard or overhead as everyone works together to revise or correct one piece, or hand out a quick teaching sheet for students actually to make those corrections on paper so they will know how to do it on their own papers.

When we conference, our textbooks become important resources as we use them to locate and learn information related to specific writing practices. This makes more sense than memorizing lists of rules unrelated to things concrete; as we pause to consider a writing question, then find answers and examples of how the rules of writing are used, we make immediate use of them, thus reinforcing comprehension of that information.

In conferencing, we talk about writing ideas, story characters, anticipated outcomes—the work "in progress," just as grown authors consider these things in their writing. We can follow up in conferences to see if students have, in fact, learned and put into practice what we have discussed.

As students, most of us were expected to write a perfect first copy. The two most important things about those papers, as I remember them, were that they had to be *neat* and the spelling had to be perfect. There was no "rough draft" or "sloppy copy," no crossing out and revising. While we wrote, we tried to keep our papers covered so the Teacher would not see any messy work as we composed. The sound of white rubber erasers moving back and forth across papers was a constant. Most of the help we received was in the form of red notes on completed papers—and few of us followed those comments and rewrote, with corrections, our papers. It was not expected that we do so.

In process writing, we help students as they write. We do not write in isolation—we work together: we talk, ask questions, encourage, and make suggestions as we work in pairs, in groups, and one-on-one to provide needed help throughout the progress of a piece of writing. Conferencing allows us to teach within the context of what is needed for any writing piece and is an important component in writing with our students. Questions about conferencing might be: How do we conference? Who does it? When do we do it? And where does conferencing fit into the steps of the process of writing?

We cannot conference about every piece of writing students produce. We do, however, need to teach and expect our students to know and follow the steps—the process for writing. This includes conferencing, particularly when they produce stories, reports, and other pieces we plan to publish for a special purpose. Conferencing is a time to teach the language of writing, and we can assure students that once they have learned it, the process remains the same, no matter their age or grade. Done step by step, it is the way to achieve a good piece of writing. Now all students can learn how to develop a good piece; it is not a secret known only by a chosen few. This gives students a sense of power, of confidence, knowing that moving step by step through the process, assisted by peer writers and their Teacher, they will have a piece of high-quality writing when they have finished.

I am a writer and I am a writing Teacher; I have taught writing exclusively for many years. In that time, I have learned many things about writing with students. Among the most important is that students should take as much responsibility as possible for their written pieces. That is how they learn, how we all can learn—by doing. At the same time, we must show them how to make their writing better; they are students, after all. But how do we do that?

Often, it is by conferencing. But that does not always need to be done by the Teacher. It can be done with other students, in large-group conferences and in small-group conferences. We can call these *writers' workshops.* Daily, I see the value of students helping one another. And in a time when demands on Teachers are heavy, we do well to allow our students to use their abilities to help themselves and one another.

One day I was writing with a group of sixth-graders. Elizabeth had written an excellent story about an old woman. All through her story she used the words, "The old woman..."

As she shared her story with a conferencing group of classmates, one of her friends said, "Elizabeth, your old lady needs a name. I want to know who she is."

"All right," Elizabeth answered, "but it needs to be an old-fashioned name." Off she went to the library where she checked out a book of names, then spent time hunting for just the right "old-fashioned name" for her character. Good advice— and from a peer.

In another conferencing group, Danielle read her rather complicated story. A classmate commented, "I really like your story, but I have a suggestion: You're introducing so many characters that it's hard to stay on track with your story. How about eliminating two or three of the characters?" Danielle could see that her friend was right. The revised version of her story, minus three minor characters, was easier to follow.

A writers' workshop atmosphere provides the setting for students to help one another, to "talk writing," asking questions and making suggestions as only writers can, to learn from one another and to invest in one another's growth as writers. How much better than to sit alone and write in isolation as we did, never to hear our peers' ideas, convictions, stories, and dreams.

Every child has important things to say. Some speak with strong, confident voices. Some speak softly. Some have little confidence in their ability to speak. Many individuals, old and young, speak best in writing.

We have learned that talking about writing and sharing ideas and experiences is a helpful, practical way for students to become competent writers. We need the ideas of other minds to jumpstart our own. We need to read, to talk, to question, to give and receive suggestions, to listen, to watch and to learn. Then new ideas come. That is why a writers' workshop setting in a classroom is important—it gives writers access to us, their Teachers, and to one another. In schools everywhere, writing has become a cooperative, social activity.

In first grade, especially early in the school year, we begin teaching students to write by composing a group story together; all the students share and contribute ideas as the Teacher acts as secretary, writing the story on the chalkboard. In one class where we had done this, writing a story about a giant together, students went on to write their own individual stories. After three or four students had shared their delightful stories, bright-eyed Andy exulted, "These books are even *better* than the giant story we wrote, because they are all *different!*" Because we were in a writers' workshop setting, sharing and listening to one another, he could see and hear that all the students in his class had great ideas and could create original, imaginative stories of their own. Even young beginning writers have good ideas, and sharing them builds enthusiasm and imagination for even more writing.

I suggest to Teachers from about the second half of third grade or the first part of fourth grade on up that they do not work on students' first (*rough*) drafts but allow students to take responsibility for those, letting Teachers deal mainly with papers that have been revised—usually, *second drafts*. Built into the process of writing is the "rough draft," which allows students simply to get the first draft, their fresh ideas, on paper. They normally revise and change that rough first draft before it is ready for sharing with anyone. The changes may come through whole-group or minigroup conferencing, as students read to one another, ask questions, and revise. *Revising* is part of the process.

Students need to learn to do this for themselves if they can. Although it is easier for students to dash off a first draft, then give it to a Teacher for "fixing," it is not as useful for students' learning. Explain this to your students. They learn by doing. They learn by teaching one another. No doubt we all have been pleased and surprised at times to discover that in teaching information to someone else, we have more firmly learned it ourselves. As students help one another, they learn too.

So, how do we help students deal with their first drafts?

We teach students that they are their own first audience. We encourage them to read aloud to themselves what they have written, to listen to it, and to see if they have truly said in writing what they intended to say.

Have you ever watched the members of a chorus or a choir cover their ears as they sing? (We have seen even the great opera singer, Pavarotti, do this on television.) They are listening to the sound of their own voices to see if they are in tune with the others.

Students can do this too as they read aloud to themselves what they have written. I call this the "ear trick." Often, after students have been writing for awhile, I ask them all to stop, cover their ears with their hands, and when I say "One, two, three, GO," they are to read *aloud*, softly, what they have written so far. "Listen," I tell them. "Pretend someone else is reading to you." Do this with your students. Be sure all are reading aloud, softly. This is an easy way of discovering how one's piece is coming along. Often you will see pencils begin to move as students see where they must make changes or additions. When they read silently, they often miss these places because they read what they *think* they wrote, rather than what they actually did write. They are more likely to notice places where changes are needed when they read *aloud*. Instruct students to continue their writing when they come to the end of what they have written so far. Ask how many discovered that they needed to add or change something. Take a few minutes to discuss what those changes were. Encourage them to stop frequently and read aloud as they continue to write.

Two fine young writers were discussing with me their success when reading aloud to hear where changes were needed. "We read books all the time," said one, "so we know just how something should sound, even if we don't remember the writing rules." The other agreed. One of the fundamentals young writers should learn is that they usually can *hear* when something is written correctly. Reading their writing aloud is important, too, in that it helps students to punctuate correctly. You can tell young writers, "Where you read a comma aloud, *write* one. Where you read a question mark aloud, *write* one." Or, if they are reading to you as you follow along on their papers, you might comment, "I heard a period there but I don't see one," and so on. In this way, students learn that good writing is a matter of common sense.

How do I introduce conferencing?
Begin by asking students to write about something they remember.

> *I Remember*
> running in a race
> visiting the farm
> when my ice cream cone melted
> my first airplane trip
> etc.

Have them brainstorm, create a list of perhaps five ideas, then choose one that might be "fun to write about" in more detail. Now they will write several paragraphs about that memory. They should tell when, how, and where it happened; who was there; and what they heard, saw, smelled, felt, and so on.

It probably won't be long before a student indicates that she is finished. Even if there is only a limited number of sentences on the paper, that's just fine: she will be the perfect person to start the writers' workshop session.

Ask her to read aloud to herself what she has written, to be sure it says exactly what she intended to say. She may make some changes as she reads and listens. By now, other students may indicate that they too are finished.

Ask everyone to stop writing. Tell them they are going to have a *writers' workshop*. Explain that this is a way for everyone in the class to get help from everyone else, a way for each student to have a super piece of writing.

The listeners (the writer's *audience*—use that term) are to turn over their papers and to pay full attention to the student who is reading. Tell them that there are just two jobs in a writers' workshop. One is the job of the student who is going to read to them. Her job is to read clearly what she has just written. If students cannot hear her, they are to raise their hands immediately; that tells her to read louder.

The second job is that of the *audience*, and it is a big, important job: They are to help her create the best piece of writing possible. They will do this by listening carefully to see if more information should be added, if there is more they would like to know in addition to what has been written.

Note: This is a perfect opportunity to teach students a bit about speaking in front of an audience—this is language too. Instruct them to walk to the place where they will stand and to hold their papers in front of them at a level where they can see over the tops of the papers in case members of the audience raise their hands. Tell them to look carefully around the room to see if all members of the audience are listening. If not, suggest to the reader that she simply look at the inattentive individual and wait until he or she is listening too.

When the reader sees that she has the attention of everyone in the room, she can begin to read. Watch to see that all students are listening. Compliment the reader at the end of her reading, then ask if there is more anyone would like to know. Encourage them to ask helpful questions: "How did he get from here to there?" "How did you feel when that happened?" The reader will answer the questions. (Sometimes, other students may want to answer questions being asked of the reader. Gently insist that the reader will answer her own questions, since the writing belongs to her.) Help the conferencing time to move along smoothly in a congenial, nonthreatening way.

While the reader is talking, it may be helpful for the Teacher to jot down questions asked by the listeners; the reader may have difficulty remembering them. When four or five questions have been asked and answered, thank the audience for their help, hand the reader the sheet on which you recorded the questions and instruct him to begin adding the requested information to his piece immediately wherever it seems to fit best. No one else will be writing, but he should revise right away while all the questions and answers are in his head.

Go on to the next reader and repeat the sharing/listening activity.

Each student should have a turn as you and your students begin learning to conference in this large-group situation You may run out of time and need to continue the next day. Generally, students enjoy this time and will look forward to more of this activity.

Allowing every student to share may seem time-consuming, but it is a most useful activity. Students learn how to ask good questions and how to give answers. They learn about one another and they gather new information. They learn to know one another's writing *voices* and the value of writing and revising, and they do what real writers do. This is a lifetime skill, and those students who learn it now will have a tool for writing they use all their lives.

Conferencing is wholeness of language at its best: thinking, writing, reading, speaking, listening. The writers' workshop atmosphere is encouraging, nurturing, learning-directed, and cooperative. It provides Teachers with opportunities to show children how to think on their feet and how to develop effective speaking skills. It lets the class learn to be an appreciative, helpful audience. It allows us all to tell one another what has been done well and encourages students to move on to do their best. What could be better than that?

In conferencing, students will get ideas from listening to one another. Every Teacher has seen students sprawl across their writing, guarding it from anyone who might "steal" their ideas. Conferencing sessions provide opportunities to encourage students to *share* ideas, to get ideas from one another. We all are richer when we help one another.

After several students have read their pieces and received feedback from classmates, you might propose drawing up some guidelines for conferences like this. Invite students to offer suggestions. These might include the following:

Be polite; be sensitive to others' feelings.
Try not to use the word *should* ("You *should* have started this way...")
    Instead, students might consider ways to make suggestions: "Have you thought of...?" "You might want to think about..." Maybe you could try..." "I'd like to know..."
Look for things you really like about others' writing. Praise what has been done well.
Clap—sometimes.
Offer suggestions in the kindest way possible.

Criticize only if you have a suggestion to make the piece of writing better, and do it in a kind way.

You may find you need to limit the number of questions asked. Maybe you will need to allow, for example, four questions for each reader to keep the conferencing moving.

Once students have a good understanding of this part of the process, you can have them work in pairs or in small groups—in miniconferences. Groups of three work well: one reader to two listeners who give feedback. Explain that things move more quickly in miniconferences, and tell students they will work in threes as they listen and help one another. I suggest changing the composition of groups rather often so students experience the knowledge and abilities of many students during the school year. I also like to assign the group participants rather than allowing them to choose their own; that way, no one is left out or chosen last—experiences that can be painful for those who are not selected. It is good for students to learn that, truly, every student in the class can give help and can get help from all the others.

You also will see that it is often the students for whom school is difficult who ask good questions and make helpful suggestions. Just as in the whole-group conferences, students are to hold their own papers and read from them, not to exchange them.

While students hold miniconferences, move around the room, stopping to listen to each group. Be sure students follow the model—asking and answering questions, telling one another what they have done well, making suggestions to help improve peers' pieces. From time to time, call a break and ask how many students have received help from someone else, how many have given help. Ask what that help has been. Point out that although it is nice to say, "That's really good!" it probably does not help the writer make his piece stronger or better. Assure students that when their final pieces are published and read aloud, they can tell one another what they like best about each piece and can clap and cheer if they feel moved to do so.

Students do not *have* to make the changes suggested by classmates; they can listen and consider what others have to say and then decide for themselves if they want to implement the suggestions. Remind them that ideas that are offered are meant to be of help; this is an opportunity for everyone to help everyone else. Once they have made the changes directly on the first drafts—crossing out, adding more information—it may be helpful to copy the papers over (second drafts) for ease in reading.

Now they may want to read their pieces again to see if they do, in fact, sound better. This can be done by partners, in small groups, or in large groups. It is important that students actually do follow through on revising; it is part of the process for working toward a final piece of high quality.

At this point, students may be ready to conference with the Teacher. I like using six chairs in a conferencing circle. If chairs are of varying heights, I sit in the smallest one so the student conferencing with me is on my eye level. Students come to join the circle as they are ready to talk about their pieces, and the student with whom I am conferencing sits beside me. The students hold their own papers, and I watch as they read and show me what they want to discuss.

As we begin an individual conference, I ask, "How can I help you?" or "How are you coming along?" Rather than telling writers what they need, I let them tell me. This is a skill, too—learning to identify in our own writing where we need ideas or input from someone else. We talk together *as writers* about each piece. When a student's conference with me is over, she goes back to her seat to continue working on the piece in progress. Another writer moves to the conferencing chair and we begin again.

Sometimes students in the conferencing circle will write as they wait their turn. Sometimes a student who has been waiting will get up and go back to her seat because she has learned what she needed to know simply by listening to my conversation with another student. Because the writers' workshop atmosphere is congenial and comfortable, students in the circle may occasionally add their comments to those of the writer and Teacher.

First-time conferences take longer. You and your students need to develop your own comfortable situation with conferences. As you improve your own skills in conferencing with students, you will find that conferences generally become shorter and that you are able to ask better questions of your writers. Give yourself time to learn this kind of conferencing. Your students will appreciate their time with you; just one idea or tip acquired in a conference may help a student put an entire piece together.

In conferencing, I try to help those who need immediate help first. If the student can wait, I might ask to see the piece overnight and will share my comments with the student in the morning or whenever we can make a few minutes together for a short conference. After several conferences with a Teacher, students begin to feel confidence, a freedom in writing because—assisted by their Teacher and classmates—they are responsible for their own work. If we allow and encourage students to take responsibility for their own writing, they *will*. If we take it all, most of them will allow us to do that.

In conferencing, we provide feedback and help to students *as they go through the steps* of the process; we don't wait until they are finished, then simply make after-the-fact comments.

When I was a beginning Teacher, I helped my students as they wrote, but I didn't do it in a conferencing circle, and I didn't enlist the help of my students. Instead, my students would line up (often in a long line!) by my desk and wait their turn for my help. The longer the line was, the more I talked and the faster I talked—after all, there were so many students wanting my advice! The process was exhausting, and stressful, and it allowed me to help just one student at a time.

I now conference in a much better way. We sit together in a circle and take our time. Students keep ownership of their writing. Instead of telling them what to do, I ask questions, listen, and sometimes make suggestions. Rather than reaching out to take their papers, I hold in my lap a clipboard or a notebook in which I jot the date and comments about each child's writing progress, mastery of certain writing skills, special areas of interest for writing and other notes that provide me with an always current record. This kind of conferencing is much more effective and much less stressful. It is part of a process where we work together to help one another.

Where does conferencing fit into the writing process?
We can conference as students work on the various drafts of their writing.

We conference at the proofreading stage; sometimes proofreading and editing are done by peers, by partners, in small groups, or with the Teacher. Sometimes the Teacher holds editing conferences specifically for the purpose of working on the mechanics of a piece.

We do not conference about the published piece; we *celebrate* it!

For purposes of continuous conferencing with all class members, a class might be divided into a specific number of students each day: for example, the same five students might have regular Monday conferences, another five on Tuesday, etcetera. They can bring portfolios containing works-in-progress to these conferences, knowing that this specific conferencing time belongs to them.

In addition, "open" daily conferencing time must be available for those who need your immediate help. Some conferences are short as students quickly get from you the help they need: others will take longer. You must decide how long these conferencing sessions will last—20 minutes each day might be adequate for some classes while more time will be needed by others. That is your decision to make.

This workshop approach to writing provides a real laboratory in which both students and Teachers learn and develop confidence in writing skills. Work is done cooperatively, and the goal is always to help one another become the best writers we can possibly be.

Advice to Teachers who conference with students

Don't offer too much advice. Students are listening to what we say, and too many suggestions given at once may be overwhelming. Working on one or two things at a time allows a student to feel the work is manageable.

Treat students as *authors*, just as you would authors of any published books. Their pieces are every bit as important.

Wait. Listen. Ask questions. Be patient. Don't try to take over students' writings, much as you might be inclined to do so. They belong to the students.

One day, before students started writing their mysteries, we discussed some firm guidelines on the use of violence in writing. Later, as a student read from his first draft *he found Chris dead on the floor*, I interrupted. Saying "Just wait a minute," the young author explained that Chris wasn't dead— he had hit his head on a kitchen counter and was knocked unconscious. I had reacted too quickly.

Always listen for what the child is saying. Putting oneself on paper can be scary. The student who says, "I can't spell" may be a marvelous writer. Be sensitive to the feelings of your young writers and point out the good parts of what the child has written. Ask questions, if that will help the child to write more. Always encourage, always be a hope-giver that, with practice, the student will be an even better writer in days to come.

As you conference with students, ask what they like best about their own piece of writing. This helps them identify and articulate their strengths, and it helps them identify areas where they need some help. This too is an important skill for students to learn.

A second-grade Teacher came hurrying in to see me before our writers' Round Table (a gathering of young authors that I was to coordinate when school began that morning). "Terry's story was just terrible," she chattered. "Look." She handed me his terrible story written in his uneven, second-grade printing on a wrinkled paper that gave indication of having been carried around in a pocket for some time. "He copied the title from another story, and I didn't like the names he gave his characters, and the story had an awful ending. I fixed it for him. Now his story will be O.K. to read at the Round Table. " She hurried down the hallway to her classroom.

Back in class, she handed Terry the story which she had run off on the computer. He came into our Round Table room, sat down, looked at his new paper and burst into tears. "This isn't my story," he said. "and I can't even read this writing!"

I assured him that his own story would be fine, handed him his wrinkled original and directed crabby thoughts down the hall at his homeroom teacher. Terry read *his* story to the students at the round table, and they praised it.

We must respect our students and their writing efforts. They are beginners after all, and writing combines complicated skills. It is not learned without great effort over a long period of time, and it is not required that beginners write perfectly.

When you are conferencing in a situation where students will give feedback to one another, let students give their feedback first; save yours until they have made their contributions because sometimes Teachers "steal" students' comments. Hold back a bit and see what students have to say—it often is every bit as useful as what we might contribute, and often kids say it even better.

One afternoon as I looked over second graders' shoulders while they wrote animal stories, I saw the first part of a wonderful tale called "Turtle's Broken Shell" on the desk of a small boy. In my adult wisdom, I immediately thought of a wonderful way to mend the turtle's shell; I bent over and whispered, "I know how you can fix his shell!"

The author didn't even look up. "So do I," he said and continued writing. His solution was far better than mine—a friendly bear came along and kindly gave some of his fur to the turtle who became the only fur-covered turtle ever to exist. So much for jumping into the plot of another author's story!

Just once I attempted to add an ending to what turned out to be an already completed story: A second-grade girl wrote of a tiger chasing a small yellow hen through the woods. She got away and the tiger went home. "THE END," read the girl. "Maybe," I suggested, "you could add a last sentence like "And that tiger is still hungry!"

"But he's *not*," said the student. I was puzzled. "But he must be; he didn't catch the hen," I insisted.

"It doesn't matter; he already has a whole bunch of them at home in his freezer," replied the author matter-of-factly. Students generally know what they are doing.

Conferencing takes time, but as we conference, all students learn at the same time. They learn to improve their own writing in many different ways, rather than dealing with only their own writing pieces. Sometimes they become so excited over peers' comments about other students' writing that they can hardly wait to read their own pieces to the class. They learn through working together both how to give and how to receive help, and they develop special sensitivity toward one another.

In conferencing, students question one another to make things clear and orderly and they learn to think of an audience, those who will read or listen to what they write. Conferencing changes forever the thought process that goes into their writing. They come to know what they can do *right* as authors.

As they listen to one another, students learn to know one another's writing *voices*. *Voice* is what gives writing personality. It's what lets us recognize one another on paper. Mark Twain's writing sounds like no one else's. If you have read the wonderful *Tuck Everlasting* by Natalie Babbitt (the prologue sets the story stage with incredible description) or *Dr. Seuss* stories, you know their writing voices. When we write with voice, we write in a way that reflects *us*, in our own special way of speaking. Children too develop writing voices.

Let your students know that when all the work of preparing to write, drafting, revising, proofreading and conferencing has been finished and the final copy is published, *you will not write on that paper*. Let them know you appreciate the work that has gone into it and how special it is. Write your comments on a separate paper attached to the work with a paper clip, not stapled; or use stick-on notes. Some of these writings can be used as unique, one-of-a-kind gifts; others will be treasured and saved. Students will appreciate your caring for their hard work. Let them know you are proud of it as they are.

Summary

Children want to write *real* things that they care about. Conferencing is an important part of the process of writing because it will help them to do that. It is what real writers do and it *works*.

If many students are waiting to conference with you, ask some of your stronger writers to start another circle, conferencing with a small tape recorder in the middle so you can listen later to their discussion.

Encourage students not to just wait to become part of the conferencing group, but to go on with another piece of writing until it is their turn. They can always go back to their idea lists for new writing ideas and start work on another piece. Professional writers usually have several pieces in progress at one time, and students can do this too.

Conferencing can relieve Teachers of much of the work of helping students correct and revise what they actually can do for themselves; that is good for Teachers as well as for students.

Conferencing gives students necessary practice in learning how to do for themselves what they will need to do for the rest of their lives; this is good for students.

Conferencing saves hours of at-home work with red pencils, which is not really communicating with students (there, the Teacher takes responsibility for the paper); it is better to work together on students' pieces, sharing the responsibility and showing students how to make improvements in their writing. This is good for students.

Conferencing makes us *helpers* in the entire process of writing. No longer are students writing to please a Teacher; the Teacher is helping the students write something to please themselves, something that they will be motivated to develop into their best work. In conferencing, we talk, not about writing in the abstract, but about each student's own writing. This is good for students.

Conferencing is language in all its wholeness, at its best; it leads to high-quality writing, to students' working to achieve excellence in writing, reading, listening and speaking. This is good for students too.

Written language crosses all areas of learning. The ability to write well gives us all—students, Teachers, children and adults—the power to say what we want, know, think and dream. And whereas in reading we learn what someone else has to say, in writing we speak for ourselves. Do we teach anything more important than this?

What differences do teaching methods make in student writing?

A study conducted in the Eau Claire, Wisconsin, public schools and reported in a local newspaper compared the writing performance of sixth-graders who received traditional writing instruction to others whose teaching centered on open-ended problem-solving/workshop methods.

Students in the workshop method approach surprised researchers by doing nearly as well on the mechanics of writing and much better on many sophisticated language skills. Workshop students were far better at skills involving sentence structure, organization, detail, vocabulary, focus, and voice.

Principal Bill Klaus told the reporter that the workshop students were "much more aware of their own processes and strategies." Traditional students depended on others to provide writing subject material, while workshop students performed much better in prewriting and revising skills.

Try it! Set up a conferencing circle in your classroom. Invite students to write, then share with classmates, to ask questions and make suggestions, to help one another develop writing competencies. Do it together. All of you will learn and find satisfaction in new ways of becoming good writers.

4 From Reading to Writing

If you want to write, read! I heard that somewhere and I know it is true. Perhaps you have memories like mine: I was *read to* from the time I could sit. One of my fondest, warmest memories is that of my father, sitting with me on the corner of my bed at night, reading to me. We read book after book, books filled with beautiful, marvelous, glorious, wonderful words. My favorite was *Penrod* by Booth Tarkington. *Penrod* was filled with intriguing, new, challenging and interesting words, the meanings of which I could only guess through the inflections of my father's deep bass voice as he read page after page about the activities of this rambunctious, troublesome boy. We also read the Albert Payson Terhune books about collies: I dreamed about having my own collie one day—and got one! There were no "limited vocabulary books" then, thank goodness, or I might have missed this incredible introduction to words. I might not have been driven to learn new words, all kinds of new words, and to strive to win our weekly schoolroom spelldowns. I might have missed hearing the phrases that caught my mind's attention, many of which are with me still, the wonderfully painted descriptions of places, characters, happenings in literature.

A love of words
Second-grader Barbara Jean, brown braids swinging, eyes sparkling, comes bouncing into our morning writing class. "Salutations, Mrs. B.!"

"What a wonderful word!" I respond. "Where did you get it?"

"From *Charlotte's Web!*" she says, grinning.

Children love words. Where do they learn them? From reading, mostly, and from listening to someone read to them. What does this say about "limited vocabulary" books? I myself love language and words. As a small child, I went straight to "How to Increase Your Word Power" in every *Readers' Digest* the minute the mailman dropped it through our mail slot. After I had learned the words, I neatly erased my own markings so my parents could use and learn them too. My hunger for new words also was fed by unlimited vocabulary words like those found in *Penrod* and in L. M. Montgomery's wonderful *Anne of Green Gables*, where Anne celebrates the "upspringing of the flowers" and where her lyrical expressions went right to my poet's heart.

I remember being rocked by my mother as she sang to me the songs I still can recall perfectly. And I remember receiving letters from my uncles who took time to write to a small girl waiting for mail from ships and foxholes during World War II. I still have those letters but seldom take them out to read them, for I have them locked in my mind's eye, the exact writing patterns and words used by each writer; I read them over and over as a child, planting them firmly in my mind.

Think of *your* childhood language nourishers. We can help to give our students this love of language. Have you heard students discussing the wonderful language in the book *Anne of Green Gables* or *The Lion, the Witch and the Wardrobe?* In *Tuck Everlasting* or *A Wrinkle in Time?* Have you ever finished reading a book to your class only to have a child rush up eagerly, desperately begging, "Oh, may I have that book next?" Then you know you have given that child something precious.

We need to feed words to our students, to use every tool, every method we can to increase students' vocabularies so they will have a deep, rich supply of good words to use.

Writing with a class of first-graders one day, I was enjoying the interesting and varied spellings they used in stories they were creating. Having read lots of first-grade spelling, I can understand most of their writing, but looking over one child's shoulder as she wrote, I was puzzled about what appeared to be something about her "horsedog." She looked up at me, her eyes serious. "I can see that you're wondering about my horsedog," she said. "That's because my dog is so big I can ride him like a horse, so I call him my horsedog." Of course! If there are such things as catfish, why not horsedogs? New spellings, new words, new names for things—a breath of fresh air! How about another: the child who likes to sit "begainst" her mother—*beside* and *against*. Lovely!

We know that a good writing program goes hand in hand with a good reading program. We must *read* to learn those good words! We must read to our children and our students to get them excited enough to read and write for themselves. This is how we give children a love and appreciation of language, of words and writing.

When I was in elementary school my best friend, Caroline, and I walked faithfully each Saturday to our old, cozy, inviting downtown library. It was built of stone, with rattling, cozy old radiators all around the walls; on wintry days we draped our jackets and mittens over these to dry and warm as we searched through shelf after shelf for just the right books to read for the coming week. And there, in the hot summers, we would settle ourselves into the cool, quiet corners to read.

Weekly, we would return the seven or eight books we had taken home the previous weekend and spend perhaps an hour gathering a new pile for the next week. We would dig through the bookshelves for the perfect books, compare our growing piles, finally have them checked out by the wonderful old librarian who had worked there forever, and then walk home, kicking through piles of fragrant, rustly leaves and rocks, observing the lawns, the flowers, as we carried our treasures back home.

At one point, we discovered the Frank Yerby books and felt so grown up as we checked them out, one a week, devoured them and then traded them for the next week. We deliberately limited ourselves to one weekly so the collection would last longer. They were our introduction to wild, glamorous romance, and to this day, we laugh when the name of that flamboyant writer comes up in conversation. During and because of our trips to that marvelous library, we were learning our love of language that continues to this day, and when we write or visit, our conversation often is of books we have discovered and want and need to share.

Often as I read, my mother would come to my room to ask, "Joyce, why didn't you come? I've been calling you and calling you!" "But I didn't hear you," I would reply. "Of course you heard me; I've been calling you for five minutes!" It was hard to convince her that I truly had not heard her: How could I, when I was off in a castle somewhere with Nancy Drew? Or wading with Laura Ingalls Wilder in Plum Creek, watching nasty, screaming Nellie Olson as leeches clung to her legs?

Teachers never should feel guilty about taking time to read to their students; in these days of homes with two working parents, of one-parent homes where there sometimes is no one who reads to children, who nurtures this love of language,

Teachers may be the only ones who have the special privilege of sharing wonderful stories and poems aloud. It is one of the most important things you can ever do for your students, whatever their ages.

D.E.A.R. (Drop Everything and Read!)

It has become popular now in some schools to provide special times during which everyone in the school—principals, secretaries, and custodians included—reads silently for perhaps 15 minutes. This kind of program says to our students that it is important that we read, that we nurture language. In some schools, a special reader shares over the loudspeaker a short portion from a favorite, easily identifiable book at the beginning or end of the school day; students drop guesses about the book's title into a collection box. Winners receive a special treat, often a paperback book.

Find some of your own favorite old books. Dig them out, some of the old classics rich in language and experiences, and read these to your students. Encourage them to ask their parents to dig out theirs too. Read to your class, books with varied and interesting language; many books published today demonstrate a great poverty of words that leaves our students poorer, not richer, in language experience for having read or heard them.

Be creative (and what does that mean?)

We cannot give our students creativity; and we can't tell them what words to write when they write. But we can create an atmosphere that allows creativity to develop in our students. In one of my favorite books, *A Circle of Quiet*, author Madeleine L'Engle says: "The creative impulse, like love, can be killed, but it cannot be taught. What a Teacher or librarian or parent can do, in working with children, is to give the flame enough oxygen so that it can burn. As far as I'm concerned, this providing of oxygen is one of the noblest of all vocations." I have to smile now, when I think of all the times I simply told my students, "Be creative!"

We can help our students to be creative by asking them to stretch their thinking—to be adventuresome with new words, thoughts and ideas. We do this by creating an atmosphere where they feel free to explore in writing, to be silly with it if they wish, to play, to have fun with it. We can provide a safe atmosphere where they know that what they write will be accepted and encouraged, never put down. We must let them know it's fine that their work will be different and special, that we don't want it to be like anyone else's.

What are you reading?

A Teacher attending a college class I was teaching told us a great story: A young woman, one of her former students, kept handwritten records of all the books she had read, together with comments about them, from the time she was a little girl.

By the time she reached college, she had determined that she would become a librarian. As a library-science major, she wrote her master's thesis on her own reading history, totally documented and ready to use.

One's own reading history can be most interesting and enlightening. On the following pages, note and make comments about some of your own current reading. In the reproducible section of this book, there is an identical sheet to be used for your students. Encourage them to record and write about what they read. Ask them to make suggestions about how this record might be kept and used.

Books I have read

Author _____ Title _____

Date _____

Comments:

_____

_____

_____

Author _____ Title _____

Date _____

Comments:

_____

_____

_____

Author _____ Title _____

Date _____

Comments:

_____

_____

_____

Author _____ Title _____

Date _____

Comments:

_____

_____

_____

Author _____ Title _____

Date _____

Comments:

_____

_____

_____

Author _____ Title _____

Date _____

Comments:

_____

_____

_____

Author _____Title _____

Date _____

Comments:

_____

_____

_____

Author _____Title _____

Date _____

Comments:

_____

_____

_____

Author _____Title _____

Date _____

Comments:

_____

_____

_____

Author _____Title _____

Date _____

Comments:

_____

_____

_____

Author _____Title _____

Date _____

Comments:

_____

_____

_____

Author _____ Title _____

Date _____

Comments:

_____

_____

_____

Good books to read

Teachers often suggest books they think other Teachers and students might enjoy reading. While lists published by libraries and professional book reviewers might contain a more balanced list, here is a compilation of favorite books recommended by Teachers attending my workshops. Many of these are old, wonderful books; others are new. Some are popular while others, though great favorites, are rather obscure.

This is not a "scientifically tested" list in terms of appropriate age levels. Reading level designations are what Teachers themselves felt appropriate; readers can make their own judgments—those may vary from what is suggested here.

This list came from classroom Teachers who love to read and share books with their friends and classes, so it is a "smorgasbord" of sorts. Choose, read and enjoy!

Author	Title	Grade Level(s)
Alcott, Louisa May	Little Women	3–9
Angelou, Maya	Wouldn't Take Nothing for My Journey Now (poetic prose)	11–adult
Archabault, Martin	Knots on a Counting Rope	Everyone
Arnold, Tedd	Bentley and the Egg	K–3
	No More Jumping on the Bed	K–3
	Green Wilma	K–3
Babbitt, Natalie	Tuck Everlasting	Everyone
	The Search for Delicious	3–9
Banks, Lynn R.	The Indian in the Cupboard	3–6
	Return of the Indian	3–6
Bemelmans, Ludwig	Madeline	K–3
Bronte, Emily	Wuthering Heights	10–adult
	Jane Eyre	10–adult
Burnett, Frances H.	Secret Garden	Everyone
Butler, Robert	A Good Scent from a Strange Mountain (stories of Vietnamese immigrants)	ESL
Cameron, Eleanor	A Room Made of Windows	4–9
	That Julia Redfern series	
Carter, Forest	The Education of Little Tree	Everyone
Cather, Willa	O Pioneers	9–adult
	Song of the Lark	9–adult
Caudill, Rebecca	Tree of Freedom	4–6
Cherry, Lynne	The Great Kapok Tree	Everyone
Clifford, Eth	Flatfoot Fox books	1–3

Corcoran, Barbara	*Annie's Monster*	7–9
Crutcher, Chris	*Chinese Handcuffs*	7–9
	The Long Journey	3–6
Davis, Jenny	*Sex Education*	7–9
Dickinson, Peter	*Eva*	7–9
Duder, Tessa	*In Lane Three, Alex Archer*	7–9
Duncan, Lois	*Don't Look Behind You*	7–9
	Five Were Missing	7–9
Edwards, Michelle	*Chicken Man*	1–4
Eiseley, Loren	*The Star Thrower*	10–adult
	The Immense Journey	10–adult
Haley, Alex	*Roots*	10–adult
Hammarskjold, Dag	*Markings*	10–adult
Hanff, Helene	*84 Charing Cross Road*	10–adult
Hassler, Jon	*Four Miles to Pinecone*	4–7
	Jemmy	4–7
Houston, Gloria	*Littlejim*	7–9
Hudson, Jan	*Sweetgrass*	7–9
Keats, Ezra Jack	*A Snowy Day*	K–3
Kingsolver, Barbara	*The Bean Trees*	Adult
	Pigs in Heaven	Adult
Knutson, Barbara	*Why the Crab Has No Head* and others	1–4 up
LaRochelle, David	*The Evening King*	1–3
Leaf, Munro	*The Story of Ferdinand*	1–3
L'Engle, Madeleine	*A Circle of Quiet*	Adult
	Summer of the Great-Grandmother	
Lee, Harper	*To Kill a Mockingbird*	9–adult
Lewis, Sinclair	*Main Street*	Adult
Lobel, Arnold	*Frog & Toad* books	K–3
Lowry, Lois	*Number the Stars*	6–adult
Lyon, George	*Borrowed Children*	6–9
Mayer, Mercer	All of Mayer's books	K–3
Michener, James	*Chesapeake*	10–adult
	The Covenant	
Montgomery, Lucy Maud	*Anne of Green Gables*	4–7
Murphy, Robert	*The Pond*	6–adult
Myers, Walter D.	*Fallen Angels* (Vietnam war novel)	7–9
Nelson, Theresa	*And One for All* (Vietnam war novel)	7–9
Noble, Trinka	*Meanwhile Back at the Ranch*	K–3
O'Brien, Robert	*Mrs. Frisby and the Rats of Nimh*	4-up
O'Dell, Scott	*Island of the Blue Dolphins*	7–9
	Sing Down the Moon	3–6
Orenstein, Peggy	*Schoolgirls*	Teens with adult guidance– adults
Paulsen, Gary	*The River*	4–9
	Woodsong	7–9

Paterson, Katherine	*Lyddie, Bridge to Terabithia*	4–7
Paulston, Christina B., and Bruder, Mary	*Teaching English as a Second Language*	Teachers
Prelutsky, Jack	*The Dragons Are Singing Tonight*	K–4
Raskin, Ellen	*The Westing Game*	6-up
Rawls, Wilson	*Where the Red Fern Grows*	3–adult
Robertus, Polly	*Dog Who Had Kittens*	K–3
Sachar, Louis	*Sideways Stories from Wayside School*	3–5
Schwartz, Amy	*Annabelle Swift, Kindergartner*	K–3
Scott-Maxwell, Florida	*The Measure of My Days*	Adult
Seuss, Dr.	*Horton Hatches the Egg*	K–3
Sieruta, Peter	*Heartbeats*	6-up
Silverstein, Shel	*Where the Sidewalk Ends* (poetry)	K–6
	Light in the Attic (poetry)	K–6
	Lafcadio, the Lion Who Shot Back	2–4
Smith, Janice Lee	*Monster in the Third Dresser Drawer*	3–4
Smith, Betty	*A Tree Grows in Brooklyn*	Adult
Snyder, Zilpha	*Libby on Wednesdays*	4–7
	Black and Blue Magic	4–7
Steinbeck, John	*Travels with Charley*	10–adult
Stegner, Wallace	*Crossing to Safety*	Adult
	Angle of Repose	Adult
Steptoe, John	*Story of Jumping Mouse*	1–3
Taylor, Mildred	*Roll of Thunder, Hear My Cry*	5-up
Van Allsburg, Chris	*Mysteries of Harris Burdick*	3–6
White, E. B.	*Charlotte's Web*	Everyone
	Trumpet of the Swan	Everyone
	Stuart Little	Everyone
Wilder, Laura Ingalls	*On the Banks of Plum Creek* (and all the rest of her books)	3–adult
Williams, Margery	*Velveteen Rabbit*	K–3
Wood, Douglas	*Old Turtle*	Everyone
Yarmolinski, Avrahm	*The Portable Chekhov*	10–adult
Yolen, Jane	*Piggens*	1–3

Also:

The Read-Aloud Handbook by Jim Trelease, an excellent guide for selecting appropriate reading material for children of all ages

Whodunnits

Most students enjoy reading mysteries. It follows that once they have been reading these for awhile, they may want to try writing their own.

Writing a mystery is a challenge. As one student said to another at a writers' round table, "It's so hard to put the parts of a mystery together so they all get to the end at the same time!"

Writing of mysteries must be preceded by reading them—not one but several.

Discuss differences in the writing of mysteries as compared to other kinds of stories—the use of "mystery" words like *villain* and *victim, clues* and *evidence*. Create a mystery word bank on the board of words that are commonly used in mysteries.

Discuss the way mysteries begin: not, "Once upon a time . . ." but, more likely, "It was five minutes past four on a cold, rainy afternoon when . . ." Have students open the mysteries they are reading and read aloud to the class the first paragraph or two from the books. Discuss and compare these beginnings. Jot information and observations on the board about these beginnings, these "settings of the stage" for mysteries.

Use three heavy pieces of rope to demonstrate to students that one "braids" a mystery together, and that at the end, the pieces all come together to form the solution.

You also can use a balloon to demonstrate how a mystery writer creates suspense, blowing the balloon until it almost pops. So too a mystery writer builds action until the reader is "on the edge of her seat."

This is a good time to discuss violence in writing. Together, set up some guidelines:

No killing, no guns or knives, no "blood and guts" stories. Together, create guidelines with which you are comfortable. Encourage students to write appropriately, to be clever in inferring, in hinting at clues and solutions. Tell your students that *anyone* can write about shooting and blood and guts—that takes no talent at all—but that it takes a good thinker, a good writer, to create a clever, challenging mystery for readers to enjoy.

A good way for young writers (I use this idea at about third grade) to begin a mystery is to follow the pattern of a *Nate the Great* story: He announces who he is and what he was doing as the mystery began.

They will enjoy creating their own identities, settings, and mysteries for this kind of writing.

To add to the fun of writing mysteries for fourth-, fifth-, and sixth-graders, I use envelopes containing three strips of paper on which I have typed information students must use as they write. These are *school* mysteries, with school settings and with staff and students used as characters. The following examples include the villain, victim, and a clue. Students must add other clues. You also might enjoy creating your own sets of information. As part of getting ready to write mysteries, we create a word bank of "mystery words," such as *evidence, scene of the crime, investigators,* and so on, for students to use as they write.

Villain:	Billy Bump, student
Victim:	The art teacher
Clue:	Green fingerprints were found on the doorknob to the art teacher's garage.
Villain:	Tom Taylor, student
Victim:	The physical education teacher
Clue:	Orange fingerprints were found on the top windows of the gym.
Villain:	Debbie Davis, student
Victim:	The custodian
Clue:	Pink fingerprints were found on the doorknob to the store room.
Villain:	Angela Shan, student
Victim:	The principal

Clue:	Yellow chalkdust prints were found on the handlebars of the principal's bicycle.

Villain:	Peter Racker, student
Victim:	The music teacher
Clue:	White fingerprints were found on the new violin in the music room.

Villain:	Mr. Donalds, the sixth-grade Teacher
Victim:	The first-grade Teacher
Clue:	Blue fingerprints were found on the empty candy jar in the first-grade classroom.

Students are not to discuss the contents of their envelopes as they begin writing first drafts. They are likely to be much more creative when they do some thinking on their own about their mysteries.

Once rough drafts have been written, groups of three students might gather to exchange ideas, ask questions, and make suggestions before students write their second drafts. As these conferences take place, remind them to ask pertinent questions. Discuss what they are finding to be difficult (for example, presenting clues without giving away the mystery).

Final drafts may be illustrated, published, and shared in a "mystery" celebration.

This is an exciting, lively project; it requires students to think and plan carefully their stories from beginning to conclusion. Be available to help those for whom this is difficult.

These examples—used for another mystery writing project—give time, place, and problem—the *mystery* in the mystery. Again, these go on papers in envelopes which are given to students.

Time:	Early in the morning
Place:	In the library
Mystery *in the mystery:*	A valuable book about animals is missing.

Time:	Early in the morning
Place:	In a candy store
Mystery *in the mystery:*	Every box of chocolate candy is missing.

Time:	7:00 P.M.
Place:	In a toy store
Mystery *in the mystery:*	Every teddy bear in the store is missing.

Time:	Monday morning
Place:	In-line skates store
Mystery *in the mystery:*	Every pair of girls' in-line skates is missing.

Using these three pieces of information, students write their own mysteries.

Suggested reading for mystery unit
This is only a small Teacher sampling of available books. Ask your school's librarian for a list of mysteries available in your own library. As your students read and prepare to write mysteries, do the same: You must be their role model, and as you

do what they are doing, you will experience much of what they are experiencing. Writing a mystery is hard work!

A comment I often hear from students who have read some of the Nancy Drew and Hardy Boys books is that they "like the *old* ones best!" (I share their feeling.) To that end, you might encourage them to shop at garage sales, flea markets, and antique stores for those older books and to ask their parents to dig out *their* old ones.

Author(s)	*Title*	*Grade Level(s)*
Adler, David	*Cam Jansen*	1–3
	Encyclopedia Brown	1–3
Bellairs, John	*House with a Clock*	5–6
	The Letter, the Witch and the Ring	
	Figure in the Shadows	
Bonsall, Crosby	All of Bonsall's mystery books	1–2
Boston, L.M.	*Treasure of Green Knowe*	4-up
	Children of Green Knowe	
Duncan, Lois	*Down a Dark Hall*	7-up
	Killing Mr. Griffin	7-up
	Dragons in the Waters	7-up
Farley, Carol	*Case of the Lost Lookalike*	1–2
Fenton, Edward	*Phantom of Walkaway Hill*	5-up
	Riddle of the Red Whale	5-up
Giff, Patricia Riley	*Something Queer in Rock 'n' Roll*	1–3
	Something Queer Is Going On	
	Something Queer on Vacation	
	and more	
Hahn, Mary Downing	*Wait 'Til Helen Comes*	5–6
	View from the Cherry Tree	5–6
Howe, Deborah, and Howe, James	*Bunnicula*	3–4
L'Engle, Madeline	*Arm of the Starfish*	7-up
Lunn, Janet	*Root Cellar*	5-up
McKillip, P.	*House on Parchment Street*	4-up
Pearson, Susan	*The Campfire Ghosts*	1–3
Roberts, Willo Davis	*Megan's Island*	3-up
Raskin, Ellen	*The Mysterious Disappearance of Leon*	4–6
	The Westing Game	
Sharmat, Marjorie	*Nate the Great* books (lots of them!)	1–3
Stevenson, Drew	*Case of the Wandering Werewolf*	5-up
	Count of Castle Dracula	5-up
Van Leeuwen, Jean	*The Great Rescue Operation*	3-up
Voight, Cynthia	*The Calendar Papers*	7-up
Wallace, B.	*Danger on Panther Peak*	3-up
	Trapped in Death Cave	
Wright, Betty Ren	*The Dollhouse Murders*	5-up
	Midnight Mystery	5-up

There are those misinformed people who do not think first-graders can write. For their benefit, we include here two stories written by beginning first-graders (pp. 34–36). In spelling, they "used their ears" and wrote down beginning, middle, and ending sounds: We call this *invented spelling/kids' spelling*. And, working mostly on their own, they produced wonderful stories that they then shared delightedly with their Teachers and classmates.

Also included are third-grader Drew's delightful piece about two hundred million years (p. 37) and first-grader Amy's beguiling Christmas piece (p. 38).

By
dimmy WiKman
One winter day
Toad wined in the
Snon to find bare to
play with Hm in
the Back yord.

Bare By axinedined
ait Toad up.

frog and cat go icesgating
by Heather Allen
One day, frog woke up
and ran to the windo.
Hrae! its snoing! he
theru his cote, squf, and
Btseont hen he ran ovre

to cats hoes. Baing!
baing! he nokt. One
minit! cride cat Tene.
She opind the door
Cmone cat lats go
icesquteing! Crid frog

One momint! crid Cat.
I do not no ho to skat.
I'll tetsh you. sed frog.
the frst time cat
trid her squatid she
flekrplobl onth ice

tatisit! crid cat
and she winte home.
the End.

,200,000,000, years ago

200 million years ago was so long ago, that the

earth was frozen...Then, as time passed,

God made dinosaurs, amphibions, and plants.

Matter of fact, 200 million years ago,

the earth was just a gigantic icecube!

Then before you'd know it, man was created.

Then the world got more beautiful then

ever. Wars were started, Dairy Queens were

made, then we had Ronald Regen.

That's how long two hundred million
years were.

Drew Harold

Amy

December 12, 1985

Christmas

Christmas is the tim whn jeses is born. God is anothr name for jeses. Jeses named

himself god beeckos it sownd mor gronop.

What about spelling?

Correct spelling should not be the primary goal in any writing program. It is important, and we work constantly at improving spelling; I continue to use my own dictionary to learn correct spellings and meanings of words new to me. But what is truly important is a student's ability to transfer ideas from speaking and from thinking to writing. We need also to be aware that frequency of writing alone, or practice, does not guarantee improvement: We must show our students how to improve, how to do those things that will give them competency as writers.

Show young writers this trick for spelling: cover one ear with a hand, then say aloud, softly, the word to be written. Then write down the sounds they hear. Tell them that their wonderful hearing sense is designed so sounds will "echo" in their heads when they cover one or both ears and speak, but they can do it softly so that it does not disturb others around them. Most students love this trick and find it works well for them. They also love the challenge of "talking to themselves" in this way in a large, exciting place such as the Metrodome in Minneapolis in the middle of a noisy Twins game!

Tips for parents

Sadly, many students today come from homes where no one reads to them. Encourage parents to make time to read to their children, to purchase gifts of books for them, and to encourage them to read.

Parents also can help their children by creating a "writing place"—a corner, simply equipped with pencils, paper, and other writer's supplies. Some may be able to purchase desks, but that isn't necessary; a clipboard works well. And with a box in which to keep completed pieces and "work in progress," any child can feel like a writer.

Encourage parents to go with their children to the local public library, get them a library card, and let them visit there regularly to bring books home. Parents can help their young children choose books. Librarians are wonderful about helping their patrons, and parents should feel free to ask for that help too.

(The next page is a handout for parents. Many parents ask how they can help their children become more competent in writing. Copy and send home the following page; it contains ideas parents can use in helping their children develop writing skills.)

PARENTS, encourage your children in written language:

Read to them! From the time they are born, fill them with good language, good stories, good pictures, good books. They take in more of this than anyone knows. Continue to read together even after your children can read. Let them see *you* reading. It shows that language is important to you too.

Go with them to the library. Let them see what a special place the library is; teach them to take good care of books.

Encourage them to own their own books. Show them your books; read them some of your childhood books. Speak of your family's books as your own "library."

Make them aware of good authors. Note the authors of their books and the illustrators. These are important people. Perhaps as you read over a period of time, your family will find favorite authors.

Ask them to tell you stories. Write down the stories together. Let the children illustrate the stories and then display them in a special place.

Create a writing place for them. Supply pencils, pens, paper, crayons, tablets, a dictionary, stationery, liquid eraser, a typewriter, a thesaurus, a clipboard, and a box in which to save writings.

Write letters together to friends and relatives. Encourage those recipients to respond. Let children help order things through the mail.

Show your children ways in which you use written language in your work. Talk about why it is important.

When your family travels, keep a travel diary; perhaps your child can have that responsibility. Share it when each trip is over.

Be encouraging; praise your child's writing efforts. Don't ever scold for what you perceive as mistakes. And do not insist on perfect spelling at an early age; that will come in time. Spelling is only one part of written language.

Support your child's teacher in his or her efforts in the teaching of written language.

Ideas for young or beginning writers

A good story can be the take-off point for students' creating their own stories. Reading of the book, *My Friend Jon* by Charlotte Zolotow might be followed by students' telling about their friends. Sharing *The Important Book* by Margaret Wise Brown might be followed by students' telling about their own "important things."

A story coat

Sew colorful pockets on a plain old coat. Into each pocket, put a story starter—a card on which are written such directions as these:

- Tell about your favorite thing to eat; make us hungry! (Not just, "I like cookies," but what kind of cookies? For example, warm, still-melty chocolate chip cookies.)
- Tell a fast, short story about a lion!
- *Continue*: If I could stay up all night long while everyone else in my house was asleep, I would...
- Tell us a sentence that begins with JUMPING.
- *Continue*: I was almost asleep when I realized that my ceiling was gone, and silvery stars were twinkling above me instead.
- *Continue*: If I found a friendly monster in my back yard, I would . . .
- *Continue*: If I could do anything in the world, I would . . .
- *Continue*: There was this boy. Usually he was happy, but . . .

Allow a child to draw a card from any pocket as you create a story with the class.

We begin writing group stories with kindergartners. You may begin by reading a "starter book" first, such as Margaret Wise Brown's *The Important Book*. Then together create a story that follows the pattern. Or you may write a story about whatever you wish. For example, perhaps you have decided to write a story about a bunny. Talk about bunnies, about how they look, what they eat, what they do. Put some "bunny words" on the board.

Ask how a good story might begin (*Once upon a time, Long, long ago,* etc.). Ask if the story should be about a big bunny or a small bunny. Let students vote by raising their hands. Encourage them to think for themselves, not to make decisions based on what everyone else is saying.

Together, choose the story beginning. Then ask, "Where was the bunny?" "What was happening?" Allow for suggestions and "vote" as final decisions are made. Comment positively on all suggestions and encourage students to remember their ideas, because they can use them later in stories they write themselves, even if they aren't used in this particular story.

Here is one bunny story, written when I visited and worked with a group of kindergartners.

Bunny Finds a Home

One cold, snowy winter night, a small bunny was out looking for a home. First he looked in a big, dark cave. But bats lived there. "Get away! This is our cave!" they yelled.

Next he looked at a grassy pile. "This is my house. Please go away, "said Jumper Bunny.

Then Bunny found a nice big hole. But Badger lived there.

Bunny was cold and tired. Suddenly he saw a big building. It was an orphanage. Lots of boys and girls lived there. The teacher saw the bunny outside. She picked him up and took him into the warm house. The children made a special cage for him and gave him lettuce and carrots to eat. Now the bunny was happy.

The end

As you write the story on the board, go back to the beginning each time you complete a sentence and ask students to read it with you. By the time you are at the end, they will know the story "by heart." Draw small figures or pictures above key words to signal to students what those words are. (For example, draw a bat above the word *bats*.)

Ask if students want to make changes; if so, name the term for changing: *revising*. Tell them we can always make changes in stories as we write them.

When the story is finished, inform students they have just written a "one-of-a-kind *original* story that no one in the whole world has ever heard or seen!"Congratulate them and identify the authors of this story by adding by "_____'s class"to the end.

Invite students to illustrate; provide copies of the story to go with the illustrations, and instruct students to take the stories and pictures home and share them with their families. They are *authors*!

Invite these young writers to create teddy bear stories—what do teddy bears do all day when we're gone?

They can write a giant story based on a reading of the book *Jim and the Beanstalk* by Raymond Briggs.

Talk with them about their "third eye," that wonderful place of imagination inside their heads.

Tell them that sometimes reading a good story makes us want to write one of our own. For example, reading a story about a monkey might make us want to write a monkey story, too. Help them learn where to find ideas for their own writing.

Here is a delightful piece about lions written by a beginning first-grader whose passion was lions:

All about Lions
Lions like to klime.
Lions are vairy men.
Lions hav lots of fun.
Lions live in the junngl.
Lions have fits sum times.
Lions don't like there emnees.
My sister dusint like lions.
I do.

And a piece about something scary:

The Dog
Ther usd to be a big dog in my bdroom.
Befor I trnd out the lits I alwas hopt it
wuod go away. Whn it was tim to go to bed
I closd my eys and peekt agan.
And one day I dcided to grow up.

Keys, keys—magic and marvelous keys!

Gather up all the old keys you can find. Tie each with a ribbon, then put them in a colorful cloth bag. Let each child draw out a key and tell a story about it. (It might be a magic key, or it might open the door to a dragon's cave, or...)

Money stories

Give each student a penny or nickel. Each is to write about where this particular coin has been before coming to him or her. Tell your students to look at the date and the letter identifying the place of origin. On a map, show where San Francisco (S), Denver (D), and Philadelphia (P) are; students may wish to use this information in their stories. How did the coins travel, where, and under what conditions? Be sure to allow sharing of these pieces. (Writing in first-person can make this a lively story.)

Take a train ride

Post a large picture of a train engine on the bulletin board. Tell students, "Put yourself in the cab of this engine and tell a story about where you would like to go."

Special words for special things

On one side of a chalkboard, draw a witch or monster. Beside the picture, write words that describe it. On the other side, draw something pretty (a Valentine, a flower, etc.). Beside it, list describing words. Then discuss how words from one list do not fit words describing the other object. Talk about how specific words are needed for good descriptions.

Bring a large and a small object to class. Help the class list words on the board to describe the large object. Then have them describe the small object. Write those words on the board. Discuss how we choose appropriate describing words for different objects.

Collections of words

Staple a brown lunch bag for each student to the bulletin board. As students come into the classroom, write down their favorite "word for the day" on a slip of paper and drop it into the bags. At the end of ten days, have students take down their bags and discuss the words they have chosen; then students take their words home to discuss with parents.

Months of the year

Ask each child to tell something special in his or her own world about the current month. Talk about colors, animals for that month (for example, robins coming back in late March or geese flying south in September). Have students look up monthly happenings in encyclopedias; help them search for new information. Encourage students to make this their own unique writing, different from all the others.

Days of the week

Ask each child to tell a favorite day of the week; they may describe days by colors, then explain why, for example, "Monday is green."

Show-and-tell writing

When your students bring pets for "show and tell," discuss color, size, shape, and other details about the pet. Talk about how it is like another pet that has already come to visit. Talk about how it is different. Write about it on the chalkboard.

The "guessing game"

Describe something in the classroom by color, purpose, or another detail, and have students guess what it is. ("Something green and shiny is sitting on the corner shelf. It grows a tiny bit each day. Can you guess what it is?") Students continue the game, with the "guesser" becoming the "describer."

Tell "all about"

Ask students to describe something about which they are experts. For example: A student who plays the violin might tell all about that activity. Another might be an expert on toothbrushing or hanging clothes out to dry. Then let classmates ask questions.

On a very WEATHERY day

Have students use all the words they can think of to describe the day as you write

them on the board. Using the words, each will write his or her own story or poem, then paint or draw illustrations when the writing is done.

Pets, pets!

Most pets are "normal household animals"— cats, dogs, fish, birds. But what fun it would be to have a different kind of pet! Ask students to choose what they would like if they could have any animal. They can tell where they would keep it, what they would name it, what they would do

with it. Then have them draw it! (I have always wanted a giraffe; now, I think I'd like a llama!)

Mother's Day

Read *Are You My Mother?* by Eastman. Give each child an eight-page blank booklet. On the cover write the title: *Are You My Mother?* Students will make a self-drawing or glue a small picture of themselves under the title. On all remaining pages but the last one, children will draw or paste pictures of things *not* their mothers (cow, dog, rabbit, etc.) and write at the bottom: *Are you my mother? No!* On the last page, they will draw or paste a picture of their own mothers and write under it, *You are my mother, and I love you!*

Book reviews

Each child will bring a favorite book from home and tell about it. Why is it a favorite? Where did it come from? Each is to draw a picture of some part of the book and dictate or write something to go under the picture.

Story bags

Sometimes when young writers have written a wonderful story, they like to carry it around with them to read over and over. Give them small zip bags (the kind we use for sandwiches) for the books; bags will protect stories from wind, rain, snow, and wear.

The three bears

Read the story of the three bears. Ask students to think up their own bear stories—about one, two, or three bears. What color are they? Where do they live? What do they like to eat? Who are their friends?

And oh, when they write their wonderful stories, DO read them! You will sometimes find spelling that just tickles you! Like the bear with the "booshytail," and the "porky pine"! And the little girl who spelled out "wozza" (as in, "once there wozza bear"!).

Sentence stretchers

(Do this orally; it involves thinking and memory!)

A _____ is red.

A _____ is red and it is _____ .

A _____ is red and it is _____ and I _____ .

Choose a color

Talk about things that are that color. Then write:

My favorite color is _____. (*Example: My favorite color is red.*)

It smells like _____. (*It smells like a rose.*)

It tastes like _____. (*It tastes like a strawberry.*)

It feels like _____. (*It feels like my sweater.*)

It looks like_____. (*It looks like my mother's hair.*)

It sounds like _____. (*It sounds like a fire engine.*)

What do we do about spelling?

"Mrs. B, I can't spell, but I like to write…may I please be part of your writing group?" The tall, dark-haired fifth-grade boy had come quietly into my book writers' classroom and stood, waiting for my answer.

"Of course you may!" I answered, delighted with his interest. From that time on, every Monday afternoon at his group's appointed writing hour, he would come into the room, greet me, pick up his clipboard and papers, and go to a quiet

corner by himself where he would write, uninterrupted, for fifty minutes. Then he would put back the clipboard, say, "I'll see you next week, Mrs. B," and leave.

It was several weeks before he allowed me to see what he was writing; one day, he was ready to share. He brought me approximately forty pages of writing, a well-told story of a pioneer family moving West, finding their land, and settling there. He was right: he couldn't spell, and many of the words were hard to decipher. He was embarrassed about that, but I told him that sometimes spelling was hard for me too. I offered to help with proofreading, and he said that his mother and older sister also would help.

By the time his story had gone through several drafts and into an attractive book cover, the spelling had been corrected. He had learned how to spell many of the words himself, had acquired a paperback dictionary of his own for assistance in spelling, and he knew that he had earned the right to call himself *writer*.

Many students will improve their spelling skills as they write and learn and move from grade to grade. Others never will spell well (many famous writers are terrible spellers) and will need all the tools and "tricks" we can give them to make their spelling acceptable. But we should never let a demand for perfect spelling destroy a student's joy in writing.

I sometimes hear stories about principals and/or teachers who require that every piece of writing that goes home with their students contain only perfect spelling. Why should that be? There are thousands of words to spell! How could a beginning writer possibly know how to spell all the words he or she knows and wants to use? Teachers need to use common sense as we share with our students the process of learning to write. Perfect spelling is not the most important thing in the world. Continue to demonstrate and encourage correct spelling, but don't let your beginning writers get bogged down with the overwhelming chore of spelling every word perfectly, of looking up every word in the dictionary; then they may come to hate writing.

When, on the other hand, Teachers are understanding and encouraging as students learn to spell and write, children will feel comfortable writing and sharing their pieces. A first-grade girl wrote a story about a **trtl** she had found. She described the color and shape, told how it moved, and so on. When she gave it to her Teacher, she said confidently, "I don't know what this (**trtl**) says to you, but it says **turtle** to me." Her wonderful Teacher, without hesitation, responded, "Well, it says **turtle** to me, too!"

Several years ago, I asked a just-turned-six-years-old girl to write, with her classmates, about her house. This is what she wrote, completely unassisted:

> A house is nice. When a big storm comes we all can be safe inside. A house at night for us to sleep and also where to bake cakes. For pets and also where to keep we (our) car and to keep (?) that's in, and to watch TV and it's also good for cuddling up to your neck in bed and read a nice book. A house is nice to cook and eat our meals. A house is nice for at Christmas time our house is so beautiful at Christmas time. And we can take nice naps. We can be nice and cool on a hot day. We can find our Easter basket. We can make a nice fire. We can hang our (Christmas) stockings on top of our fireplace. We can hang our favorite posters. We can do housework. We can play a whole bunch of games.

Anna loved her home, and she was so excited about writing about it that she didn't know she spelled like a beginning writer. Had she been told about her spelling errors in the first two or three lines, she would probably not have gone any further with this wonderful piece. Anna spelled much better the next year, and now is a fine speller who writes beautifully, descriptively, competently.

Teachers who demand perfect spelling of their young writers may do so to please parents who learned to write using only correctly spelled words. Many of these adults now describe writing as something they hate.

With thousands of words in dictionaries, with crazy rules and exceptions to those rules in our system of language, we make a choice: We insist that beginning writers limit their vocabularies and use only those words they can spell correctly, or we let them use their wonderful vocabularies and write with "kids' spelling"— invented spelling (sounds they hear as they think, cover their ears, and listen to themselves say the words). The more they read and are read to, and the more time they spend in language activities at school, the more correctly most of them will spell. And we can give them tools for spelling: for example, a small "dictionary": 8½" × 11" paper, folded in half and stapled, about 30 pages in all, with large letters of the alphabet on successive pages in A–Z order, and lines below where they can ask adults to write correctly those words they especially wish to know. We also can give them paperback dictionaries and thesauruses and "word banks" on the board as they begin writing about a specific topic.

Spelling help

Spelling help for some students may be found in asking them to close their eyes and look into their minds' eyes at a big blank chalkboard or bulletin board they have created there, to make a picture in their heads of the word as they have seen it in books written on that board. Then they can open their eyes and write it down that way on their papers. This won't help all students, but it can help those who visualize well. Tell them that in this way, they are using their minds' camera ability, their memories.

Young children can learn to spell! But consider: It may be that to mark with red pen or pencil those words that are misspelled only reinforces those mistakes. Try making corrections at the top of the paper, using plain pen or pencil. This separates the correction from the error. It helps students to "see" correct spellings in their minds.

Show your students how to recognize syllables and how to spell words syllable by syllable. I was spelling my long last name by syllables for a man who had agreed to hold a purchase for me: "You're a Teacher, aren't you!" he grinned. "Yes, I am. How do you know?" I asked. "Because you spell in syllables!" he answered. "And that's the way I was taught to spell well!"

Young writers need regular free-writing experiences. As they think and write, they add knowledge and experience to their written language skills. There are thousands upon thousands of words to be learned; their oral language usage is almost always much more developed than their written language skills. But they like to use big, descriptive, exciting words that they do not know how to spell. How do they do this? With invented spelling: "kids' spelling." We must give them permission to do this; we must communicate to parents that spelling is only a part of the writing process, that skills in spelling will develop as students read and write, and as parents read with them and to them.

Learning to write and spell is much like learning to speak; we go from babbling and experimental sounds to beginning sounds, syllables, words and sentences, and mature speech. Early writing may consist mostly of sounds that students can hear; this writing may include few vowels. Awareness of consonants comes first, and much early writing is done without use of vowels, which are heard and used later. As writing competency develops, vowels will appear, along with "silent letters" and letter combinations. Just as we encourage the development of speech, we need to encourage, to cheer, development of writing skills.

Encourage, encourage! (When a child first begins to speak, do we say, "That's wrong!" No, we say, "That's right! NANA." Or, "NIGHT, NIGHT. Listen! He's starting to talk!") We show our excitement, our delight, in the development of speech; we must do it also as writing ability begins.

Our English spelling system is filled with inconsistencies, rules, and exceptions to the rules. Over a period of time and exposure to books, reading material, and to classroom and home activities centering on language, most students' spelling skills will improve.

When we find a beginning writer's markings puzzling, we might keep in mind several things. Writing is a complicated task; the fact that symbols mean something may take longer for some students to learn than others. The fact that specific symbols mean specific things, words and thoughts is another important component of learning to write and read. Add to this the complications of working from left to right; of putting motor skills together with visual observations and stored knowledge to reproduce letters and words in a meaningful order; of letter and word placement on lines in a meaningful sequence; of leaving empty spaces that also mean something; and of discovering and using punctuation marks—it's amazing that children learn to write at all!

Very young writers may use letters simply as place holders, meaning that the letter represents a word that goes in that place. (The letter used may have nothing at all to do with the letters in the word it represents.)

A positive attitude, patience, and encouragement are the best things a Teacher can give to his or her students as they begin to learn how to read and write. The atmosphere surrounding children's first attempts at reading and writing will have long-lasting effects on a child's attitudes toward these important activities. Awareness that reading and writing do not develop step by step is most important. Children are learning on many levels at this age, and we do well to encourage beginners' efforts to acquire and develop competency in language.

Show your students the differences between words that are almost alike. Talk about the differences; show your students tricks for remembering them. One problem Teachers often have with beginning writers is that many of these children want every word spelled for them. Encouraging students to "use their ears"— giving them permission to use invented spelling—will help them become more independent writers. Explain that you cannot help 30 children at once and that you want them to work on their own as much as possible, but that you will help wherever you can. If possible, during class time help your writers create a "word bank" on the chalkboard. This is especially helpful if all students are writing on the same topic. It will give students a good feeling to be helping the rest of the class as they suggest words for the bank, and it can help reinforce correct spelling.

Correct spelling is not simply a product of development and memorization. It is learned through practice, through the acquiring of phonetic skills, through learning to listen carefully for sounds, through a Teacher's help in specific areas, through regular practice in written language, through emphasis on what students know.

Teachers attending workshops often ask, "At what point should we expect students to spell correctly?" There is no one answer. Expectations vary between school districts, schools, grade levels, and Teachers. Thus, school decisions are made on an independent basis, and the answer is not always the same. If Teachers and administrators decide that correct spelling is expected at the third-grade level, then the push for it begins there. If they opt for fourth grade, it starts there.

Children, however, begin learning early in their writing experiences that for people to read what they have written, the conventions of spelling are helpful. The desire to share their writing with others motivates them to attempt to spell correctly. Again, the more a child reads and the more writing he or she does, the more likely it is that correct spelling will be that child's own goal—the very best kind.

Remember: No matter how hard they try, no matter what spelling programs we use, and no matter how well they do on a spelling test (many can get 100 on spelling tests but cannot make the transfer to correct spelling within their writing), some children simply always will find spelling within their writing to be difficult. As Teachers, we need to help them in every way possible, let them know that there is nothing wrong with them—and give them permission to write anyway.

Another question Teachers often ask me is when to let beginning writers use dictionaries. Let me tell you a story:

I was visiting a first-grade classroom of 28 eager, bright-eyed, motivated students. Because I like frogs, we were preparing to write frog stories. We talked about frog names, frog activities, and frog places and were so excited about writing stories that we could hardly wait to begin.

"All right," I told them, "let's start!" Students grabbed their pencils, eagerly wrote their names at the tops of the papers—then reached inside their desks to pull out brand-new dictionaries. *And began looking for the first words they would write on their papers.* In an instant, they had become word *hunters*, not writers.

The exciting momentum came to a screeching halt. Now, one word at a time, students were looking up even those words they already knew. The clock hands were moving rapidly, and time was disappearing with only a few words on students' papers.

"Let's try something," I suggested. "I know you can spell lots of words yourselves, and you know the ear trick, so you can use invented spelling for many others. Let's put away those dictionaries and just write for awhile—get those wonderful stories down on paper while you have the ideas in your heads."

Slowly, rather reluctantly, students slid the dictionaries back into their desks and began to write. They talked to themselves, used the ear trick to sound out words—and soon the energy in the room began flowing again.

All except for one small boy: He sat, glaring at me, his arms crossed, anger written all over his face. I knew what was wrong, but I asked anyway. "What's the matter, Jeff?"

"I need my *dictionary*," he announced coldly. I encouraged him again to try writing without it, but he refused. Five minutes later, he still sat, angrily searching through his dictionary for the second word to put down on his paper.

I stopped beside his desk. "What word do you need?' I asked.

"*Was*," he said through gritted teeth.

"I'll bet you know that word without even looking it up," I coaxed. "Cover your ear and say it to yourself. What sounds do you hear?" I got down on my knees beside him and covered my ears too. Together, we sounded out *was*. He printed *w a s* on his paper.

"What's next?" I asked.

"*Windy*," he answered.

"Try sounding it out," I suggested. Glowering at me, he covered his ears and said the word aloud. *W*, he wrote. Then *N D Y*. "Good for you!" I cheered, then moved off to observe other students' writing, watching him from the corner of my eye. He began talking to himself, listening, writing. Soon his pencil was moving along, the wonderful story in his head now going onto paper. He looked up at me and I smiled at him. He glared back! I stepped to his desk and asked what the matter was. "I didn't think it would **work**!" he said angrily. Jeff was so dependent on his dictionary that even though it controlled and limited his writing, he could hardly bear the fact that he could write without it!

I learned something that day: First, students need permission to write, to use "kids' spelling," invented spelling, tricks, pictures—whatever works for getting started, for knowing **they can write**. Then, armed with permission to write and courage to write and the knowledge that they can write, they are ready to use dictionaries and the rules that go with writing. These tools should not *limit* students' writing but enhance it.

Keep parents informed

Communication with parents about the process of writing is important; many adults went through the school systems with more emphasis in writing placed on correct spelling than on any other part of the process of writing. Now we know that we need to encourage children to read, to write freely, and to use invented spelling in the beginning of this learning process. With this background, a comfortable classroom atmosphere, and acceptance of early writing efforts, students will be motivated to continue their early attempts and go on to become competent

A Hous is Nice
A Hou.s is Nce whtn
a big Stom comes We
all kin Be Savf o Sdde
A Hous att night for uos to Slep
and allso wene to Bake Kaks
For Pats dadall so wene to Kepwe
CaR and to kep werfert
thets in and to wech t.v.
and it's also goodfor cldll
up to uou naccahvee
deb and Red onick book
a Hous is nic To
Kok andeit aer meels. a Hous.
is nvice for at krmsms tim
aer Hous is So Beuuoytfle
at Crwmes tim
and we kin thtr nic naps
dwe kin Be nic andcol
on a viwe Hit day
We kin fin aer Etr Back
We kin make a Nic Furr
We kin hieg aer Stakes
We kin hieg aer fart Pets rs
We kin do Hous wek
on tap of ar Firre plas
We kin ploy a hol Bu h of games

writers. You may find it helpful to send parents a letter telling them these things, so that they will be more accepting of imperfect papers and understand that your students are working on *learning* to write.

A small personal dictionary—a small blank book—is a wonderful tool for first- and second-graders. *Adults* write in the words children want to know (all may choose different words), and students use their dictionaries independently, because they chose the words themselves.

From third grade on, students can keep a spiral notebook filled with their own words and spelling "tricks." For example, take the word *friend*: No matter how far away a friend may move, he or she can remain a friend to the end. And *-end* is how *friend* ends. The word *attendance* is also remembered with a sentence: "Will you *attend* the *dance* with me?" Students can draw pictures, circle words, underline them, use any marks they need to help them learn and remember how to spell. Some may wish to tab these in alphabetical order with small tags for each letter so they are easy to find.

One clever principal asked a Teacher to design two rubber stamps, then had them reproduced and gave one to each Teacher in her school. One stamp indicated that "construction" was underway—practice papers would go home uncorrected; the other, that students were "working on . . ." Each stamp was accompanied by a green or red ink pad so Teachers could stamp, then send papers home uncorrected; or unfinished and parents would understand what skills were currently being emphasized. (This also helped to show that spelling was not the only component of written language.)

Writers' round tables

One of the best ways for students to "publish" their material is to share it with other students. This can be done in many ways, but let me suggest one that has worked well in many school districts: a writers' round table. Each month, or twice monthly, one student is invited from each classroom, first through sixth grade, to bring a finished piece of writing to share at the round table. A different student comes each time so the privilege of participating is spread as widely as possible. (By the way, be prepared to explain why the tables around which you sit are not ROUND, if in fact they aren't!)

In one school, teachers of students with learning disabilities made the round tables special experiences for them. They helped write and revise, then published

these students' pieces so that when they came to the round tables, they were more than ready to share what they had written; and all the participants celebrated with them! It became one of the favorite writing activities for these students.

Round tables can begin with a brief introductory statement by the coordinator: "Welcome to the Writers' Round Table! You have been asked to come and share a special piece of writing today. Before your turn, please tell us who you are, what grade you are in and the name of your Teacher. After we hear your piece, we'll tell you what we like best about it . . . and we always like what we hear!" There might be a short discussion about "what's good about writing." Then the sharing begins. Sometimes no one wants to begin and the coordinator may simply ask a student to start. Other times, everyone wants to be first.

Round tables, including from 12 to 18 students, can be completed in about an hour or slightly less; anything longer than that usually becomes too long.

The atmosphere in a Writers' Round Table should be comfortable, friendly, completely accepting of what is shared. Suggestions for changes or improvements are not necessary, as the pieces are presented in their final form. Appropriate comments might be something like, "I really liked your description of the grandmother. I could just see her face when she was laughing!" Or, "I liked the way your story began; it made me want to listen."

At a round table, you may receive an invitation, as one group of us did, from a wonderful third-grade writer: "I am going to take you on a journey!" She then proceeded to take us into strange and lovely new places in her story. You may hear delightful descriptions, as this description of a courageous girl: "She was a high hoper and a strong dreamer!"

I always find that round tables bring out the best in those who come to share. Older students look for kind and encouraging comments to make about younger writers' pieces, even those of only three or four sentences. Younger writers like the opportunity to praise and comment on pieces of older students, as did the first-grader who had listened to an older student describe how he had broken his leg in a skiing accident: "I understand," she said sympathetically. "I broke my head once!"

Some schools give participants badges or blue ribbons that say *I Am a Writer*. These can be worn or used as bookmarks. In some schools, the principal presents a special "Writer" pencil to each student in a round table. In many schools, it is a status symbol to wear these indications that the students are indeed *writers* and possess the ability to say special things on paper.

Copies of the shared pieces often are displayed on the office window or in the halls, where all students can see and read them. Copies can be bound (you might use a spiral binder) into a "book of the month" that goes into the school library. Students enjoy reading these and take special delight in going back years later to see the books containing their pieces. (Some librarians allow these books to be checked out and provide large, laminated envelopes in which students can carry them home.)

The coordinator may be a writing or reading specialist, a principal, or a Teacher. The position of round-table coordinator should not be given to a volunteer but should remain with teaching professionals, who must be extremely sensitive to the feelings and concerns of participating students.

Coordinators enjoy the opportunity to celebrate writing with students, as in this session: A third-grade girl had shared a beautifully written story about her dog, who had been lost. "I just *knew* I'd never see her again, but my mother kept saying, 'Don't give up! Don't give up!'" The girl told how, one night, she heard scratching at the door. She couldn't even bear to go to the door; her mother went and discovered her dog, cold and wet, shivering there. "That night, Cuddles slept with me, and I woke up over and over, just to make sure she was still, really, there with me."

All 19 round-table participants and I breathed big sighs of relief. Then, simply to reinforce the fact that true stories often are wonderful to write, I asked casually, "And was this real, Amy?" Bashful Amy, grinning from ear to ear, softly answered, "No, I made it up." The entire group pounced on her. "You fooled us!" "You tricked us!" Amy, that day, knew that she was a writer!

We do not invite parents to visit round tables: These are planned to be gatherings for students who share their writings with one another. They are not meant to be "recitals" for parents. Occasionally, however, a parent may stop in to listen. When that happens, we invite the parent to sit in back and observe. Parents always leave these gatherings pleased with what they have seen and heard.

Following is an example of the invitation we use for Writers' Round Tables. These are given to students two weeks in advance of the round-table gathering.

Writers' Round Table Invitation

TO_____

You are invited to be part of Writers' Round Table for the month

of_____.

Please write a story or a special piece (essay, poetry, etc.) to share at Writers' Round Table for this month. Give your final copy (your best work!) to your Teacher by _____ so copies can be made
                                    (DATE)

Writers' Round Table will meet on Friday, _____
                                                (DATE)

at _____ o'clock in _____.
   (TIME)   (PLACE)   (LOCATION)

_____, Coordinator

....
(PLEASE TEAR ON THIS LINE)

Yes, I will participate in the Writers' Round Table.

_____

(NAME)   (GRADE)   (TEACHER)

*Teachers, after your student has signed this, please give the bottom part to your round-table coordinator. Thank you!

Information letter to parents

So that parents will know what we are doing, we send the following information home with students in a school newsletter each fall:

Dear School Parents:
Once each month, the Writers' Round Table meets at Frog Mountain School. This is not a performance or recital, but an important sharing of one's best writing, student-to-student, so that children at all grade levels can hear what other students are thinking and writing.

Each month, a different student comes from each class, so that as many students as possible can participate in this experience. It has become a popular program among our young writers.

Very young students may ask their parents for help with the actual writing of their stories, but the stories are to be the students' own. We encourage students to share at home with their parents what they will bring to the round table. It is to reflect their best efforts, and invitations are issued early so they will have time to write a first draft, then a final copy so their finest work can be shared.

Our writers' round tables are guided by an experienced teacher who invites positive comments from the young writers after each reading. We are sensitive to the fragility of children, seeking to build their confidence in writing and in sharing aloud what they have created.

This month we are sending you several examples of pieces from last May's round table. Every piece of writing was good; it was difficult to choose those for printing here. We hope you enjoy them!

Cecily P. Baker, Principal

With each invitation sent to students in grades 1 through 3, we also send a note asking parents to give any needed help with the writing, informing them that this is not a classroom activity but a special enrichment experience that may need parental assistance. We found it necessary to do this so round tables do not add more work to teachers' heavy loads.

Helping students begin

Some of the most commonly heard words when students begin a writing assignment are: "I don't know what to write!" (Does this sound familiar?)

There are many ways to help students get into their writing; one is to have students brainstorm words in a list, headed under a particular category related to the writing assignment. For example: *Neighborhood* might be the category as students prepare to write about their own neighborhoods.

Under *Neighborhood*, students might write:

trees
houses
fences
dogs
kids
streets
sidewalks
my friend's house
my house
white with blue trim
black driveway
cars
horns
crunch on gravel
birds
etc.

Once the list is complete, students may go back and, using the words in the list, begin to write. This frees their creative minds to think quickly as they write impressions, just thoughts, that can be put together later into a complete piece of writing. When students have done "brainstorming" several times, it may, for many, become a tool they will use often for writing.

Horrid red pencils, ugly red pens!

Many of us remember laboring hard and long over papers that came back to us covered with red scribbles and scratches made by Teachers who thought they were teaching us to write. Not so. More often, they were teaching us to see red, to hate red, to put into us the fear of not pleasing them, of not getting "a good grade" in writing, of not being competent writers.

To this day, any editor who marks my manuscripts with red goes on my "hit list," and that editor probably will not see another of my pieces again.

Somehow, magically, those red marks were supposed to show us what we had done wrong, and to inspire us to "do better" the next time. I hate to think of the time spent and the red pencils used up by those seemingly well-intentioned Teachers.

Now we know better; we show students how to improve their writing—we teach them there is a *process* that will help them acquire the power that comes with the ability to write competently. We become not the Teacher on one side and the student on the other, but partners in working toward the same goal—the acquisition of writing power.

I never use red pens or pencils; that old dislike of them persists. And when it is necessary to write on a student's manuscript, I use soft greens and blues, "kinder" colors. I also am careful not to write on final copies, but to make my comments on separate sheets that I paper clip, not staple, to the students' manuscript.

Does this look familiar?   I WILL NOT HIT DAVID
                          I WILL NOT HIT DAVID
                          I WILL NOT HIT DAVID

(pow!)

It goes without saying that writing anything 100 times or more has absolutely no lasting effect on behavior. It can be done "on automatic," and sometimes we see students writing an entire list of "I" 100 times down one side of the paper and the other, then returning to write "will" next to every "I," returning to add "not," etc., etc. When we ask students to write, we ought also to be asking them to *think*. This kind of *punishment writing* does not encourage thinking! It does influence attitudes, however; it causes those on whom this punishment is inflicted to hate to write. For while we Teachers know better, many students will perceive this to be "writing" and may hate it for the rest of their lives.

If it is necessary to use written language as part of behavior modification, then it is more appropriate to have the student write about how he or she was feeling when the undesirable behavior occurred, how other students may have been affected by it, and what resulted. It can be a good tool for self-analysis; but please, please, don't insist that your students write "I will . . ." or "I will not . . ." over and over again. It is wasted, purposeless time and effort.

More reasons and ways to set the stage before writing

Before attending a play, which I do frequently, we often have dinner with friends, visiting and enjoying that special time and the feelings of festivity and preparation that, for us, accompany play-going times.

When we enter the theater, we find our places, look around to see all the others in attendance, observe wonderful and unusual dress, settle into our chairs, and read the play notes. Then, finally, we are ready to enjoy the presentation. The earlier preparations are an important, anticipatory part of the evening. It would not be nearly as satisfying to rush into the theatre, drop into our chairs, and have the curtain rise, the stage lights go on, and be pushed into the mood of the evening. The anticipation is important.

Sometimes students are turned off about writing because it is just plain hard work. Sometimes it seems to encompass too many skills at once. Often students who can't spell find it unpleasant. If students do not have enough information, if they don't understand the assignment, then we must explain again for them. There are many reasons that students can be turned off about writing. One of the key reasons is often that the Teacher isn't excited about it, either. If you were simply told, as many students are, to "Write about something that happened yesterday," or "Write about something that happened last summer," how excited would you be about your writing assignment? On the other hand, if your Teacher loves to write, if he takes time to set the stage for what you are about to write, and if he writes with you, he can turn you on to your writing assignment and you will have fun doing it together. You can do this for your students.

One way of setting the stage is by sharing an activity—for example, taking your class outside to sit on the grass and listen for awhile to the sounds around them. Another shared activity might be playing a softball game or taking a walk to a special place in your community. A film presentation and discussion may precede writing activity and "set the stage" effectively for the paperwork that follows.

An interesting picture can be the basis for setting the stage for writing. For example, a picture of small children singing, dancing or running might introduce a writing assignment about some favorite activity. A quiet picture—a grandmother reading to a small child, for example—might set the stage for children to write about favorite quiet times and places. Sometimes students can work in pairs or small groups, with one picture for each group to stimulate writing activity.

Another means of setting the stage for writing can be found in good, old-fashioned storytelling. Tell your students the beginning part of something that has happened to you, that you know will make a good story. Then stop and allow them to anticipate the ending. For example, driving through a small town in early spring several years go, I saw an entire block that was one big mud puddle. In the center of this huge puddle were two small girls, having the time of their lives, stamping and splashing, obviously not about to leave the source of their fun willingly. On the edge of the puddle stood their mother, a pregnant young woman, whose pleas to come out were being carefully, deliberately ignored. How was she to get these two imps out of their mud puddle? How would the story end?

Think of situations you might share with your students to set the stage for writing. Talk about what is happening and what might happen next; then let your students write. In this way, they learn about the the high point in a story; they learn how to reach that special point and how to find a satisfactory ending. Ask them to set the stage sometimes—they will enjoy doing this. Kids' ideas for stories can be wonderful. Be sure to let them choose their own ideas often; they like and need to do this. Here are some story ideas from young writers:

The two-ton rabbit
Girl who had three wishes, spent two, and saved one for the right time
Boy who wanted to be in space; his dad brought home a huge box that made him dream
Mysterious cave that sends one back in time
New boy in town, out for a walk, meets another boy: "Hello. I was looking for a friend."
Story of the missing moon (when the moon was new)—a boy sent a spaceship out to put a light on the moon!
New endings for fairy tales
Someone going back in time; every time she sensed herself beginning to fall, she knew she was going back in time.
Story of a girl who learned how to make stars to put out in space, because there weren't enough to please her!
Boy and his father fishing on a cold, blustery day: "Just the thought of the fish kept them warm!"
A turtle who wanted to fly—so Goose helped gather feathers, glued them on the turtle's shell

Boy who tore witches from construction paper; they flew on Halloween from
   California to Maine!
What does your pet do while you are gone?
The day I slew a dragon
You think you know what happened; well, that's not the way it was!
The story of Sojourner Truth and why she sang
The snowman in my freezer (he eats ice cubes and snowballs!)

Starter books

Our libraries are filled with wonderful starter books, books that carry a pattern, or
an idea, that children can quickly understand and use in their own writing. For
example, you might read Charlotte Zolotow's delightful *My Friend Jon* before students write about their own special friends. They will quickly grasp the book's
pattern and adapt it to their own writing. Starter books can be found mainly in the
primary section of the library but are useful for writers of all ages.

How to use a starter book

Teacher reads the book aloud to class.
   Read it again, immediately or later.
   Ask for discussion and suggestions from students about what they might write,
following the line of thought in the starter book. Allow time for students to share
ideas before making the writing assignment.
   Here is what one of my students wrote about himself and his best friend after
hearing *My Friend Jon:*

   My friend likes the school's food, but I hate it; I think it's mushy and gross.
      I collect teddy bears and stuffed animals, but he cuts out pictures of girls.
      I like kittens and my friend does, too, but he hates cats.
      He likes pizza and I like macaroni and cheese; friends don't have to like the same
   thing.
      My friend is afraid of big dogs like German shepherds, but he knows that I don't
   like scary movies.
      I like to draw things, but he likes making things out of clay, like animals and bugs.
      My friend sticks up for me, but I help him with schoolwork sometimes.
      I know where the cookies are in his house, and he knows where we keep ours.
      My friend knows I'm bugged when people say that I'm small, and when people
   call my friend "egghead," I know he doesn't like it.
      My friend knows that I like a girl in my class, but I know about his sixth-grade girl-
   friend, and so we don't tease each other.

My friend is afraid of the dark, but he knows I hate to be left alone in my house with nobody in it but my kitten. But we don't tell anybody else, because we would both get embarrassed.

We get in fights a lot and don't talk to each other for a long time. But good friends do that.—by Juan

Margaret Wise Brown's *The Important Book* is a wonderful first starter book. Read it to your class. Then allow students to share orally "the important thing" about some of *their* favorite things.

The writing assignment begins with each child in class choosing a different thing to describe. List them on the board so there is no duplication.

As they begin writing, tell them they must use at least three to five sentences.

Example

The important thing about school is that you learn there. You learn how to spell and read and you can get away from home for a little while. You can see your friends there. But the important thing about school is that you learn there.

When the assignment is completed, students may illustrate their final drafts. These can be put together into a wonderful class book. It can be the beginning of your own student-written book collection; students will love reading their own books, and parents will enjoy seeing the books at home or when they come to visit.

Another marvelously creative starter book is *The Mysteries of Harris Burdick* by Chris Van Allsburg; it is a book of captioned pictures that stimulate the imagination, and I highly recommend it.

Do You Know What I'll Do? is another wonderful starter book by Charlotte Zolotow. Children in my classes, after hearing it, wrote the following:

To My Sister: Do you know what I'll do? I'll save all the leaves in our yard for a week, and then I'll give them to you to jump in.

To My Dad: when you're gone jogging, I'll get a nice, ice-cool drink of water for you, and you'll be happy. And when you play our TV game and I'm waiting for my turn, if you get hit on space invaders, I'll let you start over. And you'll get a good score and you'll be glad.

Several years ago, I was teaching a class of Teachers about writing with students. I read them Charlotte Zolotow's *Janey*, a lovely book about the lonely feelings of a girl whose friend, Janey, has moved away. Following the reading, each of us wrote to our own "Janey," someone who had been special to us but from whom we were now separated in some way. Within seconds of beginning to write, there was no sound in the room but that of pencils and pens moving rapidly across papers. We wrote and wrote, each drawn into our own feeling-filled pieces, each remembering special things about our friends.

Then we shared. There were giggles and gasps as these adult writers shared delightful, touching, and lovely pieces. And then Mary asked to read what she had written. As she began to read, her eyes filled with tears. She smiled and stopped for a moment. "I want to read this," she said. "Please just wait." She had written to a friend known to the rest of us, a friend whose serious illness meant that she would not be coming back to teach again. Mary's piece began, "I remember how the first parking space in our school lot was always empty, and your little red car would be in the second space because you had saved the first space for me." Tears slid down the beautiful face of this caring friend as she finished reading. Then, as

I was about to thank her, she turned to me. "Thank you," she said. "Until I heard *Janey*, I didn't know that all of this was inside me."

Starter books can be used by everyone!

Some starter books to use for writing

- *Alexander and the Terrible, Horrible, No Good, Very Bad Day* by Judith Viorst
- *Alexander, Who Used to Be Rich Last Sunday* by Judith Viorst
- *A Boy, a Dog, and a Frog* by Mercer Mayer
- *Christmas Is a Time of Giving* by Joan Anglund
- *Crystal Is My Friend* by Shirley Gordon
- *The Day I Had to Play with My Sister* by Crosby Bonsall
- *The Fat Cat*, Danish Folk Tale
- *A Friend Is Someone Who Likes You* by Joan Anglund
- *Frog Goes to Dinner* by Mercer Mayer
- *Frog and Toad* by Arnold Lobel
- *Hailstones & Halibut Bones* by Mary O'Neill
- *Harry and the Terrible Whatzit* by Dick Gackenbach
- *If It Weren't for You* by Charlotte Zolotow
- *Imogene's Antlers* by David Small
- *The Important Book* by Margaret Wise Brown
- *Just Like Everyone Else* by Karla Kuskin
- *The King at the Door* by Brock Cole
- *My Daddy Don't Go to Work* by Madeena Nolan
- *My Friend Jon* by Charlotte Zolotow
- *Rabbit and Skunk and the Big Fight* by Carla Stevens
- *Rain Drop Splash* by Alvin Tresselt
- *Round Is a Pancake* by Joan Sullivan
- *Sand Castle* by Ronald Wegen
- *Someday* by Charlotte Zolotow
- *A Tree Is Nice* by Janice Udry
- *Where Does the Butterfly Go When It Rains?* by May Garelick

Watch for your own starter books by searching the shelves in the primary library section. You will find many there that can be special for your own class. Ask other Teachers to recommend starter books too.

6 Learning from One Another

Teachers and students often learn from one another. Luckily, Teachers often share what they've learned with me. One idea came from a Teacher in Foley, Minnesota. When her students write in their journals, she writes in hers, and she makes hers available to them to read whenever they wish. They are always eager to see if something has been written about them and to know how she "sees" her class and their activities. (She is definitely "writing for an audience" when she writes in her journal!)

And another one: A special Teacher friend of mine called one morning to exult in the birth of his first grandson and to share this idea. He has begun writing a book for the baby already! He has written of the waiting, the arrival, their first meeting, and so on, and will give the book to him when the grandson is old enough to understand how special it is. Students might be excited about doing a similar piece of writing when new babies join their families.

Obviously, there is no definitive word on teaching children to write; we only share, suggest, ask questions, and learn from one another. Use those good tools and techniques that you already have found to be effective for teaching written language. Then add those things that you feel will be helpful to you and your students. And know that, as you write with your students, you will learn from them, too.

Writing: Time and the process

Learning to write is a lifetime process. You *will* influence your students' feelings about written language. These are attitudes they may take with them through their entire lives. The acquiring and developing of writing skills is never completed. We continue to write, to learn and to grow.

Students need to know that they write first to please themselves. They are their own first audience. As we write with our students, we develop our writing skills too. Pleasure in our own writing becomes contagious; not only will our students feel it, but other Teachers too may catch our enthusiasm for writing.

In a Teachers' class I taught one year, there was a Teacher who had just changed from fifth grade to first grade. She was not sure that first-graders could write all the things we had been discussing; she listened intently and spoke of her doubts. "Oh, but they can do it!" said an enthusiastic kindergarten Teacher. She went on to tell the first-grade Teacher some specific things to do with her students, and as we all went out the door that evening, she said again, "Try it! You'll see! You'll see!"

The next week, the first-grade Teacher came to class bursting with excitement. "It worked! They really did write!" she exclaimed. We all smiled, happy for her discovery of what we already had learned. Her students now write daily, and she celebrates constantly with them the discoveries they find in their writing.

I spoke in another town several years ago, saying much of what is contained in this book. I had encouraged the Teachers to put some of their own writings in a folder with those of their students, all without names on them, to be "critiqued." Later, a Teacher who had been there saw me at another workshop. "Do you remember what you told us about putting our own manuscripts in with our students' papers?" he said. "I did that, and you should have seen what they did to mine—they just took it apart!" He was grinning as he spoke, and it was easy to see that he had enjoyed writing with his students, being a part of what they were doing.

To write competently is to have power

It is a terrible thing to feel powerless. Children, I think, experience this feeling often. We experience it as adults also. One way of having power is to become competent in written language. When I want to say something on paper, to make changes, to make my feelings about certain issues known, I write to company presidents, legislators, senators, and the president. They nearly always respond with letters and sometimes with action. Not long ago I received a beautiful new bag sent in response to my complimentary letter written to the manufacturer of my favorite brand of bedroom slippers. A few years ago I wrote to the employer of a young man, who cheerfully and efficiently repaired our dryer, to say how helpful he had been. The employer wrote back to say such letters meant something special at his company and were always posted on the bulletin board; special awards were given to those whose work merited complimentary letters from customers.

Many years ago, when our children were small, we were traveling through California when a part from our brand-new car flew out from under the hood and rolled across the freeway. Thankfully, my husband was able to steer our car safely to the side of the road where we sat until a highway patrol car came by to rescue us. The car was towed and repaired, and we were able to continue our vacation. Upon our return home, we wrote to the president of the company that had manufactured our car, saying that we did not want our car repaired; we wanted it *replaced*. By this time, several other minor incidents had occurred with the car, and we no longer felt safe in it. We wrote politely, clearly and firmly. In just a short time, a representative from that company came to visit us and, within several weeks, we had a new car.

In other incidents, defective toys purchased for our children and unsafe foods (items with strange "ingredients" that appeared unexpectedly in the containers) were replaced, free of charge, accompanied by free gifts and coupons.

A letter to a restaurant owner following a most unpleasant incident in which a waiter rudely refused to seat us because it was "in between breakfast and lunch time," though we could see people seated and eating at nearly all of the tables, resulted in a profuse apology and the gift of a free dinner for two—and the assurance by the owner that she did not intend to have her employees treat customers in that way.

A few years ago, I purchased an expensive camera for my husband. We used it occasionally and were pleased with its performance. But within a few months, the button no longer activated the shutter. We returned it to the store where it had been purchased and were told that it needed to be sent in for an estimate. That estimate was $76! (The clerk indicated that she felt we'd be better off purchasing a new camera!) We asked that it not be repaired, writing instead to the manager of customer service at the company's headquarters. We described what had happened, indicating that our thirty-year-old box camera still took marvelous pictures and that if this company's advertising meant anything, it would stand behind its product and either repair or replace it free of charge. Customer service replied, telling us to send in the camera. Within two weeks, it was returned to us, repaired and as good as new, free of charge. For the time it took to write a letter, we saved $76! Writing competency is power!

Many of our friends and acquaintances have had similar experiences, but most of them do not feel capable of writing letters of complaint. They keep the defective merchandise, upset with the product and the company, frustrated that they have no recourse or means of obtaining satisfaction. They do not, they say, "know how to write that kind of thing."

The ability to write competently provides power that has brought a street light to illuminate our previously dark neighborhood. It helped bring citizenship to a friend immigrating to the United States, and it has changed the lives of our family members in many satisfying ways.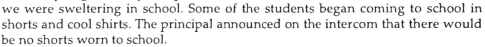

And consider how powerful my students felt several years ago. Late spring brought unusually high, steady temperatures, and we were sweltering in school. Some of the students began coming to school in shorts and cool shirts. The principal announced on the intercom that there would be no shorts worn to school.

My fourth-grade students' moans and groans quieted and their eyes began to twinkle when I quickly presented a lesson on how to write a petition. A simple, clear petition to allow knee-length shorts was circulated through the classes, and a group of students politely presented it, signed by several hundred students, to our principal. He, a fair and approachable individual, called a meeting the next morning, inviting one representative from each class. Following the meeting, students emerged triumphant: Their petition had worked! Knee-length shorts and cool summer shirts were now the order of the day during hot weather.

We educators also need to value writing as still more than opportunity for self-expression, creativity, communication. We must view composition and the composing process as a method for learning and as a resource that makes our students strong, meets their learning needs, and gives them power. Then writing will become a natural part of what goes on in the classroom, a competency that includes all areas of study, a craft with which they feel comfortable. It should not be reserved only for major projects. My own style of learning relates directly to writing; if I just listen to a Teacher, a speaker, I will retain but a small portion of what I hear. But if I write down some notes to jog my memory later, I will be able to rebuild mentally nearly all of what has been said. My learning style involves my hands, my head, the entire process of writing, thinking, then putting information into my own words.

Proofreading
The piece *Mirror, Mirror on the Wall* (p. 65) shows a first draft, including corrections and changes, and the second, final draft, written to hand in as a completed piece.

Teach your students to proofread
Proofreading is a skill that must be learned. It does not come naturally. Students learn the skills of good writing by writing, supported by reading and listening. They must develop an ear for language to proofread effectively. They also must learn the rules for good writing as they work through the process of developing competency in written language. All these things will allow students to proofread and to write in ways that are useful and satisfying to them and to their Teachers.

Proofreading is a critical skill that determines the quality of the final product. Therefore, it must be taught well, and the Teacher must present it as a positive step in writing a final product of high quality. We cannot hope that students will simply pick up the ability to proofread; we must teach them.

Proofreading generally takes place after writing a first draft, but it also must be part of the writing; that is, students must, as they write, go back to earlier parts of the writing piece to consider what has been produced already.

Teachers should insist on students' proofreading aloud. In this way, they will be more likely to hear what they actually wrote; in reading silently, they often read what they *thought* they wrote.

Proofreading is most useful and instructive when it is mainly the students' responsibility. If Teachers introduce the concept and instruction for proofreading at the beginning of the year and continue to encourage and instruct students in the process of proofreading throughout the year, that desired outcome can happen. I myself do not remember ever being shown how to proofread; how much easier it would have been for me to learn had I actually seen the process taking place.

Some students will find it helpful to proofread in two steps, reading first for language and flow, then a second time for mechanics—capitalization, punctuation, grammar, and so on.

It may be helpful to have students proofread in pairs or in small groups. Exchanging papers with other students and hearing them read aloud the writer's work may be helpful; a writer may hear where editing changes might improve the piece. When this is done, students are encouraged to make positive suggestions and comments to one another. The Teacher is responsible for setting a positive and encouraging classroom tone that allows students to help and learn from one another.

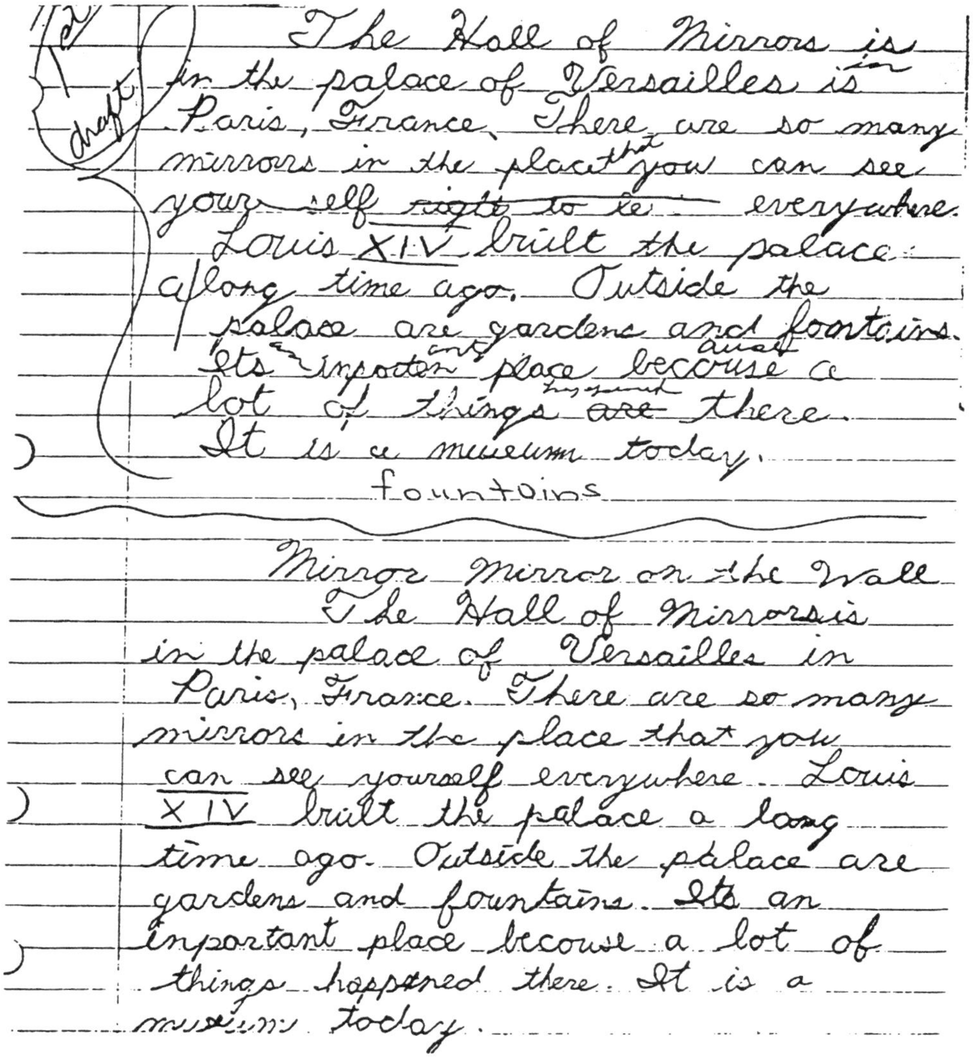

[Handwritten draft:]

The Hall of Mirrors is in the palace of Versailles in Paris, France. There are so many mirrors in the place that you can see yourself everywhere. Louis XIV built the palace a long time ago. Outside the palace are gardens and fountains. Its an important place because a lot of things happened there. It is a museum today.

fountains

[Handwritten revision:]

Mirror Mirror on the Wall

The Hall of Mirrors is in the palace of Versailles in Paris, France. There are so many mirrors in the place that you can see yourself everywhere. Louis XIV built the palace a long time ago. Outside the palace are gardens and fountains. Its an important place because a lot of things happened there. It is a museum today.

Students may find it useful, once a completed first draft has been proofread, to put it away for a day or two. A second proofreading done later may give the writer a fresh and new perspective that allows for some better and different ideas to enter the writing.

If students skip lines as they write first drafts, there will be room between lines to make changes.

Encourage students to cross out mistakes with a single line rather than to erase; it saves time and allows them to see, when they proofread, whether their changes are desirable.One first-grade Teacher cuts the erasers off all the pencils in her room so students understand it is all right to make mistakes, to cross out, and to revise as they write!

You may wish to make a copy of the following information for each of your students. It is also found in the "Handouts" section of this book.

Proofreading Information
1. Does each sentence make sense? Does it sound right? (Proofread aloud.)
2. Did I use descriptive words and phrases to make my writing "come alive"?
3. Are there vague parts of my piece that could or should be left out or clarified?
4. Have I capitalized where necessary?
5. Have I spelled correctly to the best of my knowledge?
6. Is punctuation correct?
7. Will my readers understand what I am saying?
8. If I used dialogue, is it clear who is speaking?
9. Have I chosen a good title? (Titles often are easier to choose after the story is written, and a listening partner may have title ideas.)
10. Is this the best writing I can do right now?

If appropriate, encourage students to look for these things as they proofread:

Are your paragraphs full of many short sentences? A combination of short and long sentences is most interesting to read, but if you have used too many short sentences, combine some of them into longer sentences. Leave out unnecessary words. Expand some sentences and make them more interesting wherever you can by using good description.

There is a tree by our house. It is big. It is beautiful. It is my favorite tree.

Rewrite:

The big, beautiful evergreen tree near our house is my favorite.

Have you answered questions that your readers might ask as they read? Ask yourself if you have answered: *how, why, where, when,* and *under what conditions did actions take place?*

Have you used the same words over and over? This kind of writing becomes tiresome for readers. Get out the thesaurus and find synonyms, other words, that mean the same thing. Use these to add variety and interest to your writing.

Have you used run-on sentences? These often are connected by *and, then, but,* and other words that allow sentences to become too long and uninteresting. Listen as you proofread aloud, and where you hear a period or another ending punctuation mark, *make* one. Then start a new sentence.

Remember: We are working at the *process* of writing. As practice in the process continues, the product will improve.

Proofreading: Part of the process

Changing and correcting papers are important steps in the writing process. Another way to reinforce the learning of these techniques is to print ten or twelve "spelling sentences" for the week, containing students' own errors, on handouts. The class is challenged to find and correct each error. They enjoy this, treating it like a puzzle, and they like seeing their own sentences used in a class project.

Students are to find errors and write these sentences correctly. Can you find the mistakes? Look carefully! This ( ) indicates number of errors that students must find.

1. Aren't you comeing mary. (4)
2. he's a nice guy (2)
3. I'm am going to. (3)
4. Is you'er name Tom? (1)
5. I'll rakeing up the leafs. (2)
6. I can't sleep over tonight I'm sorry Amy. (2)
7. you'll Have to eat now jenny. (4)
8. Do you no Greg in my class he's nice. (3)

There is a wonderful tool to assist with proofreading called the Daily Oral Language (DOL) Program published by McDougal, Littell and Company. This is a set of Teachers' guides from grades 1 through 12. Two incorrectly composed sentences from the guide are put on the chalkboard each day. Orally, the class finds and corrects the errors. In this way, they *see* and *hear* the corrections being made. Time for this program is just five to ten minutes daily. Conversations with Teachers who use DOL indicate that it is popular and successful with both students and Teachers. The program is not expensive and requires only a teacher's manual for each Teacher. DOL books can be ordered by writing Daily Oral Language, McDougal, Littell, P.O. Box 1667, Evanston, IL 60204. Many Teachers begin the day with DOL.

What do we do with students' papers?

Some of these papers can be used as gifts for family and friends; others may be pieces students will want to keep as their own. They will appreciate your care of their hard work. Display their writing: You might layer one copy on top of another until a student has several sheets—a collection of his or her own writing on the bulletin board. Perhaps you will help your students put their writings into book form, making covers and binding them together into something permanent.

Let them know in this way that their work is valuable and that they can be proud of it. Let them know that you are proud of it too. Several years ago I worked with a class of fifth-graders writing descriptions of their favorite places. One boy wrote of visiting his grandmother's farm, where he spent one special week each summer. He wrote of waking in the single upstairs bedroom and peering out across the farmland, of seeing deer walking through the trees, of listening from the window to the sweet birdsongs. When he finished reading his beautiful, sensitive piece to the class, I suggested that he give it to his grandmother as a gift. He smiled and looked down at his desk, a bit embarrassed. A week later as I walked through the halls of his school, I was stopped by a smiling boy.

"Do you remember me? I'm the one who wrote about my grandma's house, and you told me to give that piece to her. Well, I did, and she really liked it."

"How could you tell?" I asked.

"She cried," he said simply, grinning from ear to ear.

In our family, my children know I mean it when, responding to their queries of "What do you want for your birthday?" I answer, "Just write something for me, please." To this day, I continue to receive stories and poems from our children, now grown; they understand that I consider these treasures to be more wonderful and precious than anything money can buy. A few years ago, I wrote a poem for each of our children as my gift to them on my own birthday. And a gift to each family member from me one December was a forty-page, spiral-bound book of family memories that I had written over the years. Money is not a necessary commodity in giving gifts. And now among my special gifts are love notes written by our two small grandsons.

One Teacher friend has her students write a short composition on the first day of school and another one a few months later; she keeps them, uncorrected, and gives them back on the last day of school. Her students are always proud to see how their writing skills have developed.

Ideas! Ideas! Ideas!

It is useful for students to keep "idea banks" for ideas that that will be used later. Often when students are writing, new ideas come and students are tempted to stop in the middle of one piece to start work on another. Tell them that they can safely tuck away the new ideas by writing them on their idea list, then go back to their present writing. The new ideas will then be waiting for future use. It is not unusual to see the idea sheets of some first- and second-graders with whom I write covered with thirty or forty "new ideas" that they will sometime use for writing! You may wish to provide folders for these sheets. (See the idea sheets in the Reproducible section.)

How often should you teach writing?

Almost anything that happens, any idea or experience, can become material for writing. Writing should be taught as a thinking and learning activity inseparable from other learning activities in the school experience. We hear more calls now for cross-curriculum writing—that is, including written language as a learning activity in social studies, mathematics, physical education, music, and art. Creative Teachers find ways to incorporate written language into learning in all these areas.

Another way we can help our students learn to write competently is by using essay questions as often as possible. Even in the lower grades, one or two essay questions, which require students to put their knowledge into their own words and on paper, will help them learn the process of thinking and writing.

When our son entered junior high school, he was blessed with a Teacher who required her students to do a great deal of thinking and learning, reflected in essay writing. The next year, entering eighth grade, he came home from school shortly after the semester began, to comment gratefully, "Mrs. P. *said* that some day we'd be glad she made us learn to write all those essay questions; I just didn't think it would be this soon!" He was one of the fortunate students who had been well prepared by this fine Teacher for the more difficult work expected of students in higher grades. Many other students in his class had not experienced much essay-style writing, and our son found his background to be a distinct advantage.

As columnist William Raspberry said some time ago in the *Washington Post:* "No child can be taught to think as well as he or she otherwise might if his homework consists primarily of filling in blanks on a ditto sheet. He may get all the answers right, simply by scanning the assigned reading, without ever having the material engage his brain. The cheap, unscientific, but logical alternative is to assign the passage and require the student to summarize it in his own words. Do that consistently, and he will not only learn to write a lot better; he will learn also to analyze, evaluate, sort out, and synthesize information."

A handout I call "In your own words" provides a simple way for you to encourage your students to think and write.

Each week (or more often) write a paragraph or two on one side of a paper as shown. Students are to read the information silently, then read it aloud, talk it over with someone, and, finally, write it in their own words on the blank side. Some

Teachers have students fold back the printed part as they write; others have them cut or tear it off and throw it. That really isn't necessary: they are to think and then write it *in their own words*. It is a useful tool; the world needs people who can think and can translate information into their own understanding. Frequent use of this assignment will help students become more competent in thinking and writing down information.

The blank paper, "From the book/In your own words," is provided for you in the Reproducible sections. Run off thirty to forty of these pages at the beginning of the school year, then add your own paragraphs from books, magazines, and other written materials each week for students' use.

In Your Own Words

The next time you take a walk in the woods and think you're alone, take another look. You might be staring right into the face of a frog or a grasshopper and never know it! That's because some frogs, grasshoppers, and other creatures look like leaves. Sometimes a leaf disguise fools enemies. Sometimes it hides small animals while they wait to catch even smaller creatures. Leaf look-alikes come in many colors and shapes. Insects that spend most of their time in trees may have skin the color of fresh, green leaves. Creatures that feed near the ground, where leaves often look dry and faded, may have spotted or yellowish bodies. And ground-dwelling creatures sometimes have brown skin the color of fallen leaves. Shape can be as important as color to a success-ful disappearing act. Many butterflies and moths have leaf-shaped wings. Some grasshoppers look like small branches. And the long, thin wingless creature called a stick insect has a body that looks like a twig. Animals that hide in leaves usually mimic leaves. They stay very still.*

When should students begin to write?

A principal once told me, "We know that kindergarten and first-graders can't really write, so we don't need to spend much time with them on written lan-guage." I spoke with several kindergarten and first-grade Teachers in that school, and their students soon proved him wrong! He was invited to come and listen to

*Reprinted with permission from WORLD magazine.

what they had written and to watch them in the process of writing wonderful pieces. Later, he became one of the strongest supporters in his district of providing all students with opportunities to write.

Kindergarten is where students begin to learn what a marvelous thing is the written word. Here, they discover the relationship between the written and the spoken word, and between reading and writing.

If you teach kindergarten, as you plan the free times in your days, please include a writing table. Equip it with notebooks, pictures, pencils, crayons, and writing paper. Some children may play with blocks; some may paint or choose games to play. But there will be children who choose to write. In one school where I recommended writing centers for kindergartners, I returned a week later to find that the kindergarten Teachers had immediately set up writing centers. Their students loved to write, and the Teachers had been forced to make lists so all students would have turns using the writing centers. One student had left school in tears the day before I returned, because, he said, "I *finally* got here" (to the writing center) "and now it's time to go *home!*"

I visited a wonderful first grade where the Teacher had converted a big refrigerator box into a marvelous writing study. It had curtained windows, a plant, books, paper, crayons, pencils, one desk, and a chair. The battery-operated lamp was the final touch! Posted outside the door was a large chart on which students signed up to occupy the study for twenty-minute periods.

The power begins

During their first two to three years of life, children perform perhaps the most fantastic intellectual feat of their lives—the acquisition of language. We begin to communicate with them from the time of birth; quickly, their communication with us moves from cries and facial expressions to sounds, then to words and sentences. We happily encourage this babbling, this "playing" with language.

Sometime during that period, they may begin to make marks on paper (or on the walls!) with crayons or pencils. That is communication, too, because they intend these marks to mean something, just as we have shown them that these marks have meaning in books and letters, on signs, in newspapers, and so on. When we take small children to a restaurant, we often give them a piece of paper and a pencil. We show them how to make X's and O's, telling them that an X means a kiss, an O a hug. Many papers have been filled with X's and O's while hungry young diners wait for their dinners to arrive! In this way, we teach them to communicate on paper. They begin to create their own kind of written language, drawing pictures, copying letters that we have indicated to them mean something. And they want those mixed-up, scrawly letters to mean something. They have begun doing something new and exciting: communicating with *written language*. For the first time, they are discovering the exciting, motivating sense of power that comes with being able to communicate in writing.

As educators, we have unique opportunities to encourage that beginning, just as we encourage early speech. We can tell parents to write notes to their small children. Suggest that they leave surprise notes on pillows; children may respond by doing the same. (I have quite a collection from my own children, written when they were small!) Notes in children's lunch bags are fun; my own children always knew that with their lunch would be a special love note from me. Teachers too can write notes to students. As a regular classroom Teacher, I always have written notes to two or three students daily, tucking them into the students' desks where they will see them as they enter our classroom in the morning. Over a period of several weeks, I write a note to every student, then start around the class again.

Writing can be fun

With your students, create a time capsule at the beginning of the school year, writing together about what is currently happening and some predictions for what might happen during the year. These can be read on the last day of school. Some Teachers have their students write predictions for themselves, promising to mail these back to them in five years.

I believe that every child has something to say—*every child*. That may mean that Teachers become secretaries for some students, that we sit with a student and write the words for her or him until the child is able to do it. One of my second-grade students was having a hard time with the physical part of writing, as his motor skills were not well developed and his mind moved more quickly than his hand could write. I quietly took his pencil and wrote what he told me to say. He never even noticed that I was now doing the writing. He eagerly told his story, as I wrote it, all the way to the end. Then, grinning through gaps left by missing teeth, he reread what he had "written." Several years later, his mother reminded me of how "the two of you used to write Tim's stories and he thought he did it all himself. Every time he came home with a new story, we all listened to him read it, and it was an exciting, wonderful part of that year of school for him."

Very young children may begin by writing "All About" papers—what they know about dogs, teddy bears, and cats—and what they know about themselves. They write all about going to bed, running, skipping, jumping, walking under an umbrella, eating peanut butter sandwiches, or making their beds.

We work from concrete to abstract, and it often helps students to have something to hold, touch, and see as they begin to write. We can begin with simple things: "Look at your shoes; I'll bet they're special to you. Are they old? New? Take them off and look carefully at them. Now write about them. Make a picture of them with words."

You might tell your students that they must use two colors as they write about something, or that they must talk about a size as they describe. This is how we can help them to make "word pictures."

Short, short stories!

What do you do with a student who writes a "story" like this?

> One day I went fishing. It was fun.
> I caught a fish.
> My mother cooked it.
> We ate it. It was good.

I would tell this young writer that only *part* of a picture has been painted, not a whole picture. I want to know what kind of day it was, where he or she went, who else went, how they got there—did they drive, walk, fly? What time of year was it? What do you mean, it was fun? Why was it fun? What kind of fish did you catch? Was it big? Small? What colors were on the fish? How did it feel to catch your own fish? Do you want to do it again? Did anyone help you? What kind of bait did you use? How did your mother cook it? Did she cook it at the lake or at home? How did it smell while she was cooking it? What do you mean when you say it was good?

When our students write short stories, we can encourage them to write more by asking questions...the "good old" *who, what, when, where,* and *why* questions, and the how did it *feel, smell, taste, look,* and *sound* questions. When students use their senses, when they answer questions, then they are working toward making a complete picture that readers can "see."

Painting with words, from simple to special

One way to help our students "paint with words," a term I like to use with written language, is to teach them how to take something from simple to special. They need to know how to describe just one thing well before they can tell about many things. Bring a lemon to class. How does it taste? feel? sound? smell? look? Bring some potato chips, a flower, an orange, or an apple. Describe it in exquisite detail, making it real. Peel the orange, the lemon; let the class smell it, use their senses.

The following was written by Diana, a fifth-grade student, when she was asked to take the word *dog* from simple to special. (Watch for the wonderfully descriptive words she used!)

> This dog is a raggy, shaggy, beat-up old street dog. He has no name and he lives in an alley. His bed is a musty cardboard box and he has a ripped-up old blanket he won in a dog fight. He is very tough and he lives a dangerous life, dodging cars and dog catchers. He has no collar and he has to scrounge for his food. Fortunately, though, he lives by a bakery and he can get scraps of stale bread when they throw it out. He has a limpy tail that looks like a bent hanger, and his ears sag just like socks. His fur looks like a buffalo's fur when they shed. He is considered KING OF THE DOGS because he is the largest, strongest, and the bravest of them all. He does not live what most dogs think is a happy life, but he likes the way he lives in the big, big city.

Diana has created a dog that is special. She has made us see her "raggy, shaggy, beat-up old street dog." You will find this an effective writing assignment for your students. One Teacher, upon trying this assignment with his sixth-graders, said he had students write who had never written before in his class. At any grade level, this can be an effective and useful writing exercise. Have students tell all they can about just one subject—take something from simple to special (a door, a window, a chair). They will use colors, shapes, actions, and sounds to make their objects *real.*

Talk with your students: Why do we write?

Scarcely a week goes by without finding a newspaper article bemoaning the fact that writing skills in our schools and in our adult population are deteriorating. Employers are hiring consultants to teach employees to write. College Teachers inherit students who have had little experience with putting thoughts into order and onto paper. Many adults cannot write a clear, cohesive paragraph, using correct punctuation or spelling. As students, many of these individuals thought they were "getting away with something" when Teachers allowed them to write whatever they wished with no discipline. At a younger age, many delighted in having those Teachers whose classes were easy, "a breeze." As a result, we now see a move back to teaching written language, and the process method fills this need. Many adults, in fact, now want to sharpen their writing skills, and weekend seminars and evening adult classes in written language are extremely popular.

Along with the emphasis on written language in our classrooms, we need to talk with our students about *why* we write. We are teaching a lifetime skill; they need to learn why it is necessary to know how to put words on paper. Have your students talk with their own parents about the importance of being able to write competently and about how they use written language in their own lives. You might bring adult guests into your classroom and have them speak with your students about the importance of writing skills in their various fields of work.

As we do all these things and as we seek to have our students take as much responsibility as they are able to handle for their own work, we can ask them whose name they put on their papers—it is not the teacher's name; it is their own. They are not writing for a Teacher. Teachers know how to write. Students are learning for themselves. It is their own ability they need to develop. As a Teacher you can tell your students, "I will help you, but you are writing for yourself, not for me. Long after you leave this classroom, you will need to know how to write on your own. This is why we are working here now—so you will know for yourself how to write competently."

From the writers

I've been doing small surveys, asking people I meet and people I know about their writing abilities. People tell me many reasons for their ability to write competently, if that is the case; some people give me four or five reasons, but among them are *always* these two: at some point in their education, a Teacher (or Teachers) required that they do a lot of writing; and, at some point, they learned the rules of writing. Interestingly, most tell me that it was in eighth or ninth grade that these rules all came together and began to make sense to them. Several years ago, I was visiting with a school administrator as we walked down the halls of his building. "Something exciting happened to me this week," he said. "I finally learned the rule for correct use of the subjunctive!" I smiled. "I always used it correctly," he continued, "because I read and listened well, but I never understood it until this week!"

Something else I've discovered in my surveys is that those people who feel they write well generally like to write: they've discovered exciting things can happen with written words. Words used well together in stories and verse can make people laugh, cry and feel deeply. Consider how the diary of a young girl, Anne Frank, has affected people throughout the world. Think of other books—*Charlotte's Web* and *Where the Red Fern Grows*—and how people of all ages everywhere love these stories. Children too can write things that move us to feel deeply.

A third-grader named Laura wrote of what had happened to her the day before writing this piece (printed here exactly as she wrote it):

I thought today was just another Friday but boy was I wrong. My name is Sara and I'm nine. School was normal we had math and reading but when I got home with Joanna, Mother was crying very hard. We asked her what was wrong, millions of horrible things flashed through my mind. She told us our nine-year-old cat that was older then me had died, while we were gone. I felt a huge lump in my throat then broke out in a loud cry. I ran in my room and cried, and cried and cried. I jumped down from my bed my lips quivered furiously, I flashed my sparkling light on and off.

I started to think about my cat and how she went crazy over her catnip ball, she acted just like a kitten and how she shook when we tok her to the vet and found out she was blind and how she clung to my mother on the way out. But all never forget how she laid on my bed just last night. I had no idea this would be the very last night

with her. Then mom called for dinner. As I walked out of the room I thought that maybe she could see us now.

Laura was able to say well in writing what she never could have said aloud to her class.

Several years ago, Kelly, a former student, sent me an envelope containing her first efforts at poetry. Observe the concerns she expressed in this unique way:

Dear Mrs. B,

I've been thinking about what you said about writing poems and things and I've been working on a couple about nuclear waste and all the wars and just wishing they didn't or won't happen. Well, here they are:

A light breeze whistling through the trees
The pines singing to you
Hearing the creek rush over the rocks
Hearing the peaceful sound of a bird's cry
Knowing that you're safe
Knowing that you're still here
Knowing that you're alive

Here's the next one:

Just think of all the wonderful things
God put on this earth
Now think about all of it may not be
Here by the time you're done reading this
Poem
Just think of all the trees and birds how
Come man can be like that?

Competency in written language: Could anyone say it better?

Writing talk

A good way to begin a discussion about writing is simply to ask your students how many of them know how to ride a bike. "How did you do the first time you rode that bicycle?" (Many will want to share their "accident" stories!) "How did you get better?" (Practice, of course!) " Do any of you play an instrument? A sport? Are you better now than when you began?" The more we do something, the better we can become at it. They need to be encouraged to *practice* their writing.

Teachers must give students the opportunity to write constantly so they will become better at doing it. It is much easier for us to teach them now than for them to require help with writing in college or as adults.

Clustering: A good beginning

We need to give our students all the tools we can to help them become competent with written language. One tool I like to use is cluster writing, descriptions of which now can be found in many places. In her useful, practical book, *Writing the Natural Way*, Gabrielle Rico teaches the clustering method. Based on right/left-brain information, she shows how clustering out from a center circle allows the right, creative side of the brain to quickly put down groups of related words that can be used as a base for a piece of writing. I have found clustering to be useful even for young writers; circles are different from other writing they have done.

Working with young writers, we begin this way: I ask them to go out in their yards (or in the schoolyard) and look at what there is to see. When they go back inside, they are to write *My yard* (or *Our schoolyard*) in a circle in the middle of their papers, then cluster around the circle all the things they saw and remember.

For example:

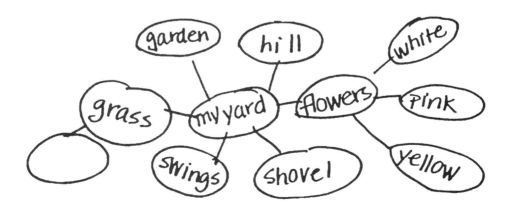

When students have finished clustering, I ask them to write some sentences about their yards, using the words in the clusters. They may wish to cross out the words in their clusters as they use them up.

Another use of clustering is the following: tell students to think what it might be like to be a bee, an ant, a ladybug, a hummingbird—something small. In the middle of a cluster, write *small*. Inside circles around *small*, ask them to write *birdbath, boy, frog,* and *lawnmower*. Leave empty places for them to insert their own ideas.

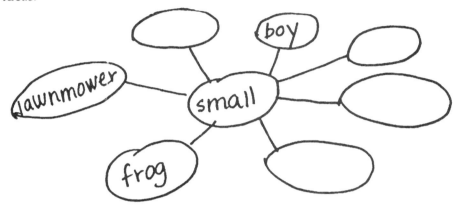

Students will use their clusters to write "If I were very small . . ."

They might begin: "If I were a ladybug a birdbath would look like a big bath tub. A lawnmower would be a very loud and scary thing to me. A boy would look like a giant!"

Ask them to think:

Where would you live?
What would you eat?
What might frighten you?
What would you like best to do?

Ask students to cluster the word *friends,* going out in all directions with thoughts about their friends, what they do together, why they like one another, and so on. Let them do this one on their own. Again, they may write a paragraph or two, using the cluster.

Some of my fifth- and sixth-grade writing students tell me they enjoy clustering, then using the clusters in their writing. Others do not care for clustering, preferring to get right into writing their paragraphs, while "brainstorming" is more useful to other writers. Be flexible; be sure all of your students try these techniques, then let them choose what works best for them.

When students are busy writing, it's nice for them to know when they finish, they will have a piece, perhaps a book, that looks attractive. In your writing center, provide materials for covers and illustrations—yarn, string, plastic or metal rings ("chicken rings" from farmers' cooperatives work well for binding books together), a paper punch, scissors, paste, crayons, markers, colored pencils, paints, chalk, charcoal, fingerpaint, various kinds of writing paper, construction paper, wallpaper pieces, and cardboard cut to book-cover size, clipboards, stickers and any other supplies your young writers can use. Ask your librarian for old photographs, books, and magazines that can be cut up and used for illustrating, too.

If your school has a laminating machine, it can be used to make a long-lasting, permanent cover for writing projects. Laminated covers will be protected from tears and wrinkles, and will be waterproof and washable. You might ask volunteer parents to laminate; they will be happy to help publish students' writings.

A writer's bag

Make a large cloth drawstring bag that can be filled with many of the above items. This is a writers' bag, made to be checked out by a student on Monday, to be used during the week to write and illustrate a special, independent piece. On Friday, the student returns the bag and shares the finished product with the class. (They may show both a first draft and published draft to demonstrate their work.) Some Teachers provide three or four writing bags for their students to use. In some schools, they are made in school colors, with the words WRITER'S BAG attached with iron-on material or stitched-on fabric. Students love to carry these home. These are popular and well-used items!

Using games to teach writing

Choose something in your classroom and write three sentences about it on the chalkboard. Do not tell what item you have chosen. Describe it by color, use, location, size, and other details. Have students watch you write. Then call on someone to name the object.

Example

On my desk is something big and red and round. It is something students sometimes give to teachers. When I get hungry, I will eat it!

Choose a student to do the same, either orally or in writing on the board.

Give each student a piece of paper on which is written a noun or you may read from a list, giving each a different topic. Ask each student to describe by color, shape, size, location and other identifiers. Students write, then share and guess what the objects are. The student who guesses correctly shares next.

Another day, assign the writing of a descriptive paragraph about something in your room or school. Encourage students to select something they think no one else will choose. They will see that they need to write about the most important features of the item they choose to describe. Again, classmates guess what has been described.

More painting with words

Students will understand the concept of "painting with words" when you write on the board a description of something at your own house that your students have not seen. Example: Something soft and furry lives at my house. It is small and black. It talks to me in a special purr-and-meow language. It sleeps on my bed. Can you guess it?

Again, the first to guess correctly "paints" the next "picture" with words, describing something at her or his house.

The writing assignment will be to describe something at home in terms of shape, size, texture, color, use, and other details. Remind students that everything the others learn about the object will come from word pictures they make. Upon completion of the assignment, allow students to share and guess.

Lost! And found!

Do you ever lose things? Glasses, wallets, pets, shoes? Everyone knows that awful feeling of losing something special.

This assignment begins with a discussion of ways to recover something that has

been lost. Students will be eager to share their experiences. As you visit, tell students that one way to recover something lost is to write an advertisement for it. Show them a lost-and-found column from a newspaper. Read aloud some of the notices.

Now tell the students to think of something in their own classroom that might be lost, and ask them to list important words that could go into a sign or advertisement in a lost-and-found column.

Their assignment will be to choose an object about which to write a newspaper ad. Remind them to mention specific details that would distinguish their lost item from someone else's.

When this assignment is completed, the "ads" should be displayed. For example:

LOST: SMALL GREEN ELEPHANT. CURLY TAIL.
HAS BLUE EYES. ANSWERS TO "FREDDIE."
REWARD OFFERED. CALL 499-0764.

Next, students will write advertisements describing something they have *found*.

Scary, hairy monster tales!

Tell your students: "One dark, rainy night while I was reading in my cozy chair, I heard a loud knock at my door. I opened it, and there stood a . . . monster!" (Or you might read a monster book first, like *Harry and the Terrible Whatzit* by Dick Gackenback.)

When you have your students' attention with this introduction, begin to write on the board as you create your own monster.

Was he hairy? scary? fuzzy? soft? brown? blue?
Were his feet gigantic? tiny? monstrous? orange?
Was he funny? frightening? lost? sad? friendly?

Tell your students, "But something was wrong—what could it be?" Solicit their suggestions. (Maybe he had no friends. Maybe he was lost.) Describe this as his *problem*. Tell them that a problem in a story usually leads to a "bump" in a story where something exciting, scary, sad, or funny happens. Usually, that is the part where, when telling about a favorite story, we say it was the *best* part, the *scariest* part, the *saddest* part, or the *funniest* part. Children understand the concept of a "bump" in a story: One first-grader read her story aloud, and we listened. Nothing really happened in it, even though it sounded like something *might* happen. One of her young listeners commented sagely, "I'd say that you're 'halfway up the hill' but you haven't got a bump yet!"

Another student read his story to the class, then observed himself that his story wasn't very exciting yet—but he would work on it. When I returned to his class the following day, he rushed up to me and said, "Yesterday my story just had a little *hill* in it. Today it's got a MOUNTAIN!"

Create a satisfying ending for your story. Then encourage the students to write their own monster stories. Remind them to create good word pictures of their monsters, to put bumps in their stories, to write stories they themselves will enjoy reading. Later they can illustrate their stories.

Here are some questions students might think about as they create their monsters:

What does he like to eat?
Does he enjoy singing?
Does he have friends?
What does he wear?
Does he like to paint and draw?
Where does he live?

Remind students that they are making *word pictures* of their monsters.

When the monster stories are completed, students may draw pictures of the monsters to accompany the stories. Their pictures must follow the written descriptions.

Allow time for reading these aloud. Then display the stories or put them into a monster book.

Drips, slides, sneaks, scurries, runs, splashes . . .

These words and many others can go on the board as you begin talking about the rainy day you are having. Turn out the lights in your classroom and invite students to come quietly to the windows to watch what is happening outside.

As students return to their seats, encourage them to think about what they saw. Together, brainstorm "rain words" on the chalkboard. This becomes a word bank.

The assignment is to write a story or poem using rain words and any other picture words that describe a rainy day. When final copies are done, students may wish to illustrate their writing. Bound together, these stories make an excellent rainy day class book.

Hat stories

A hat story can tie in with a "hat day" for your class, your grade level, or your entire student body. Each student (and you, too) might, on the final day of writing, wear a hat to school—the more unusual, the better. Have a contest to choose a favorite hat story or poem.

Suggest these topics for writing:

How and why hats were invented and by whom
A history of hats
Uses for hats
Materials used in making hats
And so on!!

Show students how to ask questions; teach them to think

A visiting college professor from another country engaged our family in conversation: "What is wrong with American college students?" he demanded. "They do not ask questions!" He went on to emphasize that all they seemed to want was "canned answers"—they did not want to _think_.

We discussed the fact that often, students who do ask questions are made to feel foolish, stupid or like teachers' pets. We also agreed that sometimes students and adults do not know what questions to ask.

The world needs people who can think—Thinkers! Few people are able to think through a problem or an idea from beginning to resolution. One way to nurture this ability is to use written language. We must show students how to ask good questions. Try this:

Give them these answers and let them create the questions! Remind them to begin each question with a capital letter and to end it with a question mark.

Set I
1. Warm mittens
2. The house next door.
3. Ice skates.
4. It fell down the steps.
5. At the pet shop.
6. In the oven.
7. Chicken and mashed potatoes.
8. It was freezing!
9. Because I was too hot.
10. The doorbell rang.

Set II
1. She said, "Meow!"
2. In the closet.
3. At the beach.
4. With a can opener.
5. It was light blue.
6. Sunny-side up.
7. I heard it on the radio.
8. From our garden.
9. I don't remember.
10. On my feet.

After these assignments have been completed, you might want to let your students write their own answers and exchange them with other students, who must write questions to go with them. Then do it again! Don't just do it once; continue to lead students into thinking!

These assignments require thinking before writing:

The Story of Ferdinand by Munro Leaf is an excellent starter book for this writing assignment. Ferdinand was the flower-loving, peace-loving bull who, while he was not a success in terms of being a fighter, was a wonderful success in the art of being happy.

When writers give unusual qualities to animals, they create delightful writing material: for example, an angry mouse, frog, rabbit, deer or lamb; or a shy lion, bear or fox.

After sharing _The Story of Ferdinand_ with your class, lead a discussion about animals and their normal characteristics. Encourage students to think about what might happen in the life of an animal if it were to be different from what we have come to expect.

Assign the writing of a story or poem about such an animal. When the writing is finished, be sure to allow time for sharing. Many students may wish to illustrate their writing. This makes a wonderful class book.

My pet is special because . . .

This may be an old-fashioned writing assignment, but it's always a winner. Every child who has a pet can tell many special things about it. Those who do not have one or who no longer have one can use this opportunity to tell what kind of pet they would like if they could choose one, what they would name it, how they would care for it, etc. Remind them to describe. What color is the pet? What is its shape and size? How does it move, sound, and feel when you pet it? And so on.

Students will enjoy illustrating their writing; some may wish to bring photographs of their pets to school. Allow a special bulletin board space for these.

Now ask students to *become* their pets and write about them from first person! Encourage them to make themselves *real* for the audience that will listen as these pieces are shared.

My special place
Where do you, the Teacher, go when you want to be alone?

What child does not have a special "alone" place? We all have our "corners," even if they sometimes must be within the hearing/seeing of others.

Allow for sharing; then assign the writing. Encourage students to make their place real for readers who will only *see* it as they read about it. Many students may wish to illustrate this one.

Winnie the Pooh
We meet Christopher Robin, Eeyore, Kanga, and all the other special friends in the Pooh stories. A woozle book is a fine thing to create. Bring in many pet-care books so students can read and learn how one cares for any pet. Point out how the book is divided into chapters about important topics related to pet care. Now the class divides into working groups to create their own "Woozle Book," which, of course, includes the choosing of a woozle, the care and feeding of a baby woozle, a place to keep a woozle—you get the idea. Finished pieces go together into a book that can be enjoyed by all. Copies might be made for each student. And, if you have an understanding librarian, the "Woozle Book" might be put on the library shelf along with those describing the care of a cat, a dog, or any other animal.

"Frog was at work in the garden, lapping up the bugs"
Thus begins a frog story written by a first-grade writer who is also a naturalist. Frog or toad stories can be simply delightful! Also, they are fun to illustrate. You might begin with an Arnold Lobel *Frog and Toad* story and let the students go on from there. Enjoy!

Writing about hobbies
Most children enjoy sharing their hobbies with others. Encourage students to bring to school something representative of their hobbies (sports, collecting, handcrafts). Allow students to show and share their hobbies.

When they write papers about their hobbies, they must assume no one in class knows how to do what they do, and they should explain in detail the order and steps involved (procedural writing).

Use story starters
Yesterday I found a lost_____.

It was_____.

When I took it home,_____.

Now, _____.

Discuss some silly possibilities before writing!

Note-writing can make people feel good!

Encourage your students to write notes to people at home—to leave notes on parents' pillows or on a brother's or sister's desk. These can be real day-brighteners.

What happened on the day you were born?

Libraries have microfilm copies of newspapers; ask students to use them to find out what happened on the day of their birth. Also, books are available that tell what happened in one's year of birth. Use this as a bonus writing assignment. (You might want students to read the book *On the Day You Were Born* for inspiration.)

Are you having a birthday?

Naturally, growing older means that students want to *do* some neat things they couldn't do before. (We're not talking about getting expensive gifts but about *doing* something new.)

Instruct students to think before they begin writing. What are some of the things they would like to do? Stay up really, really late? Go grocery shopping all alone? Bake cookies?

Students will write several paragraphs telling what they would like to be allowed to do: three good reasons for wanting to do it, why it would be a good thing to do, whether other students are allowed to do it, and so on.

Remind students to write this in their most persuasive manner. When they finish, they should look carefully at what they have written to see if it will convince others. Ask themselves: Would it convince me? This should provoke some lively class discussion at school and perhaps at home too.

Bring old buttons to school

Allow each student to choose a button to use for this assignment. They will need thinking time before writing.

Students must create a history for the button: Where was it made? Where has it been? On whose clothes was it used? Has it been lost at any time? What is it made of? How old is it? One student wrote about an old button that had "travelled to this time from the Civil War"—and the amazing adventures it had.

When these pieces are finished, students will attach their buttons to the papers, then display the papers around the classroom.

Who wants a pet?

Remember how, as a child, you cajoled, begged, pleaded, cried when you wanted a pet? Give your students a chance to write letters to their parents, attempting to convince them that they should be allowed to have a pet—a unicorn, a kangaroo, a baby kitten, an ostrich, and so on.

Allow time to discuss the responsibility of pet ownership, feeding, bathing, walking them and so on. Tell the class of your own desire for a pet when you were their age, if you wish. Students will want to discuss possible parental objections to their pets.

When completed, they may enjoy illustrating their papers.

Information gathering, Part I

Distribute to each student a volume of *Childcraft*, *World Book*, or another set of encyclopedias. Children do not choose their own; just hand them out.

Instruct students to look through their volumes to find subjects of interest to them. Tell them to read the articles. (Encourage them not to select an overly long subject: three to four pages is too much; five to six paragraphs is sufficient.)

Now they will reread the article, listing one or two main ideas from each paragraph on their papers. Use of complete sentences is required. This may sound difficult, but even students who have difficulty can do this. Be sure they are writing *in their own words* what they have just learned.

You may wish to repeat the above assignment several times or many times; it teaches beginning skills for information gathering.

Information gathering, Part II

Distribute to each student one of the books mentioned above and allow students to trade, if they wish, with those near them.

Instruct each student to look through the volume and find a subject that looks interesting. Tell them to read the article carefully. They may need to read it a second time.

Now students will write two important ideas they learned from each paragraph in the article. Complete sentences are required, and students should write this information down in their own words.

Talk with students about how the ability to gather information will be useful to them in writing reports, in learning about subjects new to them, in following directions and in many other ways. In these assignments they are learning to outline and to think, both skills of great value.

A bird story

Students will use this assignment to do research before writing. Provide a group of easy-to-read bird books and encyclopedia material for students to use.

Students will choose a bird of interest, use the bird books to locate information, then write about *themselves as birds* (first person).

Example
I am a robin. I am known as a spring bird. People know spring is coming when they see me.

Questions to be answered should include:

In what part of the country are you found? Where do you spend winters?
Where do you make your nest, and of what materials?
What color are you? Size? Shape?
Unusual identifying characteristics?
What do you eat?
What do you do that is helpful to human beings?

Beautiful and interesting illustrations may accompany this assignment. (One of my students, a girl with sparkling eyes and a terrific sense of humor, wrote about being a vulture!)

I am a . . .

Teachers often ask students to write "If I were a _____." That is sometimes difficult to imagine, and I often find that writing "I am a_____" is easier, more fun, and causes students to write more descriptively. After talking about yourself being a _____ (mouse, giraffe, tulip), tell your students that you are going to give them a piece of paper with the name of something on it. They are to write, starting with "I am a _____," and describe themselves (color, shape, size, location), telling also what they see, hear, smell, feel, taste. They will have fun doing this, and if you get into the spirit, you will enjoy it too. Be sure to allow sharing time. Following are some possible ideas to put on the papers:

(Reproducible list is included in back section. Give each student a paper with one word on it. They love drawing these words from a hat or box.)

MONKEY	BANANA	BAR OF SOAP
HORSE	DANDELION	SNOWFLAKE
PENCIL	RING	ICE CUBE
SLED	TREE	GOLDFISH
BUBBLEGUM	CLOUD	KITE
CHAIR	EAGLE	TEDDY BEAR
PAIL	SWEATER	PUPPY
BASEBALL	MOON	BIRTHDAY CAKE
RAINDROP	PEACH	PIANO

Everyone is an expert about some things

In other words, write about what you know!

When your young writers are short of ideas for writing, ask them: "What has happened to *you*? What do you know? Feel? Think? See? Hear? Write about those things that you know, that belong to you. You are an expert on those things!" Then do some "brainstorming," and allow them to write notes about those things.

Pond monsters stir imaginations!

In Minnesota, we have ponds and lakes in almost every area, many of them right in our backyards. The stories we hear about the Loch Ness Monster in Scotland are fascinating. Encourage the writing of stories about the Minnesota Monster, the Connecticut Monster (or wherever you live), found in a local lake or stream. Perhaps she comes out at night; maybe she is sighted first in one place, then another. The Pond Monster might go around nibbling in gardens when people sleep. Set the stage for writing, and have fun illustrating your monster stories!

Example

Everyone in the little town had heard stories about the pond monster. Some folks said it was dark black-green and very ferocious. One man said it had come right out of the pond one night and had eaten all the chickens in his chicken coop. Some folks said that it was very friendly and that sometimes they had seen a yellow and green pointy tail sticking up through the weeds at one end of the pond early in the morning on bright, sunny days. One boy said he'd seen it, clear as could be, through the frozen ice in the middle of winter when he and his friend were shoveling off the ice to play hockey. . . .

Have fun writing stories like this! That's why we have *imaginations*!

7 Writing Ideas for Intermediate Writers (Grades 4–6)

Some quick "bright ideas" for writing

Ask students to write down thirty things that use electricity, several bright ideas to solve a problem in school, information about a famous person whose bright idea we use today, ideas for solving pollution problems, some ways to help hungry people in our society, ideas for saving endangered species of animals or birds, bright ideas for conserving natural resources, ideas to reduce the use of plastic or bright ideas for recycling products that are otherwise not recycled. Each of these can become a topic for several paragraphs of good student thinking and writing.

Journal writing

Keeping journals may be a favorite activity for some students, but others may not like doing it. One student may write a full page or more each day; another student may find writing "Good day!" or "Terrible day!" sufficient.

Teachers may wish to encourage regular journal writing but should not always insist on it. Some students, if compelled to write daily in journals, may grow to dislike writing.

On the other hand, if journaling is done several times a week and if we help students write about things they truly care about, they may enjoy keeping journals. They will consider it their own personal writing, not merely an assignment done to please the Teacher.

Some Teachers respond in writing to students' journals. Others simply let students know they will check to see students actually are writing in them. Be careful what you decide: One Teacher, who committed herself to writing in her students' journals, became a "Dear Abby," spending several hours a day answering their problems in them. Determine for yourself how you intend to use journals in your classroom, whether you will respond to students' writing in them and what their purpose will be. If your students regularly write often in other areas of study, you may not feel a need to respond to journals. Be sure to communicate with your students so there is clear understanding about the use of journals.

Journaling ideas—Teacher's or students'?

Some educators insist that no one should ever make suggestions about what students write in their journals and that students generally like to choose their own topics. However, there are special times when all students might write about one specific topic. For example, the day after the Gulf War began, students in one sixth-grade class were invited to write about their feelings. Several excerpts from their journals follow:

> I am petrified. I prayed for one hour for the troops, civilians and myself and for my own family's well-being.

> I'm mad. I'm mad because Sadam won't get out of Kuwait. I'm also mad that the protesters are saying "No blood for oil."

> I could hear bombs in the background [on the news], and I got scared.

> If the war is still on in June, my uncle will maybe have to go and that is why I am worried mainly.

My mom was really worried—I could tell by the way she was walking. I really didn't know what to feel. I was all mixed up.

In this case, having students write in their journals on the same subject helped them express and deal with their feelings about the war.

Don't allow journaling to become boring. Ask them to write about small and big happenings, ordinary and extraordinary things. They can write about special people in their lives, memorable experiences and favorite places. If they have many ideas all at once, they can keep several pages in their journals for brainstorming ideas to write about later.

Keep a journal of your own

When your students are writing in journals, write in yours too. Model keeping a journal, the fun it can be, the uniqueness of each individual's own writing. You may wish to keep a personal journal at home, but do keep a school journal where you write about your class, your school and special things that happen during school days. You may write about a student's exciting achievement one day, about another's special experience on another. Make your journal available to your students to read. They will be pleased to know that sometimes you write about *them*.

Directions

Students must learn to gather information and to think it through and understand it. Assignments such as the following help them learn this process. When students can say *in their own words* what they have read and heard, we know they understand it.

Each week, create a handout similar to these on various topics for students to read and write about in their own words. You can find information in newspapers, magazines, and a variety of other sources.

Directions

Read the following information. Read it again carefully so you are sure you understand it. Discuss it with a partner. Then use the lines at the bottom to write this information in your own words.

Black Bears

In late summer, black bears spend up to 20 hours a day eating to put on enough weight to carry them through a five months' nap in a hollow log, small cave or in the open in "nests" made of leaves and branches. During their dormant period, they don't eat, drink, urinate or defecate. Normal waste products—which would kill other animals if they weren't eliminated—are broken down into harmless chemicals. The little water that a bear needs is produced when the stores of fat are burned. Black bear cubs are born in the middle of the mother's dormant period, but it's not known how alert the mother is during the birth. The blind, hairless cubs nurse by sensing the heat of the mother's body.—*Star Tribune,* 12/27/92

Now write on these lines what you have read and learned.

_____

_____

_____

_____

_____

_____

_____

_____

_____

_____

_____

_____

Write your observation (what you think) about this information.

_____

_____

_____

_____

_____

_____

_____

_____

_____

_____

_____

_____

Gathering information

Read the following information. Read it again carefully so you are sure you understand it. Discuss it with a partner. Then use the lines at the bottom to write this information in your own words.

Amphibious Ice Cube

To shield themselves against the cold, some frogs hibernate at the bottom of ponds or dig deep into the soil. Others, however, spend winter on the forest floor with little or no insulation. Scientists have discovered that these frogs can freeze solid and survive. Common frogs—such as the wood frog, spring peeper, gray tree frog and striped chorus frog—as well as some insects and at least one mammal may be able to stay frozen for days or weeks without suffering irreparable cell damage. Although the process is not completely understood, it is believed these animals are able to protect vital organs while allowing the rest of their bodies to freeze. Here's how it happens:

1. Ice that forms on the frog's skin triggers a chemical reaction in the liver that produces glucose, or blood sugar. The heart pumps glucose to the major organs.

2. In humans, such high levels of blood sugar could cause diabetic coma and death, but in the wood frog glucose prevents major organs from freezing, although scientists aren't sure how. (The glucose also may help to dramatically slow the frog's metabolism.)

3. While the glucose prevents ice from forming in the organs, ice fills the cavities in the body. A frog might stay with as much as 65 percent of its total body water frozen until it thaws in warm weather.—*Star Tribune*, 12/27/92

Now write on these lines what you have read and learned.

_____

_____

_____

_____

_____

_____

_____

_____

_____

_____

_____

Write your observation (what you think) about this information.

_____

_____

_____

_____

_____

_____

_____

_____

_____

_____

_____

_____

Jobs I like

Most students have jobs to do at home before or after school; some may be chores they enjoy doing, while others may be things they do not like at all.

Ask students to write about the jobs they like to do. Encourage them to tell what the job entails, how they do it, why they like it and what the result is of their having done it. (A companion piece might be about jobs they hate.)

Students may wish to illustrate their writing. Bound together, this can be an interesting class book.

Visitors bring new information

Students in your class will enjoy having guest speakers come to visit. Be aware of people who might have something special to contribute to your class. For example, invite a guest from another country to speak to your students about differences and similarities between cultures.

One year I invited a Japanese friend to speak. She brought items useful in Japan—articles of clothing, some children's games—and generously allowed hands-on opportunities for all the students.

She also presented a short lesson on the art of origami and helped each student make something to take home. The principal dropped by to visit and joined our project.

Each student might write a thank-you letter to the guest, or one student might write on behalf of the entire class. A different student should do this each time. It develops competency in letter writing and encourages the art of writing letters.

A follow-up writing assignment can be made to write about the guest and what happened during the visit. Comments can be made about similarities and differences between the United States and the guest's country of origin. These papers can be shared with parents.

Many parents are happy to come and share special interests. Let them know that you are looking for a "guest of the month." A dietician may bring information on good nutrition; a firefighter may talk about safety in the home; a salesperson may talk about traveling for work. Each visit brings opportunities for written letters of invitation and of thanks. Allow students to do as much of this as possible.

As the school year begins

Here's an excellent get-acquainted assignment as the school year begins: Ask your students to each choose one grandparent to describe and write several paragraphs telling how that grandparent is special. They will enjoy thinking and writing about their grandparent. Sometimes students are reluctant to talk about themselves at the beginning of the year, but most children like to talk and write about their grandparents.

When writing assignments are finished, ask students to share them. You may be in for some surprises. For example, one boy told of his grandpa who was missing one thumb—and of how he lost it. Others told of grandmas who were great cookie bakers. One told of a grandma who rode a motorcycle and another of a grandfather who was a rockhound. One grandmother had been a runner-up in the Miss Iowa contest many years ago! Be sure to set aside a bulletin board for essays and pictures of grandparents.

In one classroom, a student's grandfather, who lived with her family, was invited to celebrate his ninety-sixth birthday with the class. Cake, ice cream, and lemonade were served as each child presented him with a handmade birthday card. The grandfather told of growing up in Greece and then coming to the United States. He spoke of what it meant to him to become an American citizen, and he answered many students' questions. His visit allowed the class to see the loving relationship between him and his granddaughter.

Later in that school year the grandfather died. Every student in the class grieved with his granddaughter and understood her great feelings of loss—for they had known him too.

What is your specialty?

Encourage students to think and brainstorm about some of the things they do best. Some may be excellent skaters. Others may draw well or play an instrument. Some may excel at sports. Others may be good at certain games at home, and some may be good at helping care for younger brothers and sisters.

After students have brainstormed they will choose one specialty to write about. They will call this their "ALL ABOUT_____" piece. The first sentence should name the specialty and be followed by such information as how they learned to do it (perhaps a student is a good woodcarver because a parent taught her or him) and what they need to do it. They must tell exactly how they do it: They should use words like *first*, *next*, and *then*. Finally, they can tell how doing this "special thing" makes them feel.

This is an especially wonderful writing project to use for class conferencing as student "experts" write, then read about their own specialties. Classmates can ask questions and student writers can add more information to their pieces as requested.

Fairy tales are still wonderful

Refresh the minds of your students by reading several fairy tales. Then ask them to write letters from a character in a tale to another character or to the class. For example, a student might write a letter as Rapunzel's mother to Cinderella's mother, or a letter as Sleepy to the Frog Prince, telling how he felt when Snow White moved in.

Be playwrights

Remember making shoebox theaters? Most of us did that when we were small, creating pictures to use as backgrounds for the back of the box and characters that "perform" in the box. Today, students still like making shoebox theaters. Generally, students write dialogue all together on a long strip of paper that rolls off one large dowel onto another as the story proceeds. Look for library books that give more information about creating shoebox theaters.

Starting with poetry

Introduce a poetry assignment about the snowy day you're experiencing by reading some "snow poetry" aloud. The book *Piping Down the Valleys Wild* might be used. Then discuss: How did the snow begin—did the wind blow? Was the sky light or dark before it began snowing? Did it come quietly while everyone slept or did you see it come blowing toward your school or house?

Encourage discussion about what students like about a snowy day; they should think with their senses—how does snow *feel*, *taste*, *sound*, *look*, and *smell*? Invite students to begin writing. Tell them it is not important that the poems rhyme; it is more important that they write what they really want to say about the snowy day. Some may write of snowstorms and blizzards; others may write of gentle snows creeping in at night when everyone is sleeping. Final drafts may be illustrated. Soft "snow music" can be played as they write and draw.

Colorful expressions

Send your students on a scavenger hunt for colorful expressions. Have a contest for bringing in the most. Among them you may find some of the following:

as sly as a fox	wise as an owl	stubborn as a mule
slow as a snail	mean as mayflies	slow as molasses in January
good as gold	black as coal	sweet as honey
hard as rock	clean as a whistle	tough as nails
smooth as silk	selling like hotcakes	easy as pie
red as fire	cool as a cucumber	sweet as sugar

You may also find:

independent as a hog on ice	by the skin of his teeth
dyed in the wool	a wild goose chase
wears his heart on his sleeve	goes against the grain
straight from the horse's mouth	

. . . and many more.

Once your colorful expressions are collected, make copies for your class. Students will write a story including a number of those expressions. (If you can stand it, you might see who can put the most into a story!)

Have a great day!

Are your school hallways bare, dreary, or dark? If so, perhaps your class can help brighten them. Students will design their own "Have a good day" or "Celebrate" or "Smile" posters. Encourage them to create original messages.

Final drafts will be created on heavy poster-size paper. (Some businesses are willing to part with old posters—students can write and draw on the backs.)

Students do not put their names on these. Instead, they will hang these day-brighteners in the halls, a few at a time, when no one is looking. Everyone will enjoy what they have done, and your class will have the fun of doing something nice without being discovered.

Our school—a great place to be

Your class might help kick off a *school pride* campaign. Encourage other classes to join you. Create banners to show why your school is a great place. You might encourage students to write essays and poems and make posters. Provide rewards for students "caught" doing something nice for your school or for another student.

Ask your school nurse for help

Invite your school nurse to visit your classroom, and ask him or her to tell about the work of a school nurse. Students may be surprised to learn that a school nurse does more than put Band-Aids on playground cuts and scratches.

Allow students to ask questions: How did this individual become a school nurse? What does he or she especially like about this work? What advice would the nurse give to students who might like to become school nurses? After the nurse's visit, ask students to write several paragraphs about what they have learned and perhaps a thank-you note.

A biology lesson

Your school nurse can help with this assignment, too. Ask the nurse to obtain a heart and lungs from a small calf or pig (these are available for such purposes) and bring them to your classroom. The nurse can demonstrate how these organs work by blowing into them with a straw. Students may begin to understand the wonder of how this works in their own bodies. A beef heart with fat shows the difficulty the heart has in pumping blood when it is imprisoned by fat. This is an excellent way to present information about health and nutrition, the need for good foods, the importance of not smoking, and more.

Class members can ask questions about how these organs work, what their purpose is in the body, what might interfere with this work, and more. Spell difficult words on the board. Students will write papers telling what they learned about these animal organs and how they relate to human organs. They may comment on the effects of smoking, exhaustion from cars and trucks, and other pollutants on the heart and lungs.

Life in early America

As you discuss life in early America, you will find the book *Home Life in Colonial Days* by Alice Earle useful and interesting. (There are many others, but this is a favorite of mine.) The book was written in 1898 (but is currently available through Colonial Williamsburg and at other bookstores) and contains line drawings of "homes, tools, costumes, housewares and domestic artifacts of the colonial times." It is a complete, fascinating composite of what life was like in those days. This book and others can be used to do research about life in colonial America.

Create your own writing assignment about this topic. Ask other Teachers what they have done. Divide your class into research groups. Put together a colonial newspaper telling about the life of a student then, using language of that time. Write to Colonial Williamsburg, Virginia, to obtain a copy of the *Virginia Gazette*, the newspaper first printed during colonial days. Compose a daily menu. Write a diary over a period of four or five weeks. Address the unfortunate aspects—rule by England, slavery, lack of good health care, and so on—of the colonial days as well.

Join the antique collectors

Some of your students may enjoy learning about antiques. Laura Ingalls Wilder's *Little House* books are an excellent introduction. Many families have antiques that could be shown to your class, or students and their families may dig into books about antiques at the library. This is a good opportunity for parents and grandparents to bring their expertise to your classroom.

Consider starting your own temporary classroom collection. Donations, anyone? Old glass milk bottles, a rug beater, a butter churn, a washboard, kettles, utensils—all can add to learning about life in the "olden days."

Students may do research about the use of these items, their manufacture, and more. Libraries have informative books about antiques. Students can read and learn, then write articles for a school or class newspaper. All this provides interesting ways to learn about history—and families may be able to help.

Explore an old cemetery

On a field trip to a cemetery, students will find ideas for math, history, and social studies as well as writing: Students can look for inscriptions on old tombstones, search for the oldest, determine how long the lives were of those buried there, compare the language used then with current language, and more. This will be a first visit to a cemetery for many students. Talk with them about showing respect in a cemetery.

This venture can be rewarding. For example, on one very old tombstone we found a most interesting inscription:

> Behold, all you who are passing by!
> Where you are, so once was I
> Where I am, so you shall be,
> Launched from here to eternity.

That tombstone was more than 150 years old, yet the word "launched"—now associated with rocketry—was on it. What did the word mean then? Such discoveries can be enlightening.

You may wish to have students make rubbings, with drawing paper and soft pencils, of some of these old inscriptions.

Following your cemetery visit, discuss what life might have been like during the time of the inscriptions. Was it hard or easy? Did people generally live to a ripe old age or die fairly young? Why do people live longer now? Later, students can write about what they have seen and about the thoughts they had concerning this visit.

A note-taking lesson

Instruct students to listen carefully and to write down a few key words to help them remember the following story. Tell them you will read it aloud just once. Then you will ask questions about it.

The True Story of April

April was hungry. And from her corner of the farmyard, she could see just what it was she wanted to eat: the juicy, sweet, yellow pears hanging from the branches of the beautiful tree in front of the house across the street. The girl who lived there had given her one once, after she learned how gentle April really was.

April had loved the pear. It was sweet and juicy. It made her coat curl. It made her eyes sparkle. It made her tummy wish for more. Now, day after day, night after night, she could see the tree.

Sometimes someone would come out of the house and pick a basket of pears. But none of them were for April. They were all carried right into the house. April liked the grass and hay she was given to eat, but what she really wanted were more pears. Finally, she could stand it no longer, watching them hang there, waiting for her. She would just have to get them for herself!

She watched the farmer carefully as he fastened her fence shut that night. She saw him push the latch down into the catch-piece. She saw him slide the bolt into the main gate of the farmyard. She watched him go inside his house to go to bed.

The farm where April lived was on the edge of town. Right across the street and all around her were more and more houses. One by one, the lights in the houses went off.

Finally the lights in the house with the pear tree went off too. Now everything was dark.

April walked quietly to the fence and lifted the latch with her nose. She pushed the gate section open and walked to the main gate. Again using her nose, she slid the bolt back and the gate opened.

Oh, joy! At last she would have her pears!

Soundlessly, April crossed the street and tiptoed to the pear tree. The pears were every bit as good as she remembered! She began with the pears on the lowest branches. Around the tree she went, eating higher and higher. She never intended to eat them all, but they were so good!

April was so busy that she didn't notice the sun's fingers reaching up into the sky. She had eaten nearly to the top of the tree when the front door of the house opened. Out came Olivia, the girl who had given April her first pear. "April! What are you doing here?" she asked.

April stopped eating and looked at Olivia.

"My goodness, look! There's the buffalo in the Olson's front yard!" One neighbor yelled. "That's April! Look at her!"

All the school children came running outside to look at April—from a distance.

Soon a truck came roaring up the street. Some men with big cameras got out and took pictures of April eating the very last pears.

"April!" scolded her farmer. "You come home!"

April smacked her lips loudly as she finished the last pear. Then she slowly walked out of the front yard and across the street, back through the main gate and into her own farmyard. Everyone clapped and cheered for April, the pear-loving buffalo.

Later that day, two men came in a truck and dug a hole right outside April's gate. Then they planted a big tree in the hole.

When they left, April reached her big, curly black head over the fence to look at the tree. Why, the leaves were just like—just like a pear tree's leaves!

Later, Olivia came over to see April. "I hope you'll like your pear tree, April," she said. "It's a present from all the neighbors. Now you can have all the pears you want." She patted April gently. "And you won't have to cross the street to get them."

How happy April was! Now she had everything she could wish for—her own farmyard, friends who cared for her—and a pear tree of her very own.

Discuss note taking. Explain that students often will find it necessary to take notes. Tell students they do not need to use complete sentences when they take notes. Remind them to make their notes legible so they can use them later to write whole sentences and paragraphs.

Instruct students to write answers to the following questions. Be sure they have enough time to write complete sentences.

1. Who was the main character in this story?
2. What was her name?
3. Who was her friend?
4. What did the main character like to eat?
5. Where did she go?
6. What did she do there?
7. How did she feel at the end of the story, and why?

Several times during the year, read an article or story to the class, with students taking notes as you read. Allow them to use their notes during your discussions. This is an important skill to learn, one that will always be useful.

Rocks for everyone

Rocks are custom-made for children: to carry in their pockets, to study under microscopes, to rub with their fingers, to collect—and they're *free*!

Ask a rockhound (an adult expert on rocks) to visit your class. (Did you know that young rockhounds are called pebble pups?) Look under "lapidary" in the telephone directory or ask around town; rockhounds are sometimes willing to help with school projects. Create a display of rocks in your room and encourage students to bring their own rocks to share. Develop the unit as you please, but include some research in such "rock books" as *Everybody Needs a Rock* by Byrd Baylor or *Secrets in Stones*.

Create a research project by using several books to create a master sheet of questions to be answered in complete sentences. For example:

1. What is the secret of round stones? (*Secrets in Stones*, pp. 14–15)
2. Every stone is a piece of what? (*Secrets in Stones*, p. 10)
3. What are stones made of? (give book, page)
4. If a rock is made of crystals, it was once a _____.
5. What kind of rock comes out of volcanoes?
6. What are fossils?
7. Name a kind of rock that forms under water.
8. Name and describe two kinds of precious stones.

And so on.

Invite your students to create a large mural showing layers of dirt and rock and to show where there might be "pockets" of stones. Hang this in a display case as a background for rocks brought to share.

The conclusion of your rock unit will be a written assignment. Each student will write a piece from the viewpoint of a rock called "I Am a Rock." Tell them: "Describe yourself: What color are you? What size? Shape? Where are you now? Where did you come from? How did you get to where you are now? What do you hear, see, feel, smell, taste, around you?" You may wish to give each student a small rock or polished stone to use as they think and write—it is useful to have something "concrete" from which to work. Be sure students use good description and write in complete sentences.

Example

I am a brown rock. I am 112 million years old. I got to earth on a glacier. I am in a stream and I see fish go by. I like to see their shiny scales. One day a fish ran into me and he looked sad. I liked him, and so he comes to see me almost every day now. I can see he likes me too, because he comes right to me. He rubs gently against my corners. It tickles.

Many students will grasp the idea of the ages of rock. Some may write about how it feels to be thrown, to be stepped on or to be part of a building. Encourage your students to think how it would feel to be a rock. Be sure to allow time for sharing completed pieces. Many students will enjoy illustrating this assignment.

Use newspapers

Bring in a few interesting articles from the newspaper. Put a big *It's News and It's Important* (or *Current* or *Interesting*) sign on the bulletin board. Ask students to begin finding interesting articles in their newspapers at home.

Students should read the articles and discuss them with a parent or with their families. (These make good discussion topics over dinner.)

They then will bring the articles to school and tell about them in their own words—they will not *read* them aloud. Then students will put the articles on the bulletin board and fill out a report sheet containing the following information:

Name:

Credit for News Items Brought to Class (Teacher signs this)

Date:

Subject:

Does this article affect you in any way and, if so, how?

Comment on this article:

A requirement of three news items per semester might be set, with a small reward (a pencil or an eraser) for students who fulfill the assignment.

The sports section of your local newspaper contains myriad ideas for written assignments. Often students who are not interested in textbooks—and who may appear to be poor readers—are the ones who eagerly read sports sections and magazines.

For these students and others, assign the following: For one week, read the sports section daily. Look for stories of people who are experiencing first-time victories; find a story about someone with a disability who has achieved success in sports; find a story about someone who has broken a sports record; find a piece on someone who gives credit to someone special (coach, parent, or friend) for helping him or her achieve a goal; look for a feature on an unusual sport.

Students will cut out these items and keep them in an envelope or paste them into an inexpensive scrapbook. At the end of the week they will choose a favorite from among these stories and write about it. They must include information about the subject, what happened and why, how it might affect others, your student's reaction to the item and a general observation. Final copies should be shared with the class

Did you ever wonder?

When you were small, did you wonder how water towers were filled? And when? And how they worked? And how water got from the tower to your house? And why some water towers are big and others are small? The following assignment will appeal to many students.

Discuss water towers in your area. Make a list of questions about water towers. Choose a student to call the local water department for information. Someone there may agree to come and discuss the water supply in your community. If this happens, students should be encouraged to take notes during the talk; these can be used later to jog memories as students write. Other information may be found in books in your school library. Students will write reports about how water towers work.

Related topics may include water purity, water conservation, water sources, and more. This study can expand into the field of art; some communities hire artists to decorate their water towers.

Getting letters

Kids love receiving mail. Allow time for discussion of letter writing. Tell your students how you value letters and notes from special people in your life. You might share, as I do, some special ones: My first-grade Teacher still writes to me each Christmas!

Instruct each student to think of someone special to whom he or she will write a letter. What might be of special interest to that person? What would that individual like to know about you?

Students will write first drafts, revise, and write final copies. Remind them to do their best. Encourage students to mail these. (One of my students wrote a note to the doctor who delivered him—to say thank-you!) Remember, Teachers: Do not write on these final drafts.

More letters

The day before making this assignment, tell students to copy from their favorite box of cereal the name and address of the manufacturer and bring these to school.

Each student will write to the manufacturer, telling how much he or she likes the product and why, who else in their family likes it, and so forth. Tell students that some companies send recipe books and cereal samples to consumers who write such letters. (But they should not ask for these; the letter is simply to thank the company for producing this product.)

When final drafts are completed, mail the letters. (If you buy the stamps and students pay you for them, you'll be sure they are mailed.)

Next, instruct students to bring the address of a favorite toy manufacturer, book publisher, or game maker to school and write to this company. In these letters, students also should comment favorably on the product. (Teachers should take part in this too. One Teacher wrote a complimentary letter to a famous lollipop manufacturer and received a bag of lollipops—which, of course, she shared with her class.)

Answers may be shared with the class; students will be excited, waiting for answers. If a child receives no answer after a three or four weeks, encourage him or her to write to another company.

And still more!

Set up a correspondence corner supplied with stationery and envelopes, lined paper, pencils and pens, and stickers. Then encourage your students to write more letters. Provide the following resources to encourage them: a copy of *Free Stuff for Kids* published yearly by Meadowbrook Press, a library copy of *Who's Who* or another resource where students can find addresses of favorite TV or movie personalities, your state's free directory of elected officials and their mailing addresses, and a list of addresses where students can write for other kinds of information—the Dairy Council, Department of Natural Resources, Habitat for Humanity, World Wildlife Fund, and more. Students will be pleased to receive mail as a result of their efforts.

Start your own greeting card company

Have each child in your class design a greeting card. Make copies, and be sure that each child receives a copy of everyone else's card. Now they have their own stationery to use when writing letters or sending greeting cards for various reasons.

Letter friends

Perhaps you know a Teacher in another town or state or even another country who'd like to team up on a project. With some help from the two of you, students from the two classes may enjoy corresponding. Parent–teacher organizations often are willing to pay the postage.

Schoolhouse mysteries

Invite your students to write a mystery using the school for the setting. One student wrote a mystery about a school where Teachers began to disappear as they read books to their students. After several disappearances the students discovered that Teachers were going right into the books! It was a great mystery, and the entire class loved hearing the story with their Teachers and classmates written into it. (See the mystery writing section in Chapter 4: *From reading to writing*.)

Come for tea

Explain to your students that in some countries people often "drop by" one another's homes for tea. Students will write a letter to invite their parents to tea or to some other special school event. Within each invitation, each student must include directions for parents to use to find his or her classroom, coming from the school's entry. No drawings may be used. Writing directions in a particular order is called *procedural writing*, and it is important for students to know how to do this. In addition, students might include directions from the classroom to the gym if a special program is to be given.

What the world needs is . . . Part I

Here's an opportunity for students to use their creative minds: What does the world need? What kind of inventions can you think of? (Everything has not been invented yet—one student wrote of an electric toilet that flushes by itself as the bathroom door closes.)

Ask students to write two information paragraphs. The first should tell what the invention is and why it is needed. The second should describe how it works. Students will want to illustrate what they "invent" and share their inventions with one another.

What the world needs is . . . Part II

Now students will attempt to sell their inventions. Each will write an advertisement to convince others to purchase this product. As in actual advertisements, exaggeration is permitted and encouraged. Remind students to use correct spelling and complete sentences on their final drafts.

Try a recipe exchange

Every student likes certain snacks. This assignment allows students to share favorite recipes. First let them discuss their favorites. Next, ask them to write down their recipes, step by step; these must be put in order or the snacks will not turn out as desired.

Recipes should be exchanged with partners who read back to the writer exactly what has been written. This allows the writer to listen carefully, then make needed changes.

Final drafts can be put into a class cookbook and copies made so each student has one. It might also be fun to try some of the recipes in class or have students bring samples to school. Use this assignment to emphasize good nutrition.

Envelope stories

Give each student an envelope in which you have placed three slips of paper, each with one word written or typed on it. Students will use the words to create a story with a good beginning, with a problem in the middle and with a good ending. Every student's starter words will be different. Following is a list of the words I use. I type these in three columns, then give each student a word from each column. (You might wish to cut straight across the first line and include those words in one envelope—CAT, BIRD, TREE. This list is duplicated in the Reproducible section.)

CAT	BIRD	TREE
TURKEY	CORN	GOAT
FOX	WELL	GOOSE
PUPPY	DOG	BONE
ELEPHANT	POND	LION
CAMEL	FOX	BELL
CAT	MOUSE	CHEESE
WHALE	FISHERMAN	BOAT
TEDDY BEAR	FOREST	BOY
BEAR	BEAR CUB	PEANUT
PIG	CORN	FENCE
BEAVER	TREE	TURTLE
DOLL	STORE	GIRL
BEAVER	FOX	STREAM
TURTLE	RABBIT	GARDEN
CAT	MOUSE	CATNIP
MONKEY	BANANAS	STICK
TIGER	EAGLE	EAGLE EGGS
LION	CAVE	BEAR CUB
ALLIGATOR	FISH	BOY
DOLPHIN	BOAT	MAN

CHICKEN	FOX	EGGS
TURKEY	FARMER	CORN
BIRD	BELL	CAT
HORSE	HAY	FENCE
BOY	WASP	POND
GIRL	BALLOON	STRING
SLED	TREE	GRANDPA
BUNNY	FISHING NET	LADY
KANGAROO	TURTLE	MOUNTAIN

Once upon a time

Just as we loved to hear *Once upon a time* stories, so do our students.
Guidelines for this assignment:

Each story begins with *Once upon a time* . . .
Each story must have three characters.
Each character must talk to each of the others.
The story must have an introductory sentence that makes others want to
read it.
Something exciting or surprising must happen in the middle of the story.
It must have an ending that makes the reader feel that the story is at its end.
Students do not need to choose a title until the story is finished. Often, the
story itself will suggest a title.

Family traditions

Ask a student to find the word *tradition* in the dictionary and share the meaning
with the class.

What are some special traditions in your family? Share some of these with your
students, and encourage them to talk about their family traditions. Students will
talk, then write about these. Some may be holiday traditions, such as lighting the
menorah or decorating a Christmas tree. Others may be unique within a family circle. Some may have been handed down by grandparents who brought them from
another country.

Allow students to share their completed papers, and let students ask questions
that will lead to more information about others' families and traditions.

Byrd Baylor's *I'm in Charge of Celebrations* is a wonderful book to share with
your class at this time. In it Baylor creates and finds many personal events to celebrate. Use it as a starter book, then have students create their own special celebrations. Be sure you write about your celebrations too.

For extra credit: Research units

The following is a bonus assignment for those students who complete their other
work. Select a set (even an old set is fine) of *World Book, Childcraft,* or other ency-
clopedia-style books and choose from six to nine topics about which to write questions you want students to answer. Provide a sufficient number of lines for students to use as they write.

Give each student a copy of the questions. Students must answer in complete
sentences. Remind students to proofread aloud before turning in these papers.
You may wish to give a small reward to those completing the entire unit.

The following example comes from an old Book I, *Poems and Rhymes, Childcraft.*

Directions to Students
1. p. 43: What did the queen do in this poem?
2. p. 59: Read "Bed in Summer" to a friend. (Have your friend sign his or her name to item 2 on this paper.)
3. p. 214: What is this poem about?
4. p. 172: Where does this child like to sit?
5. p. 135: Name three things this child likes to eat.

The next example is from Book II, *Stories and Fables, Childcraft.*

Directions to Students
1. p. 83: Read the fable. How did the little friend help?
2. Choose a story or fable from this book. Read it. Tell about the main idea and the characters in it.
3. Read one fable to a friend. Ask your friend to write three sentences about it.

The composing of this assignment goes quickly and you'll probably learn a few things while you do it. Once it is finished you can use it for many years.

Listen, Teachers

You will see a good deal of enthusiasm as you give students the opportunity to provide you with advice. Inform your class that this is a serious assignment and that you are looking for ideas to use in your classroom. Allow time for discussion, questions, and ideas to be shared before students begin writing.

You might expect to find, as one Teacher did, everything from "A teacher should never yell at kids!" to "A teacher should throw in a surprise once in awhile. Now, you don't tell them ahead of time that there's going to be a surprise. What you do is tell them just before it's going to happen."

Students will enjoy hearing final drafts. Watch for suggestions that you can use; it will let students know that you are listening to them.

Webster defines a petition as "a formal written request"

Ask students to consider carefully any valid changes that might help improve their school. Together, choose one possible change and create a petition. Ask a group of students to present it to the individual who has the power to make a decision about the proposal.

Response to the petition may be negative or positive. In any case, this assignment—in addition to helping students learn to organize requests—will provide information and experience about making changes in an orderly, respectful way.

Let students write what they know

At these grade levels, essay questions are a practical part of every science and social studies test. Teachers should grade answers both on writing (perhaps 20%) and on content. In this way, we encourage students to think, to write what they know in their own words, and to write in a way that reflects both their knowledge and their writing ability. When we incorporate writing into the entire curriculum, we give students opportunities to write appropriately in all subjects. This shows students that writing is important and that it matters, not only in English class but in all areas of study and learning.

Group writing sessions

Groups of students can help one another write. Give a picture to each group of three or four students and let them write a story to go with it. Or each student can start a story, then pass it on. Completed stories can be shared aloud. Students really enjoy this project.

A unique book of records

Students will enjoy creating a book of records for your class, à la the *Guiness Book of World Records*. One of my students entered the information that she had won a ribbon at the state fair. A boy's mother won the lottery. There were interesting, distinguishing facts about each student and the book became a prized possession for our entire class.

Writing across the curriculum

Writing can be a part of every activity, every area of study. For math: Tell your students to discuss with their parents why prices rise—or fall, then write three paragraphs about prices, telling cause–effect information they learned at home. Encourage them to bring newspaper clippings and magazine articles to support their observations ("Meat prices rise," "Coffee prices take huge leap," and so on).

Ask students to discuss grocery and clothing costs with their families. Then have them write several paragraphs using information shared in their discussions. Math computations can accompany written descriptions, creating a useful cross-curriculum piece.

Our country, the "melting pot"

All of us, coming from different backgrounds, countries, traditions, and interests, create the United States of America. Ask students to consider, then discuss and write about the good things immigration brings to our country. (Who occupied our country several hundred years ago? Why did they come? From where are people coming now? And why?)

Plan ahead

Students should think about the future. Many of them have creative, practical solutions to big problems. How might they deal, for example, with the growing problems of safe water supplies or of gridlock on our highways? Instruct them to think, then write.

It's in the book!

Create a list of famous scientists—for example, Isaac Newton, Marie Curie, George Washington Carver, and such contemporaries as Rachel Carson and Carl Sagan. Have your students research in encyclopedias and other sources of information, then write.

Make math relevant

Assignment: Think, discuss, then write an essay relating how mathematics is used in places and situations outside of school.

Teach students to use an almanac

Using almanac information about towns and cities, students will compare populations. Find a city with decreasing population. Write about why this might happen.

Write a story as told by an unusual observer

When I did this in my classroom, one of my students wrote an exquisite story about an island populated by wild horses, pegasus and unicorns who all battled for control of the land. The story was told by an unnamed observer, whose identity, revealed in the last sentence, turned out to be an old black crow who saw it all from the top of a tree!

Point of view

Ask students to write from two different perspectives about a single event—for example, two ways of looking at a rainstorm. One might be that of a child who loves splashing in puddles, the other that of a mother who has hung her wash out to dry.

Invite students to write about other things from two points of view—a tree (one young writer told about the tree that at night was her enemy as its branches scratched against her outside wall, scaring her, but that in daytime filtered warm sunshine through her curtains), a messy room, a forest, a swimming pool, a new house, a piano, a bowl of soup, and more.

Remember autograph books?

Together with your students, create autograph books with unique, sturdy covers. These will travel around the class as students write in them two good and special things about each student and one wish for each student. This is a good activity to use toward the end of the school year when students know one another well.

Getting things done

In our towns and cities, projects always need doing—for example, cleaning up a park; providing companionship for those who are ill, old, or housebound; cleaning debris from roads, streams, and yards; or getting a streetlight installed in a neighborhood.

Tell students they can help make things happen. Instruct them to make a list of three things that need to be done in their neighborhood or community. Then tell them to choose one project they would like to see completed and to use that as the topic for this assignment. Next they will write three important reasons why their proposal is worthwhile.

Instruct students to share the idea with a classmate or with someone else, asking the listener for feedback: Is the idea a good one? Are the reasons strong and valid? Students should discuss the most important parts of the idea. Who is the proper audience (the person who has power to make changes)? Is it the principal? A parent? A store owner? A mayor? The letter should be directed to this person or group.

Students should proofread and make corrections, then write a final copy that will be sent or presented to the proper audience. If necessary, students should be prepared to help carry out their proposed project.

8 Ideas for Advanced Writers

Perspective

Ask your students to describe a place by day, then by night. What does one see, hear, feel, smell in that place during the day? At night? This is an excellent two-session assignment. Be sure to take time to discuss the assignment before writing to help students with perspective.

Be reporters: Interview

An interviewing assignment allows your students to learn many interesting facts and learn how to put that information into good order and good language on paper.

Students will interview someone at least twenty years older than they are. Interviewing someone forty or fifty years older will show the differences between "now" and "then" even more clearly.

Questions to Ask

Where were you born? If not in the United States, why and how did you come here?

What are some special school memories?

What styles were "in" during your school years?

What were some of the fads?

What were some slang expressions? And their meanings?

What new inventions were developed as you grew up?

Who were some of the most famous people?

What were some of the most popular songs?

Tell about some of the best movies at the time and your favorite actor or actress.

What were some of the best books to read?

Tell me about the house where you lived.

Describe some of the greatest differences between then and now. How do you feel about those differences?

Teachers: If possible, take your students to a retirement center and allow each student to interview someone there, or arrange for some senior citizens to come and visit your class.

Encourage the sharing of information gathered in these interviews. Your students will enjoy hearing what others have learned and may find some connections with what they found in their own interviews.

What's happening now?

The Sunday "picture" section of your newspaper can be an interesting, stimulating source of information about contemporary events. For example, "Free the Whales" was a major piece of a Sunday newspaper.

Such an issue might be used in this way: Cut up the article and mount the pictures and information on a sturdy piece of posterboard, laminating it if possible.

Create a question sheet to accompany your display, and require that each question be answered in complete sentences.

Use quotations: Students must find who said what. Use the pictures: Students must study them to find the answers to your questions. Be creative and innovative as you create these writing assignments. If you enjoy the creating, your students are likely to enjoy doing the assignments. Has there been a celebration or major meeting in your community recently? Is one coming up? Encourage students to learn and write about it:

1. Why was/is the celebration/meeting being held?
2. Who planned/is planning it?
3. What happened/is going to happen?
4. How many people attended/are expected to attend?
5. What is special about this celebration/meeting?
6. What did/will the student most enjoy about it? (learn from it?)
7. What might happen as a result of the celebration/meeting?

Help!

No doubt every Teacher, every family, has had the frustrating experience of purchasing something special after saving carefully to buy it, and then finding that the item is defective. What do you do if you cannot just return it to the store for a replacement? Discuss this problem with your students. Share something similar that has happened to you. Students will be eager to talk about their own family's experiences.

Now suggest to students that one way to get results is to write to the manufacturer, telling what has happened.

Use the letter in the Reproducible section for this discussion. Have students read and consider the letter and the results noted at the bottom. Discuss the general attitude of the letter, facts to back up the complaint, content, order in which paragraphs are arranged, "tone" of the letter, final paragraph, and so on. Discuss why the letter was effective.

Now students are to write their own complaint letter. Each letter should include the name of the product, when and where it was purchased, the price paid for it, and what is wrong with it.

Mention that surely the manufacturer would be unhappy too if this happened to him or her, and that you feel he or she would want to know if a customer experienced problems with a product.

Ask for repair or replacement of the purchase, be polite, and be sure to say thank-you for the help.

Now assign students to write a complaint letter. They can create their own problem situations if they cannot think of real ones.

When first drafts are complete, have students work in pairs, each reading to a partner. They are not to give their letters to the other student to read, but to hold and read them themselves to hear how the letters sound. Ask the other student to play the role of the person to whom the letter is to be mailed, to listen, and to decide if the letter is accurate, complete, and convincing. Then students should make revisions and final drafts. Those pertaining to real situations should be mailed.

This is a useful, practical lesson that will prepare students for times when these things happen in their adult lives.

Write from your own experiences

Students in this age group have had many experiences, good and bad, that have caused changes in their lives. Ask them to write about one of them, showing how they have grown through the experience. For example, perhaps they have found a reason to like a student they had previously disliked. Perhaps trying a difficult task has given them great satisfaction, showing them that they have grown and become capable of more than they had thought. Perhaps a tough Teacher whom they heartily disliked has proved to be the caring, helpful adult on whom they know they can depend for encouragement and support. Writing about these experiences will help students sort them out in their minds, making even clearer to themselves their own growth; students often make important discoveries about themselves as they write.

> Jennifer and her sister slept in the same bedroom, but they did not always fall asleep at the same time. So when they were very young, they made a bargain: the first one to fall asleep would wait under the "dreaming tree" for her sister.

What a beautiful beginning for a story! It was told to me by a Teacher. And it was true, for it was her sister who waited often for her under the dreaming tree. Share some special, precious things like this with your students; encourage them to do so, too. Then write about them.

Patriotism

Webster defines *patriotism* simply as "love of country."

There is no other country like ours in all the world; people from all over the world seek to come here. Why?

We are most fortunate to live in the United States. At whatever grade level you teach, you can talk with your students about our freedoms, our opportunities, our problems, our responsibilities. Cover some of these subjects, and use them for writing assignments.

> What is *freedom*?
>
> What does *opportunity* mean?
>
> What is *responsibility* (related to caring for our environment, for others, etc.)?
>
> What was *pioneer spirit*? Does it exist today?
>
> What is *community spirit*? What makes it happen?
>
> Talk about American inventors. Be sure to get current information; for example, Eli Whitney did not invent the cotton gin—a woman did.
>
> Discuss U.S. ventures into space and seas.
>
> Talk about our parks and natural resources.
>
> What does it mean to be a citizen of our country?
>
> Why do we need laws, even in a free country?
>
> Whose job is it to help keep our country beautiful? Why?
>
> Why is it important to vote in our elections?
>
> What is the meaning of excellence? What happens to a country and to individuals when they do less than their best?

Go on to create your own ideas for writing about being citizens in our country—and about being visitors in other countries. Then remind students that here, in our country, we can express our thoughts, even to our president. Together or individually, write letters to the president, to a U.S. representative or senator, to your governor, and to other appropriate individuals. (In Minnesota, one class succeeded in using letters to have the blueberry muffin designated the state muffin.) Written words carry power, and students, when they write competently, can make constructive use of it.

Mail letters that your students write. When answers return, put them on a special letter board in your room. This is an opportunity for students to see that they can be heard.

Interconnected

It is important for students to realize we are all interconnected in today's world. Discuss with your class ways in which we are interconnected with others all over the world. Students of every age can have some understanding of how happenings and situations in one part of the world affect people living in other parts of the world. Discuss how events in space, under the sea, and on earth affect us all. Allow a good deal of time for such discussion before proceeding to the writing of the paper, "We are all interconnected."

Illustrations may be done to accompany this writing—older students like to illustrate, too. Final papers may be mounted on the walls around your classroom or in the halls or on the windows of the main office of your school building where everyone can see them.

A spelling tip

Some time ago, an older gentleman who knew about my work with written language approached me. "I'm a good speller!" he said.

"Good for you!" I responded.

"Want to know why?" he asked. "Because I wanted to win the spelldowns in our class, that's why. I'm still a good speller, because I always won those weekly spelldowns!"

Perhaps you can make time for some of these too. If it motivates your students to become better spellers, it's worth the time it takes. It's also good preparation for the areawide spelldowns, or spelling bees, that have become popular again in many places.

Gathering

Gathering is the process of collecting related words. It can be used as a starter for writing and involves no special pattern or organization as it begins. Students simply gather, or list, the words that occur to them as they begin making notes about a particular topic for writing.

The example that follows was done by a ten-year-old girl with learning problems. She chose to write about the subject of baseball, but it was hard for her to get her ideas together and put them down in any kind of order.

First she brainstormed a list of all the baseball words she could think of:

Baseball

mitt x	chest guard x	center o
base x	catcher mitt x	left o
ball x	lst o	pop fly #
bat x	2nd o	steal #
shirt x	3rd o	catcher o

pants x	home plate o	pitcher 0
sock holders x	hit #	*Code3*
face mask x	homerun #	Plays = #
shin guards x	outfield o	Equipment = x
	shortstop o	Positions = o

Next we divided her list into categories and coded them before she began to write. This prewriting work was extremely useful in helping her to begin writing her piece with confidence that she had something to say and that she knew where to begin.

Next she gathered all information about equipment into one paragraph, all information about positions into another, and all information about plays into yet another. The remaining words were used as she chose.

Once her paragraphs had been written, she decided which should come first, next, and so on. She checked to see that she had a good beginning sentence for her article and for each paragraph, and she made sure she ended her piece of writing with a good closing statement.

Thus the term *gathering*—she gathered her words together, then coded them, then used all words with the same code in one paragraph or section.

Responding to controversial statements

An Associated Press article during the summer of 1988 offered the following headline: "Umpiring a Man's Job, Astro's Knepper Says." The article went on to quote Bob Knepper as saying he didn't think a woman should umpire major league baseball games because, "In God's society, woman was created in a role of submission to the husband.

"It's not that woman is inferior, but I don't believe women should be in a leadership role. I don't think a woman should be the president of the United States or a governor or mayor or police chief."

When controversial statements like this are made public, people need to be able to think them through and respond to them. How would you begin? If you want to persuade someone to do or not to do something, does that affect your beginning?

Studies indicate that one of the weakest areas of competency is in persuasive writing—the ability to argue one's position in favor of, or against, something. For example: You see another student walking down the street, drinking a can of pop. He finishes it, then throws it in your front yard. That is littering; it's in your yard, your neighborhood. What do you do? If you know that student, you might go talk to him or her, suggesting why it's important to pick up one's own trash. Do that now; pretend you are talking to that student. What will you say? Think about it; discuss it with friends.

Now take a position on a topic about which you feel strongly. Talk about it out loud at first, then write it down. What kinds of words will you use? You will use words that are strong, direct, personal, terse.

This is how we put together an argument, a persuasive statement. First you make a statement that defines your position. Then you add statements to support that position. If you do it in a logical and polite way, the other person will probably listen and consider what you have said. This is an important skill to learn and use in written language.

1. Define position.
2. Explain, giving three good reasons.
3. Back up arguments.
4. Summarize.
5. Restate position and give final statement

A world of music

Most people—most children—enjoy music. There are songs today about the children of the world and about the fact that we are all part of one world. Ask your students each to write a song to the world. Once the lyrics are complete, writers might wish to try composing music for their songs, perhaps asking the music Teacher for help. This is an excellent team project for those who enjoy working together.

Remembering

Have your students brainstorm *I remember*. In doing this, they simply write, as quickly as they can, a list of words or phrases about a designated topic. Freedom from sentence writing and composition at this point allows one's mind to take off in many delightful and surprising directions. (We began doing this in the lesson on gathering.) Students might list such things as these:

I Remember
new ice skates
jumping on ball
Grandma's candy jar
building a fireplace
trips in the car

Now tell students to choose one of those topics for writing, the one that most appeals to each of them at this time.

Inside the "frame," they will write I REMEMBER _____. (We talk about writers "making pictures" with words; we will now "paint" a memory with word pictures.)

Around the frame, they are to write any words that come into their heads regarding this memory.

When the brainstorming is completed, students will use the words to write about the memory. Sharing, of course, is optional, but most students enjoy this particular piece of writing, and as they share, their peers will enjoy getting to know one another better.

These pieces might be presented as gifts to special people involved in the memory.

Share your writing

Most Teachers allowed little or no sharing of our writing with our peers when we were in school. Rather, we wrote to please the Teacher. If he or she liked what we wrote, we were lucky; if not, we weren't. We almost never heard what our peers were writing, and we certainly didn't see our Teachers write or hear anything they had written!

Now we know that it is important to hear one another, to work together toward becoming better writers, to cheer one another on, and to help each other whenever we can. Teachers can and should be a part of this entire process.

Many students enjoy reading their work aloud to the class; others may not want to share writing about certain subjects or may not want to share at all. Sometimes they may choose to have someone else read what they have written. Go with students' feelings about their written work; allow them to share when they feel ready. Their egos can be fragile. (So can ours!) But be sure to find ways to share something written by each student at some time; each one of them has something special to say!

Students may wish to put their writing into individual books, or you may wish to put together a book written by several or all of your students. Encourage them to write some brief "About the Author" notes. They will enjoy telling about themselves, especially in third person!

Authors' Festival: A culminating activity

One school district holds a sixth-grade writers' festival at the end of each school year: It is the culminating activity in written language. Each student enters a book, covered and bound, and community volunteers—former teachers, writers, librarians, bookstore owners and employees—read and evaluate each book three times. (See the handout in the Reproducible section.) Then they celebrate the books with a big festival. Local supermarkets provide treats, the school district's cable TV station covers the event, and families and friends are invited. It is a wonderful, exciting, and popular event. Books given special recognition are entered in the state fair.

Cheerleaders wanted

We must start early to equip children with writing skills; they need to have early successes with written language. By fourth or fifth grade, the student who has not had good writing experiences may already feel that he or she is a failure at using written language. The result is students who moan and groan when writing assignments are made, who say, "I can't write!" Or "I hate to write!"

Have you thought of becoming a cheerleader? Because that's what our students need! My friend's son became a *writer* as a senior in high school because of just one Teacher who became his own personal cheerleader. Another student is now a playwright in New York City because one Teacher cheered him on. We all need our own cheerleaders; I have mine too!

A few summers ago, I experienced the delightful privilege of reading a new story of mine, "David's Bear," to my family of about thirty cousins, aunts and uncles at our annual reunion. Their approval was worth more than a million dollars to me. My nephew, Christopher, made my day with his comment, "I just loved your story, Aunt Joyce!" We all need cheerleaders—and you may be the only cheerleader some students have.

Often, when I read something wonderful that a student has written, I react almost automatically with, "Has anyone ever told you that you are a good writer?" Usually, the answer is "No." But now, having been named "writer," his or her face lights up, the student stands a little taller, looks at his or her papers— and can hardly wait to write more! It may be that a Teacher has said this before, but the student was not ready to hear it: Take every opportunity you find for genuine praise.

Let me tell you about Katie's poem, "To Winter." Katie was a third-grader in my writing class. She had finished writing a book, and we had only two class periods left in which to start and finish something new. "Have you ever written poetry?" I asked. "No," she said but looked interested. I quickly picked up a poetry book, and together we read several winter poems. Then we went to the window and looked out at the dirty end of winter; the snow was gray and ugly, the trees bare, the day dark and dismal. "How do you feel about all of that stuff out there?" I asked. "Could you write about it?"

Katie went to her seat, picked up her pencil and thoughtfully began writing. A short while later, she came to me with the following words written down the page:

> *To Winter*
> Leave!
> Go away!
> I'm ready for spring!
> I want to see flowers
> And hear birds sing.
> I want to go swimming in the lake.
> I want to ride my bike.
> I want to go camping and
> Listen to the night and
> The leaves blow
> And sing me to sleep
> Dreaming of snow.

"Is this what you meant, something like this?" she asked.

"Katie! This is wonderful!" I said. "Listen," I told the class. "Listen to Katie's first poem!" Katie smiled and read for them, and they loved it. "We'll go and make copies for your parents," I said, taking her hand. On the way, we met her classroom Teacher. "Look what Katie has written!" I said, showing him the marvelous poem.

"Wow! This is terrific, Katie!" he said. "Show the principal!"

We did. "Katie! This is great!" cheered our excited principal.

At the copy machine, we made copies for her parents, her grandparents, her sister, the principal and her Teacher—we celebrated Katie's writing. She left school that day smiling a big, beautiful smile that made her face just shine.

At the end of summer, when I saw her one day, Katie said, "Mrs. B., do you remember that poem I wrote? Well, I have written a poem every day since that first one!"

What happened? We gave her a new name: we named her *writer*. We celebrated Katie. Interestingly, Katie's poem required no rewriting; it was just right as she wrote it the first time. Sometimes it is not necessary to rewrite.

Naming students writers

Let me tell you about my own experience: I had always liked to write; wonderful, nurturing Teachers encouraged me to write, read and write some more. I wrote and improved, submitted hundreds of manuscripts as an adult and even sold some of them. Still, whenever anyone asked me what I "did," I felt embarrassed to call myself a writer. (I think I couldn't call myself a writer when no one else had yet.) One morning a dear friend was visiting me. "I want to read some of your work," she said.

Somewhat embarrassed, I complied with her request, choosing several pieces to share from the huge pile on my desk.

Quietly, carefully she read. Then her warm, friendly voice announced, "Why, Joyce, you are a *writer!*"

I heard that word. "I am?" "You are!" She had named me *writer.* From that time on, I felt comfortable calling myself a writer. It is important that we call our students writers at an early age. We must name them, and then we must treat their writing as literature, which it is. Then they will know that they *are* writers. They will feel at ease calling themselves writers as they continue to write and learn.

Jean Craighead George, author of many children's books, told this story: "When I was eight, my Teacher sent our class to the chalkboard to solve arithmetic problems. I had no idea how to do my assignment. I wrote a poem and sat down. Mrs. Clark, an extraordinary Teacher, did not reprimand me but quietly announced that I had written a lovely poem. I have been writing ever since."

Teachers' days are filled with many things—many required things. Yet I think no Teacher can make better use of his or her time than to spend much of it in helping children acquire the ability, the power, to write competently. And as we do this, we need to get beyond the technicalities, the "how to's of writing," to look for the *what*, the essence of self that students put into their writing. Expensive equipment and fancy supplies are not necessary—only pencils and paper, time to write and a Teacher who cares, who encourages and who creates in the classroom an accepting and nonthreatening atmosphere. Often in school, students are dealt with as "Mr. Dale's class," "a nice group of students," "that class!" Together, they move through the hallways, to other rooms, to the playground—through their school years. But we need to treat them, to learn about them, as individuals. Perhaps in written language we can do this best by helping them learn to think, to express themselves in written and oral language, to ask questions and to say what they know, think and feel. We nurture all this as we help students learn to write competently.

Often, when I say that I teach writing to students, people say, "Oh, you mean a program for gifted students." (Or they ask, pleasantly, "Manuscript or cursive?"!) Wrong. The student who does the most growing, the most meaningful writing, may not be an "identified" gifted student at all. What we forget is that every child is gifted in a special way. And that some "gifts" are not "identified" early. I'd hate to think that all my gifts had been tested and identified in grade school. The student who one day writes a work of art, words that sing and shout, may be the student who today must struggle merely to survive in school from one day to the next.

"Top" students—not necessarily the best writers

Some years ago, as we started our Book Writers' Room project, the administrators in our school district allowed me to plan the room according to my own feelings and wishes about how the room would work. I requested that students who *liked to write* (now we call them *serious writers*) be invited to come. Ability levels were of no importance. Thus, the classes were filled with students of all ability levels, but they were students who enjoyed writing and who wanted more help in developing their interest and skills in written language; I told their Teachers I did not need or want to know their "ability levels." What a wonderful thing this turned out to be. For some of the most wonderful written surprises came from the students who spent time in the special-help rooms! They were so motivated, so eager to be writers, that they worked to their highest and best abilities to write books, to be authors. Good writers are not necessarily the top students. Writing may come naturally to the student who finds mathematical figures a total mystery or to the student who cannot express aloud many of the ideas basic to various studies in the classroom. We need, therefore, to encourage all of our students; who among them, as among us, does not need an encourager? A cheerleader! We must fill that role. Some students may have no one else to cheer for them.

Writers need time, comfort to write

Writers need time to think before they write, or their writing may be meaningless, both to them and to others; they need to be interested or their writing, while correctly done, may be mechanical and boring. Several years ago, and it happens frequently, I presented a writing assignment, set the stage carefully and followed up with group discussion. Then it was time to write. Pencils met paper and began moving as thoughts and ideas came, but I noticed that Jana was looking around—at the ceiling, the walls, the floor, at her hands, her desktop. She saw me watching her and smiled. "Don't worry, Mrs. B. I'm getting ready to write!" she assured me. And I was reminded again—give them time—the same thing I need myself before I begin to write.

Students also need to be comfortable when they write: Do they write best with a sharp pencil? A dull pencil? A pen? Do they write best sitting at a desk? Or maybe sitting behind a filing cabinet or on an old pillow? Or in a sun-filled corner? With a clipboard? Under your desk? Allow for these differences when you can. For my own writing, I prefer to write creatively only with a black, fine-pointed ballpoint pen. For years I've done this. Only now am I finding that I can also create on my computer or electric typewriter—but only letters, reports, instructive material, not stories or poems that come from my heart. That is my own writing self—I cannot speak for others. But I do know that we need choices. I cannot write creatively on a flat-topped desk. I must use a clipboard, be comfortable in a favorite chair or corner. Nothing else allows the words to flow. We cannot be so rigid that everyone has to do it the same way. Remember, we're all different.

No one has ever been able to answer satisfactorily my question about why we put big, fat pencils into little fingers. In my classes, given choices, young students choose slim, easy-to-hold pencils that fit their small hands. Let them choose and see what happens.

Not all students are turned on by the same writing assignments. Allow for this too, and don't expect every piece from any one student to be wonderful. You may be surprised to find that some of the best writers write poorly when unmotivated by a particular topic or on a given day. And you will be happily surprised when a student who is an "undiscovered writer" says something marvelous on paper.

Some short helps for your writers

- Tell your students that, as a matter of simple courtesy, one says, "Andrew and I will go," not "Me and Andrew will go." It is correct to speak the other person's name first. This reminder, to be polite, should help them to remember.
- To show students how a writer "hooks" readers into a good book, bring a collection of award-winning books into your room. Together, read and

share the beginnings. Explore reasons why books "pull you in," make you want to continue reading. Then apply what you and your students have learned to your own writing.

- An interesting change from the normal course of writing for students is to have them write the ending of a story first, then go back to do a beginning; or have them write the middle part first, then the rest. In doing this, they must consider carefully what comes before and after and do some planning for what they are writing.

- Create a character together in class. Then assign each student an object to be used in a story with the character: Each will write his or her own story using such things as a feather duster, an umbrella, a suitcase or a flashlight. Encourage students to keep describing until the character and his or her "prop" can be seen by the others.

- In too many classrooms, dictionaries and thesauruses are on shelves far from students' desks. Encourage each student to own his or her own paperback dictionary and thesaurus, to keep these on their desks and to use them. If you model this behavior for them, and if they begin to develop the habit of using them at this age, chances are that they will always make use of these important writing tools.

How do we avoid violence in children's writing?

This is a question Teachers often ask. Perhaps there is no right or wrong answer—I can only tell you what I do.

Our world is filled with violence, and, sadly, some children experience it first-hand. Fortunately, for many, TV is their only exposure to real violence; yet it is so constant that their minds are filled with it. Violence may horrify and yet intrigue them, and we adults need to remember that perhaps they do not see it in the same way we do.

First of all, we tell children, "Write what you know." A while ago, a fifth-grader was writing about a girl who was kidnapped and placed in the trunk of a car. I wondered where she was going with her story but did not want to take control of her story from her. I asked, "Is she going to get away?" "No," the writer answered. I bit my tongue and decided to wait and see what happened before the next discussion of her writing.

The next time I saw her she had brought, not her old story, but a new one to share. "What happened to the other story?" I asked.

"Oh, I threw it away. I didn't know enough about it to write it very well," she said.

Sometimes it takes care of itself. Other times, a student will persist in writing stories filled with violence, one story after another. In such a case, after two such stories, I will encourage or instruct the writer to try a different kind of story, telling him or her that, just as we don't eat the same food for every meal every day, so we need to learn to write various kinds of material. I also direct writers of violent material to good mystery books, where they are asked to study the techniques used there. We discuss the authors' writing techniques, and the students are asked to write, using those techniques. For examples: moving a story forward with effective dialogue, and showing, not telling.

Also, I challenge the student who insists on writing about violence to infer, not tell, about the violence; usually this is a more effective writing technique anyway. The best writers show more than they tell.

And I always encourage my students to contribute something good to a world already filled with too much violence and too much cruelty. "Will what you have written make people feel better for having read it or listened to it?" I ask.

When your students write—more ideas

- When we read, we want to know what characters look like. But just as we get to know people in person, it is when we begin to know what characters think and feel that we get to know them. Challenge your students in their writing to "let us in" on the thoughts and feelings of their characters. Then they become real and believable.
- Encourage your writers to choose subjects of interest to them. Tell students to write about things they care about. Tell them to give specifics, to describe well so that readers can see them in their mind's eyes. Then they become real.
- They need to "zero in" on characters, places, and happenings. Tell students to give us a close-up look, to "get into" the story. Invite them to bring in examples of good description to share with the class. In this way, too, you will see what they consider to be good writing and can discuss what it is that makes it valuable.
- Tell them to use their senses: taste, smell, touch, hear, and see. (Also, be sure they *place* their characters—for example, by a lake. To see them, we need to know where they are!)
- Show them how action words help to make word pictures. For example, "Stamping her foot, the girl turned and ran from the room." Or "Soaring down the hill on his shiny new skis, the boy felt like a world champion." Or "Jumping was fun; he bounced on his toes and pushed himself to jump as high as he could. Was flying like this?"
- Ask students to write about something that can be done better by teamwork than by one person alone. Then write the reverse. Students will need to think carefully!

You might find it worthwhile to take time the first day of each quarter to have your students brainstorm writing ideas. These can go into a folder where they are available for use all through the quarter. Give them time to think as they jot down useful ideas.

Literature logs (lit logs, for short)
Journals might be used by students to respond to daily readings of one chapter of a book. Many teachers find this a good way to draw even reluctant students into journaling. Instruct students, "Don't tell me what happened in the story; tell me about your own similar experiences, your feelings and your reactions. Don't repeat what we've already read... now write about *you*."
Other writing ideas:
Enlist your students in the writing of their city's, town's, or school's history. (Or you may want them to write separately about each of their family's history.)
Have students write about a goal to seek in the next five years. Tell them you will keep their final published pieces and mail these back to them in five years. (I know teachers who assign their students to write about a goal for the next ten years and then send these back a decade later.)

Have students write a description of someone very old and of someone very young. Have them compare and contrast as they write.

Write a letter to a younger brother or sister to be used as a gift for that individual.

If you had a twin who was your complete opposite, what would he or she be like? Write about him or her.

If you could trade places with anyone, anywhere, and anytime, with whom would you trade, why would you do it, and what might it be like?

Where would you go if time travel to the past were possible? Why? Write about it.

The incredible _____ bucket

Bring a shiny new bucket to class. Tell students they will now do some "technical writing."

They must:

Create a name—for example, Incredible, Handy-Dandy Hold-All—for this new product.

Describe it—all of it—in great detail.

Write about the purposes for which it might be used.

Create an advertisement to sell this wonderful product. (Who will your audience be?)

Write instructions for its use.

Students will enjoy using their creativity and their originality—and will find it fun to share when the writing has been finished.

How do we help?

If we're going to have students do a lot of writing, how do we handle revising and editing all those papers?

* Accept anything beyond a first draft. Expect students to do their own first reading *aloud* and to revise as they read.
* Let students help one another by working in partnerships and in groups.
* For every three or four papers, have students use the whole process of writing to complete a final piece of high quality.
* When you observe the same problems appearing in the writing of several students, take time to point them out on the overhead or chalkboard. Discuss and teach that particular skill. Follow up to see that students have learned and are using that skill correctly.

Remember: Teachers must make it possible for students to write.

9 Evaluating Written Language

Why do we evaluate?

A principal asked me if I might want to contact several school districts to see what they were doing in terms of evaluating students' written language. "We're looking for new ways of evaluating students' writing," she said.

I agreed to do as she asked and began calling districts around our state. Something interesting happened: Every individual I contacted, once I explained the purpose of my call, asked immediately, "And what are you doing in *your* district?"

Everywhere, educators attend workshops, contact other districts, and read every kind of information they can get their hands on, trying to find the right answer to the question: "How do we evaluate students' writing?" There is no single answer. Just as districts and schools make their own decisions about goals and outcomes for their Teachers and students in other areas of learning, so they must make decisions for themselves about evaluating writing. Some create new and innovative programs for this purpose; others fall back on A, B, C, D, and F grades.

When we ask the question, "*How* do we evaluate students' writing?" we must ask another question: "*Why* do we evaluate students' writing?" We must work with *purpose*, after all.

Obviously, the purpose is to observe what writing skills a student has acquired, to seek evidence of the student's growth as a writer, and to determine what skills remain to be learned for the student to write competently.

Assessments/evaluations must meet instruction, both developmentally and individually. We have become aware, in this time of language instruction and learning in all its wholeness, that there are other, better ways to tell what students know than letters and number/percentage grades.

We also have learned that as programs for development of written language change, so too must the role of the writing Teacher. In many classrooms today, the Teacher writes *with* students, modeling in actual classroom practice the process of bringing a piece of writing from brainstorming to drafting to publishing; this provides a "writers' workshop" classroom atmosphere.

Evaluating the process way

Instead of the old *product* method where students wrote to please a Teacher and thereby earned a good grade, we now use the *process* method. Teachers show students how to use steps in the writing process to take their ideas to final written form. We take time to get ready and to set the stage for writing; have them write first and perhaps second or third drafts; then revise, proofread, and edit until the final product reflects the value of the process.

We tell our students to listen to what they write: Does it make sense? Does it hold your attention? Does it *sound* right? The answers to these questions help our students evaluate and improve their writing.

Nationwide, we hear of the wholeness of learning and of cross-curriculum instruction, where many areas of study are interrelated and where students read, speak, and write in science, geography, social studies, physical education, music, and art—as well as in language class. This is a positive change, but it is not new. As we so often observe in education, "Everything old is new again." This is what was done years ago in one-room schools, where students wrote down what they knew and what they were learning. There were no workbooks. They learned to write with purpose and moved into new learning experiences as they were ready for them.

Accountability is a vital part of the writing process: Are students, in fact, learning to write competently using these methods?

Questions about evaluating and grading students' writing remain: Do we grade for spelling? for content? structure? paragraphing? creativity? effort? audience reaction? use of imagination? Must or can grades reflect students' ability to produce high-quality written products? Can a child's writing skills be measured on a test that requires no writing? How does that measure the creativity, the originality, of the child who writes about her *horsedog*? Or the child who writes about loving to sit *begainst* her mother?

It is difficult to relate a letter grade to a piece of writing in which a student has poured out his or her excitement about a past or coming event, sadness about a heart-breaking loss, or careful description of the petals of a newly opened flower when we also want to recognize the emotion, the effort, the growth demonstrated by a given piece of writing. Is that worth an A? a B? Or, if the piece contains many spelling errors despite the fact that it brings tears to the Teacher's eyes, does that mean it deserves a D or an F? (Technically perfect writing can be cold and dead!) Is a letter grade or a number the best way to describe the quality of a piece of writing or to indicate a student's *progress* in learning to write competently? It would seem that the more important question is not what *grade* a student earns, but what *progress* a student is making.

More than one way to evaluate

As we seek to provide evidence of students' growth as writers, it becomes clear that a single grade is generally a poor indicator of writing development. Evaluation should indicate students' knowledge and use of steps in the writing process, and of being active participants with other class members—talking, writing, listening, revising, and completing high-quality pieces. It is clear we need to use more than one way of indicating development in such a wide range of writing activities. Some alternatives are provided here.

In some districts, writing samples are taken in fall as school begins and again at the end of the school year. Both times, each student drafts a piece of writing on a given topic. Following the spring sampling, each student evaluates those two pieces, noting progress made. In some schools these samples are sent home for parents to record their observations and comments.The samples, evaluations and parent comments are placed in a cumulative writing portfolio/folder that remains in the school, providing evidence of a student's writing development and parent involvement.

In other districts, holistic assessment accompanies folder/portfolio-keeping programs, with trained writing Teachers placing the samples in rank-order. Rather than making absolute grade or number judgments, these Teachers preselect certain papers to establish criteria for good writing, then independently rank student writing samples according to criteria such as the following:

Of special quality:
Outstanding (6)
Very good (5)

Acceptable:
Minor changes needed (4)
Major changes needed (3)

Unacceptable:
Poorly done/incomplete (2)
No attempt made (0–1)

The Minnesota Department of Education Office of Assessment and Evaluation has created guidelines for holistic scoring used in ranking pieces of writing. Individuals who do the scoring undergo intensive training, resulting in unusually high correlation results (.01 variation) among scorers. They have granted permission to reproduce that information here.

Scoring Guide, Grade 6

6

Writing at this level has a sense of engagement; the writer is engaged in the topic, which then engages the reader. The writer is in control of the elements all the way through. Papers are thoroughly developed, with vivid details smoothly worked into context. Information and ideas are all well shaped and balanced (the scene, the writer's self, feelings, events, people, action, etc.). The organization is so smooth that the reader often doesn't notice any particular pattern; unusual patterns may occur. The writing possesses a sense of complexity, in contrast to simplicity, and has a strong sense of personal voice. The writer has achieved his or her purpose in addressing a specific audience. Good command of sentence structure with variety is present, along with good vocabulary effectively used. Grammar, punctuation, mechanics, and spelling are strong.

5

This is a very good paper, though not as impressive as a 6 because of a lessening of either control or engagement. An excellent execution of the assignment, but it lacks the voice, engagement, and sense of language that would carry it to a 6. Well shaped and well developed, this paper contains good details worked smoothly into the text. Any organizational approach is well handled, with the "traditional" method more common, and the writer does *not* become sidetracked or lose the main idea. Indeed, the complexity of information is handled well, although not with the consistency or control of a 6. Sentences are well formed, though they may have less complexity and variety than the 6. Rules of punctuation are generally observed, and the grammar, mechanics, and spelling are generally strong.

4

This is good writing, with some omissions or exceptions, which reads easily because control still exists as a dominant characteristic. Not as vivid or well developed as a 5 or 6, the paper is nonetheless structured with a beginning and developed main idea that may or may not be finished, ending abruptly. The writer may focus on his or her own reaction to the topic rather than the topic itself. It may be a catalogue of qualities delivered in a newsy manner and, as a result, less engaging. The writer often "tells" rather than "shows." The writing is often characterized by ordinary language. Sentence structure is probably unvarying or has less variation and less success with variation. Problems arise occasionally with word choice and/or usage. Spelling errors are evident. Sentence formation and punctuation may not always be complete or correct. Verb forms/tenses may also be in error occasionally. Conclusions usually are weaker than beginnings, or there may be no conclusions. However, in this paper, the strengths outweigh the weaknesses.

3

Two major things happen here. The paper lacks development, because it lacks extended discussion even though it contains a good number of discrete details, often list-like in nature. A second characteristic is that more errors appear in sentence formation, grammar, punctuation, spelling, verb tenses, and/or formation of plurals than in papers rating a 4, 5, or 6. Errors tend to distract the reader. While the paper demonstrates a clear topic and purpose, not much is done with them. There is often a pattern of reportage, a recitation of qualities without amplification or depth. The paper does meet minimum standards.

2

Typically, these papers are short. The number of errors offsets attempts at development. The paper gives an overall impression of simplicity. Real problems exist with two or more of the following: sentence structure, grammar, mechanics, punctuation, and spelling.

1

This paper has an overwhelming number of problems. These papers are usually very short with *more errors than a 2*. Problems with development, sentence formation, usage, and spelling are so severe that the reader's knowledge must assist, to a marked degree, the writer's attempt to deliver the message.

Scoring Guide, Grade 9

6

This paper is impressive, going beyond what a writer typically learns in school. It gives the reader a sense of a real person writing about real people. With a definite, real voice and style, the paper possesses a clear, strong pattern of organization, although the approach may be unique. Facts, details, and examples are wisely chosen and well developed. Style and content work complementarily to create a unique, personal approach to the topic. The writer is able to observe the experience from a dual point of view, both engaged and detached, participant and observer. The confident tone conveys the sense of a knowledgeable writer, comfortable in displaying her or his skill. This is a mature writer at work, producing a smooth paper. He or she displays mature vocabulary, effortlessly used. Word choice is vivid, and the writer may display a sense of play with the language. There is excellent control and variety in sentence structure, grammar, mechanics, punctuation and spelling. Occasionally, a writer may lose her or his balance as a result of "reaching" a bit too far, but the paper is impressive overall.

5

Less memorable than a 6, this paper is well shaped, with a real voice, though not as evident as in a 6. It is well structured, with a good introduction and good conclusion. Indenting of paragraphs may be missing, although it is clear that the writer is organized and structured the information well. Examples are extended and discussed. The writer takes a consistent point of view. Some variety in sentence types is present, along with good command of sentence structure, grammar, mechanics, usage, and spelling. This paper may be excellent but not convey the same confidently mature tone as a 6, and/or not display quite the same flair for language. There may be a smattering of errors. Occasionally a writer may reach too far and really not be able to carry it off, but the knowledge of this writer is superior.

4

This writer is in control of all the elements of writing, but *not* in control *all* of the time. The paper exhibits a sense of structure with an introduction, body, and conclusion, but the introduction and conclusion may each consist of only one or two sentences. Specific details are present and the paper is developed but not to the degree of the 5. Writer displays sense of good sentence structure, development, and use of explanation and details. This paper may contain shifts in point of view, particularly from first to second and second to first. There may be a number of fragments or run-ons indicating trouble with sentence formation and/or punctuation. Homonym confusions may be present along with slang spelling. Problems with grammar also occur. Nonetheless, strengths outweigh weaknesses.

3

At this level, weaknesses begin to overtake the paper. Usually both introduction and conclusion are present, although some papers may not have a conclusion. Paragraphs can contain a jumble of ideas not clearly connected, much like development by free association; focus can be a problem. Some of the papers that rank a 3 will be a catalogue of events or people, list-like. This paper has a generic quality that creates a sense of shallowness. Some will be very short and therefore inadequate in terms of development, but adequate in terms of grammar, sentence structure, and punctuation. Others may be as good as a 4 paper, but quality will be offset by serious shortcomings in other areas: sentence structure, organization, usage, grammar, mechanics, punctuation, and spelling.

2

A 2 paper might be long but contain a number of problems and or have fewer but severe problems. It can be arranged into blocks of often unrelated information. Many of these papers are essentially generic lists of statements. Most likely, they will be short and undeveloped. Occasionally they will be wordy. They will contain serious errors in two or more of these areas: development, paragraph structure, sentence structure, word choice, punctuation, and spelling.

1

At this level, papers exhibit serious shortcomings in three or more areas: development, paragraph structure, sentence structure, word choice, punctuation, and spelling.

Scoring Guide, Grade 11

6

This is an impressive paper with a real voice; it engages the reader, drawing him or her into a feeling for the real, living people presented. With an original approach, the writer perhaps creates a mood or an atmosphere as a part of her or his message before moving into the topic. The paper is original and excellent without making unusual demands on the reader. More than a recounting of the friendship/person, there is a sense of reflection about the person/relationship. Excellent development is smoothly accomplished. The writer exhibits a mature quality in tone and style, yet is not necessarily somber. The reader smiles with the writer rather than at the writer. There is an excellent use of language. Sentences are excellent, both in structure and variety. Excellent grammar and mechanics contribute with the other characteristics to create a sense of impressive quality.

5

Somewhat less memorable than a 6, this paper is nonetheless engaging. Often a "constructed" paper, more than a journal entry, it demonstrates knowledge and control of language tools (rhetorical choices, sentence structure, word choice, mechanics, etc.). The introduction may open in an original way. The paper is well organized, well structured, and well developed. Good use of language occurs, including metaphors and similes. It is less mechanically perfect than a 6; special-effects punctuation may be used. The style is less accomplished than a 6; there may be some repetitiousness in sentence patterns and types. Word usage and word choice errors may occur. The writer may have problems with spelling or mechanics. While an excellent paper, a paper earning a 5 is less authoritative and less impressive than a 6.

4

This paper has a more generic quality but with a glimmer of something special, though it is not sustained. There is more "telling" here. A 4 is a very solid paper with quantity of detail, well constructed though less well developed than a 5. It may be the competent, ordinary "school paper." This paper contains a clear sense of structure in organization, which may be simple, obvious, and often chronological. The introduction and conclusion may or may not be effectively developed. The paper may have real strengths in terms of sentence structure, grammar, usage, mechanics, and punctuation, but lacks the vividness of a 5 or 6. It may seem empty and contain errors in the above areas. Strengths do outweigh weaknesses.

3

Weaknesses outweigh strengths. Lower half papers in general display a generic quality; the papers could be about anyone. They may be very general, lacking specific examples or details. These papers may be long but exhibit less control, with less development, weaker paragraph structure, poorer sentence structure, and weaker punctuation. Longer papers tend to wander and lose focus. Shorter papers may be mechanically well done, but empty. Occasionally, mechanically troubled papers do possess rhetorical structures and vivid details, but the problems overwhelm the positive features; one gets the sense that if this paper were well edited, it could have been an upper half paper. Many papers are typically declarative rather than engaging or evocative, much like journal entries. Organizational patterns tend to be simple. Papers may be repetitious and may contain shifts in point of view. They may be choppy and immature in style. There may be problems with forming the possessive or distinguishing plurals and possessives.

2

This paper contains simple sentences and is almost childlike. It displays weaknesses in two or more areas: focus on the topic, development, paragraph structure and development, point of view, sentence structure, mechanics, verb forms/tenses, and punctuation.

1

This paper contains weaknesses in three or more of the following areas: focus on topic, development, paragraph structure and development, point of view, sentence structure, mechanics, verb forms/tenses, and punctuation.

Provide expectations to students

Criteria for given writing projects should be shared with and demonstrated to students so they are aware of expectations, goals, and possibilities for their own work and that of classmates. They need to know what the expectations are before they can endeavor to meet them. Discuss and show students, for example, a high-quality paper on the overhead. Show them papers that would be described as acceptable and unacceptable. Discuss what qualities determine these descriptions and how changes might be made to improve them; this is information they need to know.

A unique and important step is taken in some districts: Students are surveyed (in writing) to determine their attitudes toward writing. They are asked how they feel about their own writing and the school's role in helping them to develop as writers, what they feel the schools are doing well to help them, and what more they need from Teachers to learn to write competently. Most students take such surveys seriously and offer good insights into the writing instruction they are receiving. Most are well aware of their own writing abilities and performance. Interestingly, one of the common pieces of feedback from students is that they want daily blocks of uninterrupted writing time. Recently, young writers, responding on evaluation sheets to group sessions at young authors' conferences, praised those presenters who "let us write—that's what we came for!" When asked how schools could best help them write, all asked for at least thirty minutes of uninterrupted writing time each day—and "don't use it for anything but writing."

Sample comments from fifth- and sixth-grade students:

> Writing is a very important part of a student's curriculum. Having specialists is important to make sure kids are using their full potential in writing and doing it properly.
>
> I think that one way the school district could help with the writing programs is to have Teachers do more writing in their classrooms. Some classrooms hardly do any writing.
>
> Instead of having all the computers in the TV studios and computer labs, sell the computers and use the money for more WRITING programs and writing Teachers!
>
> I think we should have writers' clubs and writers' round tables. It gives us a chance to share our ideas and get comments from others. You need to be a good writer to get good grades. These programs reinforce our skills. There also should be a writing Teacher at every elementary school.
>
> I think all schools should provide more writing and teach writing skills for the future—especially how to write reports and tests for college and special themes. To me, writing is my future. Maybe some other kids don't, but I need help for the future.

These students know what they need, and they are right!

How do other Teachers do it?

Many Teachers require students to keep writing folders/portfolios in their classrooms. These contain completed pieces, works-in-progress, and Teacher comments, and they may be accompanied by journals, writing notebooks, learning logs, and idea sheets for future writing. In addition, Teachers keep weekly/daily records based on Teacher observations of student writing activity.

Some Teachers collect monthly writing samples, evaluate and conference with students about the samples, and determine together the strengths demonstrated by students and the areas in which more work is needed. One or more of these may be selected as a "major piece" on which a student will spend more time developing/publishing a piece of excellence.

Contact with Teachers and administrators from many parts of the country indicates that schools everywhere are doing their best to create useful and comprehensive methods of record-keeping and evaluation. Individual Teachers are seeking methods that are useful and effective. But the evidence is clear: *Few writing Teachers are content to use A, B, C, D, F grading*—just one way of evaluating—to assess and comment on students' writing development, and most are seeking more effective ways of indicating student achievement and progress in written language.

Some Teachers find it helpful to give *points*, rather than a grade, for each step of the process demonstrated in a piece of writing:

Example

Prewriting	3 points
First draft	4 points
Revised, improved draft	6 points
Prepublished draft, edited	4 points
Possible total:	25 points

A friend who teaches students with learning disabilities says she simply gives *credit, not grades* to her students, whose writing crosses all areas of learning. Her students earn credits in various ways, one of which is revising/rewriting a first draft after conferencing with classmates and the Teacher. Their revisions are tangible proof of learning and of effort—and they deserve credit for their hard work. The more successes they have, the more confident and competent they become. Encouraged by a supportive Teacher and cheerleader classmates, they are motivated to do their best work.

An interesting observation by her is that these students often must draw first, then write about a given topic, because they have trouble visualizing. The drawing gives them something concrete with which to begin.

She says grades sometimes can be good for these students as they push them to learn more. At the same time, tests and grades can be devastating because dyslexic students, for example, generally don't do well on tests. They cannot read and write an entire passage on their own. While an obvious physical disability would be considered in tests such as this, test scores do not allow for these hidden disabilities; they are not fair to these students.

One classroom Teacher had demanded that her learning-disabled student *write an essay*. He was to be graded in the same fashion as the other students in her classroom. The classroom Teacher had absolutely no understanding of this child's disability. The special education Teacher talked with her about what was important in this assignment, about how insurmountable this task seemed to the student who knew he simply couldn't do it, about the fact that if it was to be done correctly, someone else would have to do it *for* him. What was the goal of the assignment in this student's case?

If the student was to *learn*, then it was necessary to modify this assignment so he could have success in his attempt. The student was able, with assistance, to read the required information. Then he dictated to his special education Teacher what he had learned, and she wrote it down in his own words. The purpose of the lesson for this child had been accomplished.

Using conferences to evaluate

One of the most practical, effective tools for communicating development in written language is the Teacher–student writing conference, where Teacher and student together read and evaluate current pieces of writing to determine which skills have been developed and which remain to be learned. Here, the student retains ownership of the piece and the Teacher acts as mentor, asking questions, making suggestions, and advising the writer on how to improve the final product. Sometimes such conferences take place one on one; other times they take place in small-group settings, with other students learning as they listen, observe, and even offer helpful suggestions and comments of their own.

Teacher–student conferences allow students to take responsibility for writing and improving their pieces. Such conferences are more useful than a Teacher carrying home piles of writing, red-penciling them, then returning them to students who simply follow directions for changes indicated—if, in fact, they actually do this. The Teacher then has assumed responsibility for final products.

Peers can help

Peer evaluation of writing can be an effective, practical, and useful means for helping students to improve their writing. The Teacher, in a whole-class demonstration, shows students that two jobs exist in this cooperative effort: the job of the author/reader, who reads aloud his or her piece-in-progress, and the job of the listeners, who give their full attention to material being presented.

Listeners are instructed to help determine where clarification or additional information might be needed, to suggest appropriate ideas and to ask questions that might help make the published piece clearer, more complete and more interesting. After listening to the reader, listeners give him or her feedback so appropriate changes can be made. The goal in this situation is for students to help one another publish the best pieces possible. Students can teach one another and can learn from one another, often more effectively than from an adult.

Parents can conference too

Another helpful tool in the process of evaluation is the Teacher–parent (and perhaps student) conference, which allows Teacher and parent(s)—and in many cases, the student—to discuss the student's growth in written language. These conferences allow Teachers and students to show parents what is meant by *evaluation* and how it is done to best help students learn.

In a conference it is possible for the Teacher to indicate that, while the student is having trouble with compound sentences, for example, and must learn to combine sentences to write clearly and effectively, she is marvelously creative, has a wonderful vocabulary and holds bright promise as a young writer. These conferences offer excellent opportunities to discuss parents' experiences and attitudes about language and to share ideas for helping and encouraging a student to develop these skills at home as well as at school.

A magnum opus

In one district where I worked at length with students and Teachers, we invited sixth-grade students to select, with the help of their Teachers, up to forty pages of their best writing from the school year. Students' pieces, printed by computer, were collected in mid-May. Each student's collection was put into a spiral-bound, permanent book with an attractive, sturdy cover that indicated this was his or her *magnum opus* (with thanks to Charlotte of *Charlotte's Web*), the greatest written work of the year. Bound copies were given to students to keep. Our young writers were pleased and proud to see these special pieces put together into a permanent binding.

What do letters and numbers tell us?

Because common sense tells us that letter grades and numbers do not inform us adequately of what we need to know and do not convey to students or parents truly useful information, other varying methods of assessing student growth in writing are growing in usage nationwide.

The most useful evaluation of a student's writing is done by a competent classroom Teacher who observes and interprets what is taking place daily, weekly, and monthly; who can ensure that samples are collected; and who, with the students, can discuss and determine goals and progress in written language.

As we evaluate and measure a child's progress in writing, we need to ask the following questions: Can this child think? Can he or she move a thought, an idea, in an orderly direction and bring it to a logical conclusion? Does this student work at expressing himself or herself on paper in the best way possible? Does the child revise, rethink, revise some more? Is the child growing as a writer?

Tests can give us guidance in improving curriculum and can show us where we need to develop areas for further study. But test scores do not explain what a student has learned. The seas and the mountains and the things that grow are far too complex to be reduced to numbers on test papers. As William Raspberry, the insightful and articulate columnist for the *Washington Post*, has said:

> No child can be taught to think as well as he otherwise might if his homework consists primarily of filling in blanks on a ditto sheet . . . he may get all the answers right, simply by scanning the assigned reading, without ever having the material engage his brain. The cheap, unscientific but logical alternative is to assign the passage and require the student to summarize it in his own words. Do that consistently, and he will not only learn to write a lot better; he will also learn to analyze, evaluate, sort out and synthesize information.

Most tests indicate passive recognition knowledge, not active, useful knowledge. They require only recall of small bits and pieces of information; they do not require an orderly, thoughtful process of thinking or of putting knowledge into a *whole*. Therefore, we must create opportunities for students to show us what they know. We do this with writing, with speaking, with reading, and with answering questions. A test score is just one piece of many available to us to show what students are learning. We cannot overlook the others.

Students need to participate in assessments

Students must learn to identify their strengths and those areas in which they need more help and more work. That is why carrying home students' writing each night, correcting it and handing it back is neither a time-effective nor teaching-effective effort; it leaves the child out of the assessment/evaluation and learning process, and keeps already overworked Teachers carrying what should be a shared responsibility.

This is why we need to conference with our students as they write—to listen to them, to talk with them about what they know, and to show them how to develop their abilities in written language.

It may be that fifty years from now, this same controversy will continue and Teachers will still be required to record innocuous letter grades to indicate development in written language. Common sense tells us, however, that many of the methods of evaluation described here and other similar methods will tell the real story.

Evaluation ideas from classroom Teachers

Teachers in one of my workshops were asked to write about their evaluation of students' written language. Here, described by Cindy Whistler, a first-grade Teacher, are some comments about her evaluating process:

First grade

In my school district we use a writing folder to keep samples of students' writings and to check their progress. In the classroom, each student has a two-pocket folder for daily work. Inside, we keep journals and samples of writing from any area of the school day. We include webs [also called *clustering*] we've worked on together, lists or brainstormed ideas from science or social studies, writing responses to literature and creative writing activities. Drafts of pieces that have been written into a class book or published are also included, although we do not edit every piece written during the school year. Each piece is dated with a rubber stamp—a great investment.

At the end of the first quarter, each student selects his "best piece" and I select the piece I consider to be his or her best also. Sometimes they are the same piece. We do this each quarter and at the end of the year, the first- and last-quarter "best pieces" are put into a permanent folder that was begun by the kindergarten Teacher with kindergarten selections inside. I use the kindergarten samples and the first-quarter, first-grade samples at the first conference to show progress.

In first grade, we do not use letter grades but instead use a scale of 1, 2, or 3. They do not equal the letter grades, and an explanation of each number is on the back of the report card. I would love to get away from grades altogether and use checklists for reading and writing that I have at school to show progress. Since grades are required, I generally grade on content, organization, and mechanics.

For content, I explain to the children that we are looking for their idea—is it interesting, is it explained and is it developed in the piece or are there lots of little ideas that never gel together. I look for signs that the child has proofread.

For organization, I explain that we are looking for how it is put together. In the beginning, when we are writing one sentence, is the writer trying something new, or is it something we have already done? Does it make sense? And later, when [we are] writing several sentences to make stories, is there a beginning, middle and end? I also consider readability, neatness, spacing between words—all parts we have noticed in books that make it possible for a reader to read and understand.

For mechanics, I like to see them using things we have learned in Daily Oral Language—capitals and periods in the right places, sentence order, subject-verb agreement (although we do not call it by that name) and some relationship in the spelling of their words that shows progress. We study word families—for example, *-an, can, man, pan*, and so on—and when using a word in their story that has an *an* in it, can the child put that part of the word in, even though the rest of the word may be incorrect.

I look for a progression in their writing and spelling in this manner:

1. Beginning writing may be just drawings. The child tells me about the picture.
2. Next, the child draws and makes scribbles underneath to represent his story.
3. The drawing will soon have scribbles with one or two words that the child *knows* how to spell, such as *Mom* or *Dad*.
4. After that step, a sentence form may appear, with beginning sounds recognizable.
5. Beginning and ending sounds may be next.
6. Comfortable with beginning and ending sounds, often a few vowels may be added, not always correctly, but the child knows there is "something else."

Some representation for different syllables begins when students begin to notice vowel sounds.

7. Soon, sentences are very close to accurate spelling.

I often show parents a sample of their child's writing and where it falls in this scale. They enjoy checking the writing samples when they return for the next conference to see what has changed.

Several times during the year, I use a writing evaluation with smile faces for the students to evaluate themselves. The writing-partner-evaluation checklist we do at times when I ask students to read their pieces out loud to other students. We do not do this checklist in written form but we do discuss what to listen for as the writer reads and how to help the writer with parts that are missing.

Part of the evaluation process in my classroom also involves reading pieces out loud to the group. We cannot do this every day but we do it once a week at least. We sit in a circle on the floor, pieces in front of our laps, and one person is in the "hot seat." We include everyone, and no one may add on to their piece as they hear others read since we are not at our desks. They really like to read their stories to the group and we always clap afterward.

High school

Deb Rothenberger, a high-school Teacher, shared information about her methods of evaluating students' writing:

With each term-paper assignment I conduct student–Teacher conferences to check the students' progress and mastery. For each assignment the student receives certain percentage points. For example, a sentence outline may be worth 10 percent. With these points per assignment the total is 100 percent. Points are deducted for late assignments. Ten bonus points are given for a term paper turned in before the due date.

The student may also contract for a daily grade of an A or B for the amount of work put into the paper. For example, the A contract requires a minimum of twenty-six note cards, five sources, and 7 to 10 pages typed.

For journalism articles, I do not look at first drafts. The articles are to be typed. Then the student and I read the article aloud, and the student proofreads his or her own paper in pencil for possible erasures. He or she corrects errors and revises on the computer, then shows me the next draft. This process continues until the paper is nearly flawless.

For objectivity, I ask the students to write their names on the back of their completed essay so I do not see the author's name as I am critiquing.

For literary analysis, I have the students write the paper cooperatively. The group decides which components the members will analyze. The individuals return to the group on day two and discuss, add or delete data/support for each component. (This assignment must be typed.) The members critique until the final product has been turned in.

My biggest frustration in evaluating writing is lack of time versus requirements. Writers need to rewrite and to be evaluated and then to rewrite again. As a Teacher with 160 writing students and numerous assignments required, I cannot physically manage the "ideal" of the writing process.

Because evaluating writing is so subjective, I try to manage subjectivity by giving students the opportunity to be responsible for their grades (for example, term-paper assignment points and contract). I also let the students know my expectations with student models of the writing assignment and with a grade criterion (for example, term paper). This criterion we call a *rubric.*

Evaluation is based on following the requirements for the assignment: for example, a personal narrative (something happened that developed centered on the author's thesis), plus organization, clarity and mechanics and spelling.

Setting goals together

It is important for Teachers and students together to create and share goals for students' writing and to discuss expectations for competent writing in any given area. When we were in school, few Teachers informed us what composed a good piece of writing or demonstrated what they wanted from us. It was a mystery: the Teachers knew a good piece of writing when they found one, but the important question for me was always: How could I ensure that mine would be one of them?

We must talk with our students about why they must learn to read and write competently: There will be many times in their lives when they need to write about feeling sad, scared or angry; about feelings of boundless joy, quiet peace, about ideas and opinions; about reality and dreams. They must be prepared to fill out résumés that will help them obtain jobs, then to do any writing those jobs require. No one will be able to do it for them; they will be expected and required to do it themselves.

They may need to write effective letters of complaint to companies that sell them defective products and complimentary letters to businesses that serve them well; they may want to write about memories, to write stories and poems that tell what is happening in their lives.

Furthering learning through evaluation

We must let our students know that through evaluation they will further their learning. In our own school days it seemed grades were meant to show us how many things we were doing *wrong*. Remember how we always asked, when papers were handed back, "How many did you get *wrong*?" When we did get a good grade, we usually considered ourselves *lucky*, not *competent*.

If we truly are trying to reach and to teach each individual child, we need to ask not what *grade* but what *progress* a student is making and to help the student move on from there.

As we talk with students about their writing, we can discuss the following questions: Does this piece of writing fit the criteria of the assignment and the needs of the audience for which it is written? Will your reader understand clearly the purpose of your piece? Is there enough content to tell what you intend the reader to learn? Are the applicable writing rules demonstrated correctly in this piece? Is this piece organized so that it makes sense? Does it have a strong beginning, a purposeful goal and a satisfactory conclusion?

Teaching methods now in use—process writing, with its step-by-step movement toward achieving a high-quality piece of writing—give us as professional Teachers opportunities to be the best we can be and to use our knowledge, ideas, enthusiasm and skills to help students learn. We no longer have to depend on dictates from publishers; it is a good time to be a Teacher.

Grades? More ideas from Teachers

It sometimes is useful to give an achievement grade and an effort grade.

You might want to set a limit on errors for a C grade, for example. When you have marked five *x*'s in margins for major errors in a prepublishing draft, you may stop and let the student correct the errors in a different pen color. This allows the student to learn, to make his or her own changes and not to feel overwhelmed by a huge number of errors in need of corrections all at once. When the work is again brought to the Teacher, the student should be able to explain the reasons for the corrections/changes. When students can explain—teach—why quotation marks, semicolons, and commas, for example, must be changed, we know they understand and have learned what they need to know.

At upper elementary levels, sometimes you may wish to grade the prepublishing draft rather than the final draft. Then you will be able to see what your student has done on his or her own and with the help that has been provided in conferencing and class work. If you always grade solely on the final published copy, the grades will chiefly reflect all the help the student received. At the same time, you will be helping that student prepare for final publication.

Using the writing process

How do we motivate students to use the writing process and work toward excellence in writing? For starters, use a variety of paper, perhaps colored, lined paper for the first draft; different paper for revisions; then publish the piece on better paper using students' best handwriting, a computer printer, or a typewriter.

Encourage the students to write on every other line of a first draft so there is space between lines for changes/corrections. Insist that students read *aloud* to themselves and then to a small group/partner/class as they revise. Show actual first drafts, second drafts and final copies to students. Point out how much improved the final published copy is: It *is* worth the effort! Students should keep several sets of papers that demonstrate use of the entire process from brainstorming through published piece; these are good evidence of the value of working through the process.

Make available all necessary supplies for the publishing of final drafts. Create a classroom writing center and provide there a wide variety of forms for publishing: books of all kinds of students' writings, raps, display writing where all can see, plays, songs, audio/video tapes, pictures with writing pieces, games, game shows, pop-up books, mobiles, charts, cartoons mounted pages with "readings" for other classes, parents, illustrations, posters, greeting cards.

Tell students that, sometimes, what they write in the first draft will be much like their final product, but that that will not necessarily be true as their writing abilities become more advanced.

Talk about favorite books: every book is probably the product of twenty to forty or more revisions. That's what professional writers do to be published.

Discuss the inner satisfaction we feel over writing something unique and meaningful.

Show students how following the process of writing will lead to a much better piece than rushing to finish.

Always remind students to write to please themselves; they are their own first audience.

Ask students to identify the following: What do you like best about your own writing (identifying skills already owned)? What are you doing well? What do you need to practice (looking ahead)?

For less able students, provide a modified curriculum so they too can experience successes. Every child has important things to say.

When first drafts have been shared in writers' workshops and classmates have asked questions and shared comments to be used in revising/writing succeeding drafts, be sure writers share *final* drafts so they can see the value of going through the full process toward a final draft that represents their best work. Show students that following the steps of the writing process *works*.

Teachers must write

Teachers who themselves write are modeling competencies and attitudes for students. Writing a résumé or completing a job application form, persuading a company to replace a defective product, writing a poem—the work these tasks require is understood by those who actually do them. Teachers who write a short story or a personal essay before instructing their students in doing so (or during the time their students write) will use skills needed for their completion and thus will be able to help their students meet these challenges successfully.

Writing is one part of *all* the language arts—thinking, writing, listening, speaking, and reading; they all go together. The more opportunities we provide for our students to learn any of these skills, the more we ourselves practice them, the more proficient we all will become.

Good writing leads to speaking skills

Students need opportunities to speak in prepared situations and to present their own written material. They also need opportunities to think and to speak "on their feet." Teachers often ask in workshops about those students who are always reluctant to share their writing. It is important that students begin early in school to feel comfortable reading aloud what they have written. The child who continues to evade that learning opportunity will only become more afraid as time goes on. There are times when we must allow students to "pass," to respect their need to not share. However, the child who constantly avoids such opportunities in first and second grade will be more resistant to share by fourth grade and terrified by sixth or seventh grade. He will be the adult who never speaks up because he "can't speak in front of people." Self-esteem is affected in many ways because of such a lack of language skills.

We need, therefore, to find ways to make students comfortable with sharing what they write. That may mean inviting such a child—and a friend—to share with you in an accepting, nonthreatening situation during lunch hour, for example. Once the child is comfortable doing this, invite him to share in small-group situations, then with the whole class as other students do. Find ways to ensure that all your students have opportunities to stand before their classmates and share their writing. They may find they thoroughly enjoy having an appreciative audience for their writing efforts. Everyone needs competency in speaking before others—another important lifetime skill.

To help students learn to write, in brief

Share your own enthusiasm for writing and your own writing efforts with students. Attitudes are contagious.

Preteach and review those tasks students are likely to encounter in a writing assignment. Give examples. This lets students practice writing correctly those things of special note in a given writing project and makes them feel competent as they begin.

Teach students to proofread their own papers by reading them aloud—in other words, by listening to their writing as someone else might. Give everyone identical papers on which to practice proofreading and work on these together. (Daily Oral Language fits wonderfully here.) Remind them that it's O.K. to cross out, correct, and revise; that's what real writers do. Their final piece will reflect these earlier efforts.

Allow students to work in twos or threes, carefully editing one another's papers, then returning them to the owners to do suggested revising. A good way to begin these miniconferences is with whole-group conferencing (writers' workshops).

When you are reading students' papers containing many errors, you may need to mark for correction/revision those things that are of greatest importance. Students who are overwhelmed with too many correction marks may simply give up. (Use a "friendly" marking color—not red.)

As you conference with students and observe their writing practices, take time for minilessons on common problems. For example, if you observe several students using *and, then,* or *but* to create run-on sentences, demonstrate to these students or to the entire class that a sentence of four or five lines may be too long. On the board or the overhead, show how to divide and improve the sentences. Ask students to check their own work against the example and make changes as needed. (It is helpful to collect examples of writing problems to use for these demonstrations; watch for these.)

Be sure students follow through with revising where it is needed; only in actually revising will they learn the skills they must know to become competent writers. Be sure they understand that this *is* the writing process: prewriting, drafting, revising, proofreading/editing, and publishing. Following these steps will lead to a good final piece.

Help students identify their writing strengths: in doing so, they also become more aware of areas where they need practice.

Remember: Our teaching goal is to help our students so that eventually they will be fully responsible for their writing. We must give them as much responsibility for their own writing as they can handle, then teach more, moving ahead until they are able to meet that goal.

10 *Keeping Portfolios*

Portfolios are in

When most of us were students, we knew nothing of portfolios—of organized, purposeful collections of writing. We simply took our papers home, maybe showed them to our parents, then probably threw them away. Unless a parent or student saved papers, there was rarely any effort made to put students' writings into any meaningful kind of collection.

What is a portfolio? How is it used?

Now we combine learning into a *whole* and the terms often used for it—*whole learning* and *whole language*—explain what we are doing as all areas of study and all parts of language are taught and learned together. As part of this movement, schools everywhere are saving collections of students' writings in portfolios designed to give an overall view of each student's progress. This is a helpful, practical part of helping students learn to write. In some schools, portfolios take the place of grades on report cards: A collection of writings demonstrates student competencies better than a single grade on a report card. Portfolio assessment began in Vermont in 1989 when a group of Teachers set out to find an alternative way to assess student writing. In testing, the only piece of evidence remaining once tests are returned to students is a single grade on a report card. In portfolio assessment, we read what students actually *write*—in all ways a much better indication of students' knowledge, writing history, and progress. This was the goal of the Teachers who first began using portfolios as evidence of students' writing competency.

In a portfolio, one can read students' writing and see if the pieces, in fact, meet the expectations of competent writing: Is there clear purpose in this piece? Is there organization—a logical progression of ideas? Is the writer in control of his/her writing? Is there a focus? fluency? cohesiveness? Are details clear and effective? Is there consistency of voice and style? Are grammar usage and the mechanics of the piece correct? Process writing includes each of these criteria. Pieces in a portfolio can give evidence of whether a student's writing is meeting these expectations.

Portfolios provide Teachers, parents, and students with a concrete picture of the work students have done, the skills they have acquired and a general view of some of the learning they have yet to do. Portfolios also can show Teachers what has been mastered and what they still must teach.

If it is determined at your school that Teachers will keep student portfolios, parents should be informed early in the year that students will accumulate portfolios of their writing at school and that these will be available to parents when they come for conferences. This will help parents understand why some papers do not accompany their children home. They will look forward to seeing the portfolios during conference times at school.

Better than a test

Tests do not tell us how children *think.* They are only transient indicators of a student's ability and do not show us what children really know and can do. Tests tend to show us what is *wrong,* what students do *not* know. Emphasis is on the number of errors and on the grade at the top of the paper. A portfolio gives us an overall picture, emphasizing what students *have done* and *can do*. Most teachers now feel it is more important to ask what *progress* a student is making than to ask what grade he or she has earned. A portfolio shows that progress.

Because of changes in philosophy about teaching and changes in teaching methods, many Teachers and administrators are searching for different ways to demonstrate students' writing abilities. Portfolios—collections of students' writing—have become major tools in showing what students have done and can do, just as professional illustrators' or writers' portfolios demonstrate what they can do. They give us a picture of students' progress that represents the *whole child*. A test score indicates performance at a given time, while a portfolio can indicate progress for a semester, an entire school year, and more. Portfolios provide real documentation of students' learning.

Some time ago, I was expounding with enthusiasm on some ideas about schools and learning to a friend who is head of a college department of education. She agreed with me but said, "You have to understand that for many people, education is not a priority." She was right. Yet we need to do all we can to *make* it a priority if our students are to equip themselves with the skills they'll need for living long after they leave our school systems. Emphasis on what students can do, shown in a tangible way in portfolios, can help create self-esteem and interest in learning not only for students but for their parents as well.

Keep a portfolio of your own

Teachers need to keep portfolios containing their own writing. Only then can we know what our students experience as they write—drafting, revising, proofreading, editing, and publishing final drafts. Let students see that you too keep a portfolio. If students draw designs on their portfolios, draw designs on yours too. If you find a unique portfolio for your work, show it to your students and let them know that you consider it to be a special possession.

If it is decided that your students will keep portfolios, some practical decisions need to be made: Why will portfolios be kept? What kind of portfolios will be used? How will they be used? Where will they be kept? It is pointless to keep portfolios if they merely grow dusty in sets of office files. How many papers will be included in them? Will they be kept just for the school year, then sent home—or will they be sent to the student's teacher for the following year? These are decisions that must be made by individual staffs and districts. There must be purpose in keeping portfolios, and those purposes should be determined by those Teachers and students who will create and use them.

A portfolio may take many forms: an accordion-type folder for each student, a three-ring binder, a box, or some other unique and practical holder. One teacher obtains pizza boxes each year from a pizzeria whose owner is happy to provide these for use as portfolios. Whatever works best for you and your students will be fine.

Who chooses portfolio selections?

A college freshman in one of my college classes was talking about the portfolios students were required to keep during her junior and senior years of high school. "The Teacher chose the pieces to keep," she said. "We had nothing to say about what went into our portfolios, and what's more, we never got to see them once our pieces were put into them. That wasn't fair—we wrote those pieces and they belonged to *us!*" She was right. Students *can* and *should* help choose pieces that go into portfolios; that collection of pieces will reflect the uniqueness of the student whose work it is. Included in useful portfolios should be numerous samples of students' pieces that show writing activity and development. As creators of the writing and as owners of those pieces, students should help to select that representation.

What goes inside?

It may be useful for each student to keep several portfolios. One, in which pieces are mainly chosen by the student, might show final copies of only the student's favorite pieces. The student owns this portfolio, and there is no expectation that it contain examples of all kinds of writing. This might be called a blue-ribbon portfolio or "The best of..." portfolio.

A skills or demonstration portfolio

The second portfolio might be called a *skills* or *demonstration* portfolio. This portfolio is created by the student and Teacher together. It will show samples of various kinds of writing done over a period of time, evidence to back up grades, and comments about students' writing. This portfolio may contain personal narrative pieces, fiction, informational and persuasive writing, poetry, and any other writing that demonstrates a student's ability in a variety of areas. Be selective: Together, choose pieces that demonstrate specific writing skills. On a record sheet attached to the portfolio, list skills represented on papers contained in the portfolio and the dates on which those skills were demonstrated in writing pieces. It is also suggested that the first, revised, and final drafts of a specific writing assignment be included to show how the student has used the steps of process writing to produce a high-quality piece.

Be sure to date pieces and document them with sticky notes or labels. Dating writing pieces allows for an orderly recording of students' skill development.

Documentation attached to these pieces might contain information gathered during Teacher/student conferences: *David chose this piece because he felt it was the best descriptive writing he has done in fourth grade.* Or, *David said that at the beginning of the year he had problems with dialogue, but now writing dialogue is easy for him, as shown in his story,* Jeremy and the Lion. Teachers also may note their own observations about various pieces: *David's competency in developing a tighter story plot is shown in his piece dated Jan. 3.*

A works-in-progress portfolio

A *works-in-progress* portfolio, or a working portfolio, is exactly that—a folder of current writing. It can contain writing related to all areas of study and might include stories, poetry, essays, research, persuasive writing, and more. That portfolio should be kept by the student so he or she has ready access to those pieces. Frequent "cleaning out" of these portfolios may be necessary, with many of these pieces going home to be shared with family, then kept in a collection there.

Students will find it interesting to learn that most writers work on several writing projects at once. It is not always practical to work exclusively on one piece until it is finished. Students may find it enjoyable to have several works in progress at one time.

Kindergartners can keep portfolios too. Theirs will need to be big ones, as these children often draw and write on large paper. This collection of beginning writings and drawings will document students' early writing development. In addition, keeping portfolios is exciting to kindergartners and their parents as students learn to take ownership of their papers and feel pride in these written records that show what they know and can do.

Sharing portfolios with parents

To learn about their child's writing development, parents need to look at more than grades on a report card or on the student's papers. They need to read each piece in a portfolio and take time to enjoy and listen to their child's stories, poems, essays and reports—the child's own words. A perfect time for doing this is during parent conferences. An effective way to demonstrate their child's progress to parents is to have the student present the portfolio.

It works!

A recent article in the Twin Cities' *Star Tribune* describes a fourth-grader speaking to his parents at a parent conference. "Every week we write a story," he says. "Right now we're working on getting an exciting beginning and a problem in the story." A student in an elementary school where students, not teachers, lead conferences, this young writer goes on to explain his lessons and his progress to his parents, demonstrating with samples of his work collected in his portfolio throughout the school year. In such conferences, Teachers sit with their students, supporting and adding information as needed, but the student is clearly in charge.

"We decided that it's really silly to have conferences and talk about the kids and not have them there to...give their point of view...," says a student adviser from another school. Students practice for the conferences before they take place, role-playing the part of a parent, with the Teacher as student, and then as themselves. This ensures they will feel more comfortable when they present their work to their parents.

Teachers allow parents the option of meeting alone with them, but few parents choose to do that. Conferences with students present and in charge obviously are useful and meaningful to all participants.

Some schools have eliminated report cards completely, and in their place hold three parent conferences each year where students and their teachers present documentation of learning experiences, competencies and challenges yet to come. Teachers from one school where this practice has been in place for many years indicate that the practice results in great satisfaction among Teachers, students and parents.

At such presentations, parents are impressed with their children's insights into the quality of their work, the skills they have learned and their knowledge of the tasks they anticipate learning next. Students understand they have responsibility for their work and take pride in meeting that challenge.

At the end of the school year, Teachers should encourage parents and students to keep the portfolios to enjoy for many years to come. Suggest that students ask their parents if they have kept any of their own writing and, if so, request that the parents share it with them.

Teachers also benefit by having students' writing collections in portfolios: Looking through the cover list of skills taught and learned, reading through the pieces contained in a portfolio, Teachers can see where certain skills may need more emphasis or where others have been mastered by nearly everyone in class.

One teacher requires that her high-school seniors keep scrapbooks all year long, working on them at home and in class, filling them with poetry, stories, pictures and illustrations. What wonderful portfolios these are!

In the keeping of portfolios, as in so many areas of teaching and learning, there is no one correct method. Continue to ask questions. Experiment to find what works best for you and for your students. Ask other teachers what they are doing, what works best for them. Adapt the most appealing of those ideas to fit your students' own needs.

11 Poetry: A Special Way of Speaking

My first-grade writers were busy publishing final drafts and pasting together their animal story books. I had purposely delayed the morning's poetry reading until our books were finished.

"Mrs. B!" called Steven, wildly waving his hand, "aren't you going to read poems to us today? I just looooooooooooove poetry!"

Our volunteer mother helper looked from Steven to me and grinned. She knew that rumors of children "not liking poetry" were untrue. These kids *loved* poetry. We stopped the book project to indulge in a few minutes of poetic whimsy, then returned to book publishing.

Steven's waving hand is a metaphor for children's feelings about poetry. Children instinctively know a lot about poetry—the language, the similes, the metaphors, the rhythms, the music held in a poem. The earlier they learn the language of poetry, the more they will enjoy, love, and use it as their own.

My feeling is that children who "don't like poetry" simply haven't heard it. The world is filled with poetry, and I find that children who experience it, like it. Children who like it want to write their own, for children carry poetry within them.

When I go into a classroom as "poet in residence," either the Teacher introduces me and our writing topic or I introduce it myself. Because students can quickly tell that I have fun as we learn together, they feel free to moan and groan when poetry is announced as the hour's writing topic. "Oh, no! *Poetry!*" they may complain, though in a good-natured way. And then we begin.

We talk about poetry—what it is, what it isn't, how we start learning our first poems—nursery rhymes—as babies. We discuss and put on the board those things that make poetry different from other kinds of writing. We listen to poetry written by students who are like these students. Then we write our own. Every time, students amaze themselves and me by writing wonderfully lyrical, deeply thoughtful, fantastically funny, or incredibly touching poems.

I think a poem is like a song we sing, often from deep inside us. Sometimes it is a joyful song. Other times, it is like the poem a little girl wrote while we were working together. It was about her grandmother who had just died. "This is my sad song about my grandma," she said quietly, as she prepared to read it aloud to her classmates.

A poem also is like a sculpture. As the sculptor warms and shapes the clay, pulls and pushes it into its intended form, so a poet uses words in much the same way, working until the poem says exactly what the poet intends it to say.

Often things can be said only in poetry. Nothing else will say it.

The Summer He Left Me
My friend and I were friends forever until
he left.
I was happy all my summers but one.
I remember hiding from people
in the big dipper on my
8-shaped block.
I remember the smell of summer that
wasn't even a smell.

I remember the sound of summer that
wasn't even a sound.
I remember when we used to talk about
what we were going to do
the next day.
I remember going to school and talking about
how our sisters are weird.
I remember me sitting alone and
my friend coming to get me out of
boring.
I remember him coming to my house
to play—that's when he told me he was
leaving.
I was
shattered.
He was leaving our place on
the earth
that was only a speck
on the
map.
—Sean Molin

We play with poetry, but gently; poetry is not poetry when it is pounded together with a hammer. Sometimes the compulsion to rhyme takes away from what needs and wants to be written. We must let our students know that poetry does not have to rhyme. It is more important that we say in a poem what we want to say than it is that the poem rhyme.

Not long ago, a friend was angry when a young acquaintance, having turned in to her Teacher the poem over which she had labored lovingly, received a big red *F* on her paper along with the notation: *This does not rhyme. It is not a poem.* It made us both angry and sad that the Teacher sought only form but did not look for what the student was saying—the most important part. Please do not grade poetry! Share poems, discuss them, celebrate them, and encourage your young poets—but do not grade them.

As you choose poems to read to your class and as you read your students' poetry, remember that our interpretations and understandings of poetry vary greatly. Children are not adults; they cannot and do not see the world as we adults see it. And they will interpret each poem from their own perspective. For example, a poem by a famous writer about selling one's sister, which adults may think is hilarious, was considered to be a "really sad poem" by a little girl who loved her sister very much.

Is this poetry?

Skiing
The thought of
skiing
down a hill
on
two polished fiberglass
skis
sends thrills
through my body
Skiing is an

adventure
full of
daring stunts and
breathtaking jumps
that's what skiing is.
—Brett Huneke, grade 5

Sometimes poems rhyme so naturally, so effortlessly, we hardly notice it. That is perhaps the best way to write rhyming poetry.

Sing of rain,
And butterflies' wings
Think of everything
That sings
Think of the voice
Of the fifth-grade choir,
As the off-tune notes
Climb higher and higher.
Think of crickets,
With whispering wings;
Oh, isn't it peaceful
To think of what sings!
—Meredith Reiches, grade 5

Moon
My moon
is where I go
when I want my own special time.
It's the place I go when
I'm feeling sad.
It's where I go when I want to fly
like the birds.
It's where I go when
I want birthdays all year.
My moon is my place.
—Steve Garretson, grade 5

One of my favorites
Behind the old, wrinkled face
and withered hands
there is YOUTH.
If they were in shape
they would do what
any young would do—
roll down hills,
climb trees,
jump down into piles of straw

Maybe they do that
when we're not around.
—Nicole Mari Oetjen, grade 6

How do we begin?

We bring books filled with poetry into our classrooms and we read lots of poetry to our students—all kinds, from many sources. We give our students access to poetry and we let them go, reading aloud, reading silently, talking and writing in groups, in pairs—whatever works for our students.

We encourage them: "Now write some of your own poems. " And we tell them, "You can't do it wrong. Whatever you write will be just fine. " For, just as painters begin to paint by following the examples of fine painters, so we model our beginning poetry after what we hear and see. Shel Silverstein, Maya Angelou, John Ciardi, Nikki Giovanni, Cynthia Rylant, and Valerie Worth—and Juan, Tiffani, Jason, Rosa, Troy, and Meredith—are all poets. It gives us a place to begin. It is important that students hear poetry written by other students; they learn that if other students can write poetry, so can they.

Show your young poets that often the power of a poem is found in the last line, as it is in this poem:

> *Roller Coaster*
> Heart beating, nervous
> The car is going up and up and up.
> My stomach is against the safety bar
> I look down at the bottom
> I scream.
> I'm going on it again!
> —Anon.

Have your students write original comparisons—poets constantly compare.

> Clouds are like pillows that won't fit in my bed.
> The rain was like pins falling through cotton.

Have them write contrasts—poets often make contrasts.

> He was tall and twiggy;
> she was short and round.
> Her face was long, serious,
> his a merry
> circle of laughter.

Teach them about similes:

> Her laughter was like bells tinkling merrily.
> The piano is like a monster with big black and white teeth.

And metaphors:

> Some people are drained batteries; he was jumper cables!
> The piano is a monster with big black and white teeth.

Pocket poetry

Several years ago I started the following project, which is self-explanatory. I share it with you because results have been wonderful. I made copies of the following:

> Dear Teachers:
>   This is the beginning of a new personal project, designed to encourage the enjoyment of poetry in all its wonderful shapes and forms. Will you help?
>   I am making copies of some of my favorite poems, giving them to students and friends, and asking them to return to me one of their favorites. They may copy their

"trading stock" from poetry books, use nursery rhymes, write their own—whatever. The idea is to encourage the enjoyment of poetry. Students may carry these around in their pockets, and I encourage them to "learn them by heart," for it is satisfying to know poems from memory.

Meanwhile, for you, here is one of my favorites, written by Myrtle Sylvia Johnson, a sweet woman I knew when I was a child. She was crippled by arthritis, yet her heart sang poetry.

Invalid's Longing
I am waiting for the springtime
When the fruit trees are in bloom,
When I'll see them from my window
And breathe their sweet perfume.
And I'm waiting for the summer
When the air is filled with song,
When the flowers grow profusely
And the days are bright and long.
Oh, I love all nature's seasons—
Each one has its special charms.
But the budding, blooming period
I await with open arms.

Often, students or Teachers hand me lovely poems to carry in my own pockets—this has become a special way to share our enjoyment of poetry.

Repetition in poetry
We've all heard children singing the same words over and over again; they enjoy repetition. Sometimes one line is repeated throughout a poem.

I hear the birds singing in trees outside
When I go to bed.
I hear my mother's feet down the hall
When I go to bed.
I see curtains gently moving,
And shadows on my wall
When I go to bed.

Word "banks" for writing poetry
As we set the stage for writing poetry, we might brainstorm with our students some of the words related to a single topic—for example, *fog*. Words for use in a *fog* poem might include the following: curtains, blankets, windows, gray, wall, misty, swirly, hiding. Sometimes it helps beginning poets to have "banks" or collections of words ready to use as they write.

Your name: A poem!
Just for fun, a poem can be written using one's name or a word written down the left-hand side of the paper, followed on each line by thoughts:

Winter snowflakes play outside by my window.
Inside, I watch and listen.
No footprints mar the white blanket
There.
Even the birds
Rest and watch today.

Imagery

Talk with your students about the word *image*. It is related to **imagination**, that wonderful place inside us where we can see and hear things, taste and smell and feel them. Good descriptive writing can make pictures in our minds; poems often convey images or pictures to readers.

Instruct your students to close their eyes as you take them on a walk through a deep, dark forest in their imaginations. Listen for the birds calling down from the trees, for squirrels chattering as you invade their private territory. Smell the damp, wet floor of the forest; feel its softness, the slippery pine needles under your feet. This is *imagery*. Sensory details, the pictures that make something real in our minds, are *imagery*

A detailed description of hot buttery popcorn just out of the popper can actually make mouths water, sending some students home at the end of the day so hungry for popcorn that they can hardly wait to make some!

Descriptions of what we can see, hear, feel, taste, and smell can be so real that we actually experience the reality of those senses. That is why imagery is so important to poetry

Some days I am sour milk;
Stale, milky-blue, old, terrible.
Other times, I am champagne,
Bubbly, light, new, wonderful!

or

Today I am an icicle
hanging
all alone
hard and cold
from the roof of our
schoolhouse

Encourage your students to use specific describing words in their poems for effective imagery.

I am...

"I am" can be an effective beginning for the writing of poetry:

I am something small or big, perhaps an animal: *Today I am a lion with golden eyes and a beautiful soft, cuddly mane—would you like to come and pet me?* or *Today I am a skyscraper, strong and tall!* or *Today I am an old, worn-out, cozy red sweater.* I am a color: *Today I am blue like the sea.* Brainstorm your own "I am" ideas with your class. Encourage them to go on to "tell more," to describe even more clearly.

"I am"

Read the following descriptions to your students. Each line begins with *I am*. Read each numbered line, giving students time to write a line related to the description. Read the examples given for the first three lines. Encourage students to *describe* as they write their "I Am" poems.

1. I am...something small, but not alive.
   (*Ex:* I am a small gray stone sitting out in the rain.)

2. I am… something you might find in your yard.
   (Ex. I am a long brown worm, crawling underground.) etc.
3. I am… something to wear in winter.
   (Ex. I am old, cuddly bedroom slippers with the fur wearing off at the toes.)
4. I am… something used for celebrating.
5. I am… a kind of weather.
6. I am… an animal or living creature.
7. I am…something that moves that cannot be seen.
   (Ex: I am the spirit of my grandmother)
8. I am…something that makes music.
9. I am…something big and strong.
10. I am…something soft and gentle.

Kids love the challenge of this and may want to create their own categories; several student suggestions have been:

I am something that…
is sticky
is furry.

I am…something to be opened.
a stuffed animal.
something with a label on it.
something in a forest.

This is a good way to begin writing poetry: It invites wonderful description; it discourages pointless rhyming; and it encourages students to include personal ideas to create effective lines of poetry.

We were using this poetry writing lesson in a Teachers' workshop where a young teacher shared his poem written from the lines given. All of his "I am" poem was lovely, but it was the last two lines that we will always remember:

I am a Dad. (9.)
I am a Dad. (10.)

How do we encourage students to write poetry?

We talk, share examples, enjoy the work of other poets, turn out the lights, and *imagine*. We take walks, lie in the grass, slide down playground slides, swing on swings. We become other things: birds, flowers, dolphins, airplanes. We play with words, move them around until they say exactly what we want to say. We give ourselves and our students permission to be *poets!* And when we are finished, we can share or not share these very personal statements. We celebrate our poems in different ways—publishing them, saving them, perhaps giving them as gifts, or maybe even simply putting them away in folders or pockets, knowing that we have said something in our own unique way.

Then and now

In my student days, most of the emphasis on poetry was directed at how many lines in a cinquain or quatrain, how to write iambic pentameter—the forms, the rules—not on the wonderful language of the poems and the joy of hearing them.

Though I recall my kindergarten teacher reading poetry to us, most of my own love of poetry came after my school days. It was revived by the gift of a book of poetry from a young friend, and again was stimulated by hearing one of my daughter's college professors read her favorite poems each year at the mother–daughter college weekend. Now I read poetry every day of my life, and my head is filled with wonderful words, with colorful images covering an entire range of emotions. When poetry becomes part of one's very being, something special happens inside: new/old feelings, emotions, thoughts come together in unexpected and important ways. For now, don't be concerned with the technicalities; be concerned that you and your students hear, enjoy, feel see, taste, smell, and know the *language* of poetry

A book like this can give only some simple ideas about writing poetry; do your own "homework"—check out poetry books from your school or public library. Bring a *poet in residence* to your classroom to talk with students. Check your own language books to see what might be of use to you and your young poets. Find poetry anthologies. Read and learn about poets. Buy yourself a book of poetry just for the sheer enjoyment of it. Search for poems, find some favorites and read them over and over until they are committed to memory. Share your own enjoyment of this wonderful language form with your colleagues and students. If you host a luncheon, find some delicious poems to read to your guests. (Phyllis McGinley's poetry is super for this—her "Ode to the Bath," for example.) At a dinner, invite each guest to bring a favorite poem to read. This special kind of language is to experience, to share, to treasure; it leaves us richer once it becomes a part of us.

12 *Just for Teachers*

Some years ago I was in the Teachers' lounge of a nearby school having a quick cup of coffee between presentations when a representative from a publishing company breezed in, her expensive gray winter coat swirling airily behind her.

"I hear that you're presenting a writing program here," she said, smiling professionally. "And how many steps do you have in *your* program?"

I looked at her, puzzled.

"How many steps in your program for writing? We have *five*," she said, pleased with her knowledge, counting off each one neatly, cleanly on her beautifully manicured fingers.

I felt like a dummy. I had never counted them; I just *did* them—the process, moving from step to step; it was nothing new for me. I'd always done it with my classes in all elementary grades. As she swept on out the door again, I raised my own fingers and tried to count the steps in "my program." I'd never even thought of counting "steps" before! It was hard, because one slid into the next, blurring the lines between them. I'd heard of other programs with steps, too: seven, four, nine. These professional publishers of writing programs really were organized!

Later that night, having beaten down my guilty feelings over teaching a whole writing program without a well-defined number of "steps," I began to write about my process for writing—nothing new, really—and it isn't even "my" program; it's just what we *do* in process writing.

Writing: The process

We start by setting the stage, by *getting ready to write*. We do it by talking, perhaps by listening to music, looking at a picture, taking a field trip, telling a story, reading a book, sharing some experiences or brainstorming. All of these activities help to give writers ideas from which to work, and they provide motivation for getting started. We call this setting of the stage for writing *prewriting*.

Next we write a first draft. Hopefully, this paper will reflect good first efforts, and it is fine for words and sentences on this draft to be crossed out, to contain scribbles—we often call it a *rough draft* or a *sloppy copy*—to reflect thinking, changing, revising. Teachers write too while helping those who need assistance. Writing on every other line leaves space on this *first draft* for making changes more easily. (Sometimes Teachers write first drafts before students do their writing, allowing Teachers to anticipate difficulties students may encounter, and so discussing these areas before students actually start to write.)

We *proofread* aloud, listening to the sound of our writing, deciding where changes, additions or corrections are needed. We may read the paper a second time, to make corrections of mechanical errors—spelling, capitalization, punctuation, grammar. The Teacher or other students may help with this by conferencing in pairs, in small groups, in a whole-group situation, or in the conferencing circle. This first draft becomes a *revised first draft* as changes and corrections are made. It may be recopied, becoming a *second draft*.

Finally we recopy or publish the paper in final form, doing our best to have a neat, well-written paper that pleases us, the writers—one that we will feel comfortable sharing with others (our *audience*).

That's it: the process of writing. It's simple, logical. It makes sense. Into the process we can add brainstorming, story starters, minilessons as needed about skills and information pertinent to a given piece of writing, other skills as needed and understood, and questions to help clarify the writing. All of these are concepts and activities to help our students become competent in written language. We conference with our students to see how we can be of help to them; we give them access to one another to create and share; and we help them take responsibility for as much of their own writing as they are able to handle.

Once we do these things enough times to know the process, we have no need to tick off "steps" on our fingers; the concept will be within us and we will move easily through the writing we wish to do with our students. We want them too to understand the process so it will be a natural part of their writing, no matter what subject matter is being covered. We can assure our students that this—a "recipe" to follow for producing good pieces of writing—will always stand them in good stead, from first grade through high school and college and throughout their working lives. Writing pieces in this way will always work. The terms students begin learning in the primary grades—drafting, revising, proofreading, etcetera, and the proofreading marks—will always be correct.

As you share written language with your students, be aware that in the last few years, there have probably been more writing programs created than were published all together in the years before. Remember: Publishers are in business to make money; Teachers are in business to help children learn for a lifetime. An enthusiastic, caring, alert, participating Teacher will do more to teach writing effectively than any book. *You* are the key. Few students remember the language textbooks used in their early years of writing; they do remember the Teachers who taught them, who encouraged them, the classroom atmosphere, the way language was taught.

We must name each child *writer* when he or she is young. Name yourself *writer* too. The satisfactions of writing are many: confidence, self-esteem, a sense of power that can make things happen—that can make readers laugh, cry, think, feel. What does it do to a student, to an adult, to see a reader laughing or silently weeping over something we have written? In writing, we may discover new things about ourselves, make discoveries about others and about the world in which we live.

For many years, I wrote at Christmas to my own wonderful first-grade Teacher, Miss Wilcox. She wrote back to me. I called her when I visited my old hometown and we discussed curriculum, students, schools, teaching and learning. To my constant amazement, she remembered the names of all the students in our class, as she did of each of her classes, year after year. I told her *thank you* for the important role she played in my life. She died not long ago, and I treasure the friendship that lasted long after our roles were that of student and Teacher. She knew the special influence she had on my life.

Now that I am older, I myself know the joy of hearing a former student say he or she has been nurtured through something done in our classroom. Recently a letter came in the mail; the return address was that of one of my former second-grade students, now in her last year of college and ready to step into the world of teaching. "You made me want to be a Teacher," she wrote. She will never know how much her letter meant to me. What pleasure it has brought me to learn that some of my former students are now Teachers themselves.

Perhaps you have some *thank yous* to say to your own former Teachers. If so, then do it. Don't wait. Several of those dear Teachers in my life have died, but I had written to them and thanked them before that happened. We shared memories, and they knew they were important to my own development as a person, as a Teacher. That, they said, gave them great satisfaction. The writing, the saying of my thank-yous, made me feel good too.

I recently walked back through my old elementary school and there, in memory, in the basement classroom of Mrs. Borrey, I was again in fifth grade, gathered with my classmates around the old round table that held a globe. I remembered turning, turning, turning it and looking at all the countries and seas in the world, marveling, as she encouraged us to do, at how big it all seemed. She was the Teacher who first encouraged us not to sit silently in our desks in neat rows, but to get up and move around the classroom, to talk to one another, to do "hands-on" learning. She also was the one who occasionally allowed us to climb up out the window rather than going out the door at the end of the day—something she herself had probably wanted to do! I thanked her as I stood in our old classroom.

Some writing ideas for you

Teachers who teach writing must themselves write. Here are some ideas for you to use for your own personal writing. Give them a try—each has worked well for me. You will find new things popping into your head and old memories coming back as you enjoy this craft of writing.

What I have learned

We all learn daily through our teaching, through our personal lives. Take time to write some things you have learned: Perhaps you have learned, finally, that you really are a good Teacher. Write about it. Maybe you have learned how to handle stress, how to be a good listener, or perhaps how to relax, to save some time for you, to celebrate. All these things are important. Write about them.

Coming back to teaching

One of the best things that happened when I returned to teaching as a substitute Teacher was that I went from class to class and room to room, and almost every day I saw someone else's ideas in use, ideas that were new for me. It was a great time of learning; Teachers were happy to give me copies of their ideas, to let me make samples of my own, following their patterns. Ask other Teachers to share their ideas; volunteer to share with them what has worked for you. Teachers' days are filled with activities that leave little time for sharing, and we all need every good idea we can get.

Brainstorm to create your own list of "I remember." Let your mind relax, slow down, take time to recall memories. Then begin writing in detail some of your own memories, perhaps one each week. Do a rough draft, revise, then finish it so it says exactly what you want to say.

One of my childhood memories was of our house and yard filled with guests, no one taking particular notice of me, a four-year-old wandering through the back yard with a large, brightly colored ball of red, green, blue. It seemed to demand that I do something with it, so I jumped on it, bounced right off and landed on my back. Stars flew through my head as I stood up, wobbled my way through the grass and up the steps to our back door where I knocked, then waited for my mother to come. I saw her face at the door, said, "Mom . . ." and promptly blacked out. Doctors had terrified me, as I had experienced painful treatments on my hands for a skin problem, and I remember hearing the words: "Call the doctor! Call the doctor!" as I lay on the couch in our living room, unable to get out any words but wanting so much to cry, "No! No! I'm fine!"

My brainstorming begins:

big ball
I remember
many colors
many people
jumping
falling
stars
walking to French doors
Mom!
fainting
being carried
on couch
can't talk
"Call doctor"
NO!NO!NO!

Brainstorming, I can feel myself jumping on the big, beautiful ball, can feel the bouncing backwards, the stars exploding in my head; can feel myself getting up slowly and walking like a zombie to the porch, up the steps, knocking on the door and seeing my mother's face as she opened the door and looked out at me, puzzled at the strange expression on my face. Everything moves in slow motion in my memory.

My finished piece begins:

I remember the big red, green and blue ball lying on the lush green grass in our back yard. It was shiny and new, a gift.

Our yard was full of people gathered for someone's birthday party—not mine, and no one was paying any attention to me.

So off I ran, then jumped on that beautiful ball, bounced right back off and landed on my back. Stars flew around inside, behind my eyes, as I slowly, blindly, stood up and wobbled my way through thick grass to the steps leading up onto the porch, where I knocked on the door, then waited for my mother to come. . . .

Another memory, that of roller skating down the Summit Avenue hill just a block from our house, comes back as I brainstorm:

roller skating
cracks
jump
rush
fly
free
corner
swing around
driveway
Cottons

rest
again!!
skates
key
click
stroke, stroke
hill
climb
slow
turn
top
down

I begin to write my happy memory:

I remember roller skating down Summit Avenue.
   I carry my shiny key on a string around my neck—the precious key to roller skates that will give me freedom to fly like a bird just moments from now.
   The bottom step of our small front porch provides the chair as I clamp my skates to the soles of my shoes and stand, ready for flight. (Writing this, I can feel the warm key in my hand, feel my fingers turning it to tighten the four clamps that will lock the skates to my sturdy shoes.)
   But first, the climb. For one always soars from the top of something in flight. Up the hill I move slowly, steadily, one foot in the grass lining the long, straight street curb, one foot on the gray, smooth sidewalk, my legs pulling me to the top of the hill. Only vaguely do I sense that cars pass by and people walk on the other side of the street.
   At the top of the hill, I turn and pause, peer down to the bottom, remind myself to jump over the cracked section of sidewalk in the middle of my flight path. And then, with two strong strokes of my powerful legs, I am off, flying down my hill, a joyful bird free in flight. Swoosh! Jump! Over the cracked squares of sidewalk near the top I go, faster and faster. Passersby see only a blur of skates and clothes as I swoop to the bottom, swing powerfully around the corner and curl up into Cotton's driveway. Only a moment to catch my breath, and I begin the climb again. For flight is addictive, and I do not want it ever to end.

Having completed this writing, and because I plan to have my students write in the third person soon, I rewrite my skating story in third person, take the position of an observer watching the girl skate. This too is enjoyable writing, but it does not make me breathless, as does the first-person piece.

Writing can bring special people back into our lives. Remembering my beautiful grandmother one day, I began brainstorming about her, and my writing developed into a picture of her, bringing her back so clearly that I could see her beside me:

I remember my grandma's face, always gentle, often smiling, nearly impassive in hard situations, not showing the emotions that surely she felt inside. Sometimes my face is like that too. Sometimes, entertained by one of her performing grandchildren or her outrageously wonderful, funny daughter-in-law, my aunt, her face would turn red and smile crinkles would gather around her hazel green eyes as huge tears of laughter rolled down her face, her entire body shaking with laughter. But mostly, it is Gram's lovely profile I remember, as I take my small self back in time to sit in the fragrant wooden pew beside her in church. I see her behatted head, her silvery-blue hair done up in a bun. I hear her voice, mostly a sweet monotone. And I see her face as she sings joyfully, "Ponder anew what the Almighty can do." It is one of my most real, most poignant memories. I can call it back at will.

Try it! Go back into memory and brainstorm. Let your mind move quickly, and see what surprises brainstorming might hold for you. People who go to therapists for help in solving problems, in changing behavior, often are told, "Write it down." We can use this tool ourselves to bring back memories. Don't be surprised if sometimes a sad or hard memory comes back, a frightening one, a funny one, a dear one. This is a way of taking a look at it, perhaps of growing through writing about it.

Brainstorming is an effective way to speak on paper in different ways too; here I used it as a technique to write poetry as I remembered my father and his big, strong, well-tanned hands, working to create a kite from brown paper, straws and string on my cousin's farm in the early spring:

Kite
paper sack
cloud
straw
string
tail
control
fluttering
pull
farm
lift
Dad
free
Uncle
cousins
blue sky

To My Dad
When I was small
and Easter took us to the farm,
your magic hands turned
plain brown paper sack and
fragrant yellow straw to
strong brown and yellow kite.
Small strips of cloth
made ruffly tail.
We ran and
wind took Kite to sky
to dip and soar,
to cut through clouds
and nearly pull me
off the ground.

I wanted to be
Kite, carried
free, soaring high—
Fly, Kite, fly!
And yet,
close to you

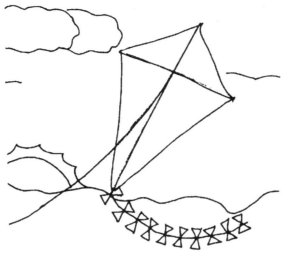

so brown and strong,
my safe Ground,
was an even better place to be.
Now I fly
bright-colored
plastic
manufactured kites,
slick, shiny, perfect,
with children of my own
and dream of you and magic hands
that turned paper sack and straw to
strong and wondrous
flying kite.
I have no magic hands.

Just as we tell our students, write what you know.

I am so thankful for those Teachers in my own life who helped to create a hunger in me for words, for stories, for books, then helped to fill that need by supplying those things and by going on to show me how to create my own stories, happenings, word pictures. They have made it possible for me to write such things as this, a small happening during the time I was reentering teaching in the role of long-term substitute in a first-grade class.

Becky (Notes from a Sub)

"Mrs. B, I only have one friend left at my house now."

Puzzlement.

"What do you mean, Becky?"

"Well, my mother told me last night that she doesn't love me any more.

And my brother doesn't love me. Only Daddy is going to be my friend now, forever and forever."

The small, earnest face looks up, waiting, crossed eyes peering at me through thick glasses.

"Oh, Becky, I don't think she meant it—maybe she was just angry."

"She meant it, all right. And now I only have one friend."

What do you do? You put your arms gently around Becky and hug her to try to fill the emptiness inside her. And you gently kiss her cheek.

"Becky, I'm so very, very sorry. But you have at least two friends, because I love you too, and you will be my special friend for always."

Anger. How could a mother say such a thing to her own daughter? Later you learn that yes, indeed, this mother speaks thus to her daughter who clearly reflects the father for whom the mother has only contempt.

One, two, three days go by. Large, sad eyes wait every day for the hugs, the reassurances. Small One stands, sits close by whenever possible.

Finally, one morning it happens. Joy bursts in the door.

"Mrs. B! My mommy loves me again!"

"Oh, Becky, I'm so glad, so very, very glad!"

The last day of school, no child escapes without a hug.

Giggles.

"I'll miss you!"

"Have a good summer!"

Becky straggles, tears in her eyes. "Bend over, Mrs. B."

I bend.

Arms hug my neck and a large, wet kiss is planted on my cheek.

"Remember the day my mother didn't love me?"

"Yes, I remember."

"And you gave me a kiss?"

"Yes."

"Well, that was it!"

And she scurries out the door, love returned a thousandfold.

And I weep in thankfulness for Becky.

Exercise, exercise!

Do you have trouble making your characters real? Here's a way to begin: do the eye exercise. Write descriptions of at least four pairs of eyes:

> faded blue but kind, gentle eyes, old eyes
> sparkling brown eyes flecked with bits of green
> snappy brown eyes that matched her short, curly hair
> small blue eyes looking straight ahead at something he seemed not to see

You will find that real eyes, the eyes of family, friends, acquaintances, come into your mind as you write. Thus you are describing real eyes to make your writing real.

Follow this with a hand exercise, a foot exercise, a hair exercise, and so on. You may wish to do this with your students.

Make time to write just for you

Here are some things to think and write about:

> How do you want to be remembered?
> The last time you cried
> The secret you that nobody knows
> I am waiting for . . .
> I always wanted, but never got to have . .
> If I had my life to live over . . .
> My life's color right now is . . .
> Some of the best things happening in my life right now . . .

A journal of your own

Keep a journal, even if you write only once a week; record feelings about your students, your school. Make notes about ideas that have worked well. Record happenings that touch you in a special way. Start with one day at a time and don't feel you must write every single day. Take your own writing seriously and value it when you finish. A few notes written on paper several times a week or month, saved in a box or folder, can serve as a journal and can be of value to you as you read them over at a later time.

My wonderful uncle died from Alzheimer's disease, that terrible illness that can change personalities and wipe away memories and knowledge of what *is*. In the middle of his illness, I visited in his home for several days. During that time, he said some dear and precious things, some funny things. I listened carefully and wrote them down.

After his death, I shared my notes with his family. We could almost hear him speaking. He had a terrific sense of humor, and some of the funny things he said during his illness were much like the hilarious comments he made before he became ill. Without the journal notes, we might not have remembered those special words, those precious happenings.

Your writing as a gift

Another special way of using written language in our own lives is as a gift. Many Teachers have parents who celebrate fortieth and fiftieth anniversaries. By that time in life, most people have all the material things they need. Short written pieces relating special feelings, thoughts, memories of children, grandchildren, and other family members can be the loveliest of gifts.

When I returned to visit a school where I had earlier presented a workshop, a Teacher came to talk with me. "Remember how you suggested that we write special memories for our parents' gifts?" he asked.

"Yes, I do."

"Well, our family did that; we put together about fifty pages of special writings," he said. "And our parents loved it."

"I'm so glad," I answered.

"But that wasn't the best part!" he said, tears filling his eyes. "My Dad, who had been in perfect health, died of a heart attack just a couple of days after the anniversary. And the best part was not just that he had loved our gift; it was that none of us now feels bad for not having told him how we loved him—because we did tell him! And we're all so glad for that."

More writing ideas

Your room when you were a small child
Your early memories
Your grandparents, aunts, and uncles
Something you've wanted to try but have not yet had the courage to do
Finish: "I feel like a professional Teacher when . . ."

Write a note to someone in your school building who needs a compliment, a word of encouragement. Often, it is especially meaningful to have a note that one can read over and over. Perhaps your principal can use an encouraging word; there's only one of him or her in your school, and many Teachers. Sometimes, being a principal is lonely. Put it on paper.

Dream

We often ask small children, "What do you want to be when you grow up?" It isn't only children who need to dream, to think of things they would like to do: We do too! Write about your own dreams, your hopes. One of my big dreams is to swim with dolphins—and I fully intend to do it some day.

When you feel that you have to do it all

"Feed the stream."

Several years ago, I visited with a dear Teacher friend, one so conscientious about his own work that he was upset by other Teachers who, he observed, did not work as hard as he, who spent much of their time in the Teachers' lounge—who, he thought, did not take their teaching jobs seriously enough. We had another friend with similar feelings, one who cared so much that he poured all of himself into his teaching, leaving nothing inside himself; emptied, he took his own life. Now my friend said, tears in his eyes, "I work so hard, all the time, and I'm never done, and I'm so tired."

Teachers are expected, more and more, to be superhuman, to cope with many more things than we feel able to handle. The task sometimes seems impossible, and we get the feeling that we are doing nothing in the midst of trying to do everything. Most Teachers tend to be hard on themselves.

When we begin to feel overwhelmed, we can remember a beautiful saying I once read somewhere: *Feed the stream.* To me, as I explained to my caring friend, it means that as the stream continues to flow by, we put in whatever good we can, knowing that other Teachers too will add their teaching as the stream of students moves along. The stream does not stop and wait for us to fill it; we are not expected to put in everything. We just add our own best, counting on other Teachers along the winding of the stream to do the same. This knowledge can give us peace as we work hard at the tasks that come to us as Teachers and can help to keep our own work in perspective.

When you share what you write

If you have occasion to share what you have written, simply share it. Never apologize for what you write; it reflects thinking and hard work. In the same manner, tell your students not to apologize for their writing. A writer who prefaces sharing with, "This is really dumb," may find that the audience actually *likes* what he wrote. Such a statement reflects uncertainty, but we all have that feeling sometimes, and it's all right to feel uncertain. (Have you done the best you can do? Then it isn't dumb!)

When you finish writing a piece of your own, stop to ask yourself what it is you like best about it. Similarly, remember to ask this question of your students. It's important that we recognize our own writing strengths, that we enjoy our own writing.

Like our students, we may work on something for awhile, but discover that it just doesn't work. Then we start over. This is an important part of learning to choose our own topics and make them work for us. Give yourself permission to make mistakes, to scribble and cross out, start over, to fail as well as to succeed.

Each summer, I teach a college workshop for Teachers who help children learn to write. And every year, there is at least one Teacher in our class who comments at the end of the week, "I discovered this week that *I can write!*" Somewhere in the years of schooling, many individuals are told, or are made to feel, that they are not writers. This deprives them of an incredible amount of satisfaction, of joy, of power. Perhaps you too have been made to feel like a nonwriter. With encouragement, perhaps with even your own conscious self encouraging your inner self, you can rediscover that power, that voice and give yourself permission to use it, to enjoy it. Just as you encourage your students, so you need to encourage yourself, to surround yourself with cheerleaders of your own.

We learn to know good authors and their writing through reading their books, not merely by hearing about them, talking about them. We do not become good writers by talking about writing; we learn to write just as our students do—by writing.

Teachers too need to read. Ask colleagues what they are reading. Find a bookstore where you feel at home, where the owner and salespeople can get to know you and your reading preferences, then treat yourself to an occasional new book. Ask for their recommendations—call them with questions about books; you will find them happy to be of assistance.

Become a patron of your local library. Ask questions—keep up on new authors, but indulge yourself with some poking around in the shelves for old "goodies" too. Then go home, find a cozy chair and *read*! You'll never be sorry for any time spent reading good books—they can provide the vacation you may not be able to manage in any other way. And in the winter, if you live where blizzards cause unexpected snow days, don't spend them cleaning closets or the basement—without also giving yourself the gift of reading time.

It is when we feel filled, accepting ourselves, that we best can give to others what they may need from us. Many people need things from Teachers every day. We must be gentle with ourselves, sometimes, to do the difficult but wonderful work we have chosen.

These are the things I would say to you if we could sit down for a long visit. This is not a curriculum guide; nor is it the answer to everyone's questions about writing. It is just what I have learned, what I know to be useful, in my work with children. I hope you have found some things here that make sense to you, that will prove helpful to you in your life as a Teacher.

13 *Writing Rules for Students*

Writers have power
Everyone is special, unique, different from everyone else in the whole world. That is why only you can say what you know; the things that have happened to you have happened to no one else in exactly the same way.

When you write about what you think and know, your writing will be your own. It will be different from what anyone else writes. And yet, we are all alike in many ways. That is why others can understand what you write. Sometimes your writing will make people smile or feel happy inside; sometimes, it may make them feel sad, remembering how they have felt during a sad time. That is why we can say that people who know how to write have a special kind of power: When you can write what you know and think, when you read it back to yourself and feel pleased with what you have written, when others read what you write and can understand it, then you feel that special kind of power.

Writers are artists: They make pictures with words
When writers paint pictures with words that are clear and colorful, readers can see in their "minds' eyes" what the writers are painting.

We do this by using good describing words. When we write about colors, sizes, shapes, actions, and when we write about how things look, smell, feel, taste, and sound, then we make them real, like pictures that can be seen.

When we write, we try to spell words correctly so that others can read what we write. There are some other rules that go with writing too. They help to make our meaning clear so our readers, our "audience," can see in their own minds what we are saying.

This handbook contains ideas to help you write well. It contains some of the rules used by writers so that you can look them up whenever you need them. We hope it will help you as you write.

Writing words
The first line of your writing is called the *lead sentence*. It should get the attention of your audience, and should give some idea about the writing that follows. Ask yourself: Will this sentence get the attention of my reading or listening audience?

Good writers paint pictures with words. Ask yourself: Will my audience be able to "see" what I have written?

Certain words point out when things happen in a piece of writing. Ask yourself: Did I use *when* words that will help my audience to know what happened first? next? last? Some of these words are: *after, next, then, later, finally, first*.

1. Get readers' attention.
2. Paint pictures with words.
3. Use *when* words.

When you edit or proofread, read aloud and look for these things:

1. Did you capitalize wherever it was needed?
2. Did you use the correct punctuation marks at the ends of sentences?
3. Did you spell as carefully as possible? A pocket dictionary will help you with this; you'll probably want to buy your own.
4. Does the work on this paper represent your best work?
5. Is your paper ready to be put into a final draft?
6. Did you use quotation marks where needed?
7. Did you "paint pictures" with your writing?

Sentences

A *sentence* is a group of words that expresses a complete thought. It contains a subject and a predicate (see next page). When a group of words is not complete, it is called a sentence *fragment*. Usually, we write and speak in complete sentences. A sentence starts with a capital letter and ends with a period, a question mark, or an exclamation point. In a complete sentence, the speaker completes what he or she started to say.

There are four basic kinds of sentences, depending on how they are used:

1. A *declarative* sentence makes a statement. (*Jill carried a book.*)
2. An *interrogative* sentence asks a question and expects a reply. (*Can you come with me tonight?*)
3. An *imperative* sentence gives a command or makes a request. (*Please leave the room immediately.*)
4. An *exclamatory* sentence expresses strong feeling. (*I can hardly wait to begin!*)

Subjects and predicates

The *subject* does the action described in the *predicate*. (*She jumped.*) It answers the question *who* or *what*.

The *predicate* is the action described. (*He jumped.*)

The simple subject is the word(s) about which something is being said. Modifiers are not part of the simple subject. (*The little girl ran home.*) (*Ten-year-old Danny dropped his books.*)

The complete subject is the simple subject with all its modifiers. (*The little girl ran home.*) (*Ten-year-old Danny Jones dropped his books.*)

When a subject has only one part, it is called a *single subject*. (*Michael walked to the store.*)

When a subject has more than one part, it is called a *compound subject*. (*Linda and Jack walked to school.*)

The subject parts can be joined by the conjunctions *and* or *or*. (*Danny or Shawn will clean the corn.*)

More about subjects (and phrases and clauses)

A single subject needs a singular verb. (*Mary is walking home.*)

A plural subject needs a plural verb. (*The girls are walking home.*)

A compound subject needs a plural verb. (*Mary and Susan are walking home.*)

Singular subjects that are joined by *or*, *nor*, *either...or*, or *neither...nor* are singular and require a singular verb. (*Judy or Janice ate the cookie.*) (*Neither David nor Ronald wants to go.*)

Sometimes phrases are used as subjects: (*Rowing a boat can be fun.*)

Sometimes clauses are used as subjects: (*Whatever you choose to do will be fine with us.*)

Simple, complete, and compound predicates

The *simple predicate* is the verb that expresses action. It does not include modifiers. (*I carried the box home.*)(*Jack was carrying the box.*)

The *complete predicate* is the simple predicate with its modifiers. (*I carried the box home.*) (*Jack was carrying the box.*)

A *compound predicate* comprises two or more verbs that are usually connected by *and*. (*Judy played volleyball and ran the low hurdles.*) (*David reads, writes, and studies Russian.*)

Subject complements, predicate nouns, and pronouns

A *subject complement* is a word that completes the meaning or action of the verb. It renames or describes the subject.

There are several kinds of subject complements: Words that rename nouns or pronouns are called *predicate nouns* or *predicate pronouns*. (*Matthew was the speaker.*)

Predicate nouns and predicate pronouns are the same as the named person or thing in a sentence and can usually be interchanged with it.

The speaker was Matthew.   *Matthew was the speaker.*
He was the director.   *The director was he.*

Words that describe nouns or pronouns are called *predicate adjectives*. (*The girl was surprised.*) (*The boys were happy.*)

Direct and indirect objects

A *direct object* completes the action of a verb and answers what or whom after an action verb.

He threw the ball first.   *Marion liked him to visit.*

An *indirect object* names the person to or for whom something was done or said. (*We took our new neighbors some cookies.*)

Phrases

A *phrase* is a group of related words that does not express a complete thought; it has no subject and predicate. *(under the bed) (after the storm) (inside the cave)*

A phrase by itself does not make sense; it creates questions but does not answer them. *Writers*: Check carefully when you proofread to be sure you have written complete sentences, not phrases.

Prepositions and prepositional phrases

A *preposition* is a word used to relate a noun or pronoun to some other word(s) in the sentence. (*The rabbit in the garden ate the carrots.*) (*The bird on the fencepost was singing.*)

A *prepositional phrase* starts with a preposition and is used to modify other words. (*The children ran through the house.*)

An *adjective prepositional phrase* modifies a noun or pronoun. (*The cover of the book was ruined.*) (*She ate the popcorn with butter on it.*)

An *adverb prepositional phrase* modifies a verb, an adverb, or an adjective. If it modifies a verb, it answers *how, when, where,* or *why*.

*He dug the carrots **with the shovel**.*
*The ship docked **after sunset**.*
*The girl jumped **out of the tree**.*
*He went home **because he was tired**.*

Adjectives, adverbs, and clauses

A *modifier* describes or makes the meaning of a word clearer.

There are two kinds of modifiers: the *adjective,* which describes nouns or pronouns (**new** car) and the *adverb,* which describes or modifies a verb, an adjective or another adverb (ran **quickly**).

Adjectives usually come in front of the word they are describing. (*The **blue** book was interesting.*)

Adverbs usually come after the word they are describing. Many adverbs end in *-ly.* (*The girl ran **happily** to her mother.*)

Adjectives like *good, real, sure, most,* and *near* are not adverbs. (*She sang good.*) (*My dad was real angry.*) *Good* and *real* are used incorrectly here.

Correct use is: (*She sang **well**.*) (*My dad was **really** angry.*)

A *clause* is a group of words containing a subject and a predicate. It forms part of a compound or complex sentence. The group containing the main idea is called the *main clause,* or the *independent clause,* because it can stand alone, usually as a simple sentence. (***She sang a song** that brought tears to their eyes.*) (***He carried a book** that belonged to his friend.*)

A subordinate clause depends on the rest of the sentence for its meaning; it does not express a complete thought, and it cannot stand alone. Its attachment to the main clause gives it meaning. (*She will compete **if she feels well enough**.*)

The subordinate clause is of less importance in a sentence than the main clause, or the main idea.

Simple, compound, and complex sentences

A *simple sentence* contains one main clause and no subordinate clause. (***Sally ran to the playground**.*)

A *compound sentence* contains two or more main clauses and no subordinate clause. (***Sally ran to the playground, but David went home to eat.***)

Main ideas in a compound sentence are joined by conjunctions like *and, but, or,* and *for.*

A *complex sentence* contains one main clause, or idea, and one or more subordinate clauses. (***The umbrella sheltered the girl who huddled under its bright colors.***)

In this sentence, *The umbrella sheltered the girl* is the main clause, or idea; *who huddled under its bright colors* is the subordinate clause or idea.

Subordinate clauses, or ideas, in a complex sentence are joined to the main clause, or idea, by words called *subordinate conjunctions*—words like *if, because, although, when, since,* and others—or by words like *who, whose, whom, which,* and *that,* called *relative pronouns.*

Parts of speech

There are eight parts of speech; the placement and use of words in a sentence determines their classification.

1. A *noun* is the name of something. (*The little **kitten** ran home.*)
2. A *pronoun* takes the place of a noun. (*David gave **him** a book.*)
3. A *verb* shows action; it tells what someone does or that something happened. Every complete sentence must have a verb. (*It **has been raining** since last week.*) (*Dawn **is** my special friend.*)
4. An *adjective* describes or modifies a noun or pronoun. (*The book is **new**.*) (*It is **exciting**.*)
5. An *adverb* describes or modifies a verb, an adjective, or another adverb. (*The man sang **loudly**.*) *Loudly* modifies the verb *sang*. (*The dessert was **especially** delicious.*) *Especially* modifies the adjective *delicious*. (*Why was he working **so** hard?*) *So* modifies the adverb *hard*.
6. A *preposition* relates a noun or pronoun to some other word(s) in the sentence. (*She gave the candy **to** her little brother.*)
7. A *conjunction* connects two or more sentence parts. (*Monica **and** Tabitha are best friends.*) (*Shawn ran fast, **but** he missed the bus.*)
8. An *interjection* is an exclamatory word used to express strong feeling. Interjections are usually used in dialogue. (***Ouch!***) (***Fantastic!***)

Punctuation information

Punctuation is used to separate words and sentences into meaningful information. Without proper punctuation, what we write would not make sense. With correct punctuation, our writing is easier to read and understand.

End punctuation marks

A *period* (.) is used at the end of a declarative or imperative sentence. (*I am tired.*) (*Pick up your books.*)

A *question mark* (?) is used after a direct question. (*Why did you do that?*)

An *exclamation point* (!) is used after a statement expressing surprise, fear, or disgust (*Oh! You surprised me!*) (*A monster is coming!*) (*Yuck! What a mess!*) It also is used at the end of some imperative sentences. (*Go to your room!*) (*Stop that right now!*)

Exclamation points should be reserved for special emphasis; too many exclamation marks weaken your writing, causing it to lose power.

Inside punctuation marks

Commas (,) are used to separate words, phrases, and clauses. Next to end punctuation marks, the comma is most helpful to a writer and reader seeking for clear meaning. (*Lee Hickerson, the teacher with the bushy beard, loves to write.*) (*Even in his winter underwear and snowsuit, the boy was cold.*)

When you proofread aloud, listen for places where you pause briefly; those places are where you may need a comma.

Quotation marks (" ") are used to enclose the exact words that come out of the mouth of a speaker.

(*"Please hurry!" she yelled.*)

They also are used to set off the title of a short story, a poem, a song, a magazine article and a TV show. (Book titles are underlined.)

Quotation marks often are used to set off a word or group of words for emphasis. (*My favorite poem is "Fog" by Carl Sandburg.*) (*Mrs. Greenway is a real "self-starter."*)

A *colon* (:) is used after a statement to call attention to what comes next. (*He wanted only one thing: a horse.*)

It also is used after the greeting in a formal letter. (*Dear Ms. Johnson:*)

A colon is sometimes used to clarify long lists. (*My dad asked me to go to the store with him to get these things: nails, a hammer, wood screws, glue, and staples for the staple gun.*)

A *semicolon* (;) is used between clauses not connected by *and*, *but*, or *or*. (*Michele wanted to learn to fly; it had always been her dream.*)

An *apostrophe* (') is used to show where a letter or letters have been left out in a contraction. (*I can't do that.*)

An *apostrophe and s* ('s) added to a singular noun show ownership. (*Susan's dog was lost.*)

An apostrophe added to a plural noun ending in s shows group ownership. (*The boys' room was picked up.*)

Clarification: Who owns or has something?

(*The children's hats are over there.*)

(*Joan's dog is fluffy.*)

(*The girls' clubhouse is empty.*)

Does that word end in s? If so, add an apostrophe. If not, add an 's.

Capitalization rules

Capitalize the first word in a sentence. (*Please come right now.*)

Capitalize the first word and all important words in the title of books, stories, songs, plays, or magazines. *The, an, a,* and *for* are not capitalized in titles unless they are the first word in the title. (*My favorite book is* <u>A Wrinkle in Time</u>.)

Capitalize the first word in a direct quotation. (*"You can write if you try," he said.*)

Capitalize proper nouns and usually words derived from them, including names and titles of people, and the pronoun *I*. (*Mr. Harrison Jones*) (*Princess Mary*)

Capitalize a name preceded by a word showing family relationship. (*My favorite relative is Uncle Buddy.*)

Capitalize names of cities, states, and countries. (*He lived in Toronto, Ontario, in Canada, but he traveled in England.*)

Capitalize days of the week, months of the year, and holidays. (*Thursday was her favorite weekday.*) (*She was born in October on the day before Halloween.*)

Capitalize abbreviations of titles preceding or following a name. (*Dr. Davidson*) (*James Lewis, D.D.S.*)

Capitalize names of special organizations of people. (*The Girl Scouts met in the school gymnasium.*)

Capitalize names of races and nationalities. (*Black, Caucasian, and Asian peoples all over the world seek peace.*) (*Swedes, Norwegians, and Danes are all Scandinavians.*)

Capitalize titles referring to God. (*The Bible says that the Lord is God.*)

Capitalize *Mom*, *Dad*, *Grandma*, and *Grandpa*, for example, when used as their names. (*I rode home with Mom and Dad.*)

Be aware of capitalization rules as you write. Words that should begin with small letters are considered misspelled if they are written with a capital letter, and words that should begin with capital letters are considered misspelled if they are written with a small letter.

One special thing to do with written language is to write letters. When you write to a friend, we call that a *friendly letter*. The form of a friendly letter is this:

```
                                        (Heading) 1422 Cardinal Drive
                                           Plymouth, Minnesota 55447
                                                   October 10, 1994
          Dear Amanda, (Salutation)
          I am so happy that you are coming to visit! My mother says she
          will take us to Lake Minnetonka to swim on Wednesday. We can go
          to Valley Fair on Thursday. It has lots of fun, scary rides. On
          Friday, she thinks we might like to just play at home.
          I'll be waiting for you to come.

          [Body of letter)]

          Love, (Closing)
          Allison (Signature)
```

A *business letter* is a bit more formal, with the entire business address written just above the greeting:

```
          Ms. Jennifer Carrier
          Sunnyside Professional Services
          1259 Valley Road
          Robbinsdale, Minnesota 55409

          Dear Ms. Carrier:
          . . . .
```

Spelling

Spelling is an important part of writing! It is something at which we continue to work all our lives. If you find some words difficult to spell, buy a notebook and write those words in it, together with their meanings and any "tricks" you need to help you remember them. No one but you ever needs to see this helping book for spelling.

Ask your teacher his or her tricks for spelling. Share your own tricks with your friends. Here is one you can use: When we are friends with someone, even though that person may move away, we remain friends always—friends to the *END*. (fri*END*) *END* is at the end of FRIEND. (One more trick: Will you attend the *DANCE* with me? atten*DANCE*)

Dictionary, thesaurus, and proofreading

Make use of the dictionary to learn how to spell and use new words. A good vocabulary (words you know and use) is one mark of an educated individual. You will find a pocket dictionary a helpful writing tool—handy to carry and easy to use.

A thesaurus is an excellent tool to use in writing. It contains words that have similar meanings. Using other words, instead of the same word over and over again, can make your writing more interesting. You may want your own thesaurus and dictionary.

Proofreading is an important part of your writing. When you proofread, you look for corrections and changes that must be made to make your writing clear to your readers or listeners (your audience). This increases your power in writing.

Proofreading aloud lets your ears help your eyes. Your "ear for language" will help you to know if it sounds right.

Here are some questions to ask yourself as you proofread:

1. Does each sentence make sense? Does it sound right? (You will need to read it aloud and *listen* to know.)
2. Did I use good descriptive words and phrases to make my writing "come alive?" (A thesaurus is handy here!)
3. Are there parts that do not relate to my writing piece? (*I like going for walks in the woods. My mother swept our kitchen this morning. The woods are filled with trees and other growing things.*) Sweeping the kitchen doesn't relate to walking in the woods. Leave out: *My mother swept our kitchen this morning.*
4. Is the punctuation correct?
5. Does this answer all the questions my audience might have?
6. If I used dialogue, is it clear who is speaking?
7. Have I chosen a good title?
8. Did I use the same word over and over in my writing? (If so, perhaps you can look it up in the thesaurus and find another word with the same meaning.)
9. Remember! The more you practice your writing, the better you will become at doing it. (It's like practicing the piano or learning to play basketball.)

If you are unsure of some grammar rules not discussed here, refer to a grammar book or to a dictionary in which these rules are given. Usually you can find grammar rules in the front of a dictionary.

When speaking of others and yourself in the same sentence, put yourself last. Not only is it correct, it also is polite.

He and I helped with the program (not *I and he*).
Mr. Jones gave the books to her and me (not *me and her*).

If in doubt, separate the sentence parts to check for correctness: *He helped with the program. I helped with the program. He and I helped with the program.*

A lot is two words!

Say all of *a* sudden, not all of *the* sudden. (*Suddenly* is even better!)

When you write a first draft, skip every other line so that you have spaces in which to make changes or corrections when you proofread. Paper with alternating blue and white or green and white lines is excellent for writing first drafts. You can write on the colored lines, for example, and make revisions on the white lines.

When you write a first draft, don't erase; if you make a mistake or wish to change something, just draw a single line through it. It's faster, easier, and allows you to see what you wrote first as you look back over your work.

Remember: It is your name that goes on your own paper. It belongs to you, and it is for you yourself that you are writing. When you have done your best, when you have pleased yourself with your writing, when you have made pictures with words that others can "see," then you are that wonderful someone we call *writer!* Congratulations!

Here are some proofreaders' marks for you to learn. A mark is a quick way of showing you that you need to make some changes or corrections in what you have written.

Lower case	*lc*
Start new paragraph	¶
Move to left	[
Spelling	(sp)
Delete	℘
Use capital letters	*Caps*
Close up space	⌒
Insert space	#

14 *Reproducible Handouts*

Suggestions for use of handouts

Page	*Grade levels*	*Title/Topic*	*Use*
172	1–up	Portfolio record	Attach copies to covers of student portfolios and use for recording information about writing pieces saved there.
173	1–3	Good books to read	For students to use for recommending good books to others to read—keep these lists available/posted so your students can actually *use* these recommendations
174	1–up	Conference record	Use this piece to record the date of student /teacher writing conferences and comments you and/or your students make about each student's writing. It provides a "running record" of students' development in written language. You may wish to keep these on a clipboard or to spiral bind them together.
175	1–3	I am a . . .	Teacher should reproduce this list, then cut apart the words. Let students draw a word from a hat, basket, etc., and describe it, as in the "I am . . ." lesson/small print list in Chapter 5.
176	1–4	From the book/ in your own words	This is a blank copy /write a paragraph on the left side. Students are to read it silently, read it aloud, talk it over with a friend, then write what they have learned *in their own words*. This is designed to help students begin learning to gather information, learn about it, then

put it into their own words. When students can explain something in their own words, we know they understand. This is a good assignment to do weekly, using a new piece of information each time—from newspapers, magazines, etc.

177	1–3	Some things I know	It is important for students to validate that they do know many things. Each student should have several copies of "Some things I know." On it they can write things they do know. On the following sheet they can list some things they would like to learn, following up by doing research—asking questions, reading, interviewing until they have learned about those things in which they are interested.
179	1–3	Ideas! Ideas! Ideas!	Students can keep these in folders where they can add writing ideas whenever they think of them, using them in writing projects throughout the school year.
180	2–up	Books I have read	Copies of this may be made for students to use in keeping records of all books read during the school year, or even during several years in a row. They are for the students' own use, though Teachers may want to follow students' reading by checking through them from time to time.
181	2–up	Animal story	Self-explanatory
183	2–3	Persuasive writing	Students will write letters to parents, asking for exotic pets. Have fun with this as students learn the useful art of persuasion. Write your own letter, too! You might have fun by asking parents to write back saying why students can/cannot have the pet they want.
184	2–4	Good things to eat!	Self-explanatory

Note: Teachers, create your own handouts or assignments on the board, following these patterns. Begin with simple sentences; allow students to enhance them with description.

197	4–7	Dialogue	Copies may be made for each student. Discuss the problem presented by this section of a story—who is talking? Does the dialogue move the story along, or does it need some help? You may ask students to make changes and corrections right on the papers, or you might prefer making an overhead, with everyone working on this together. Other changes are needed in addition to dialogue revisions—spelling, punctuation, and so on.
198	4–7	Persuasive writing: Getting started	Make a copy for each student to use in writing a letter to make a positive change. Discuss purposes for writing persuasive letters; have students share their letters and ideas with one another as they work on these all the way through the process of writing final copies ready to be *used*.
199	4–12	When you write persuasively	Things to keep in mind as students write letters to make positive changes. Make a copy for each student to keep.
200	5–8 Teachers Evaluators of books written by student	Evaluation of book	This form is for the purpose of evaluating students' books (complete with cover, illustrations, etc.). Be sure evaluators are knowledgeable about what makes a good book. Their individual comments can be very helpful for young writers, who should see these evaluations when they are completed.
201	7–12	Mr. Philippe A. Phrog	This letter (disguised) is a copy of a letter of complaint sent to a real bank. Students are to read and discuss this letter and the reason for its success in obtaining the various satisfactions listed at the

bottom. Their assignment is to write their own letter of complaint, based on either a real or imagined incident. Student letters then should be discussed and evaluated in terms of persuasiveness and successful writing. Role-playing may be done between the letter writer and the recipient

| 202 | Parents | Parents | Make copies, send home with/to parents |

Portfolio Record

Student_____

Date   *Title/Topic*   *Skills emphasis*

_____

_____

_____

_____

_____

_____

_____

_____

_____

_____

_____

_____

_____

_____

_____

_____

_____

_____

_____

_____

_____

_____

_____

_____

_____

_____

_____

_____

_____

_____

_____

_____

_____

Good Books to Read

Name_____

Title   *Author*   *grade level*

_____

Why should someone else read this book? (Not just because "it's good.")

_____

_____

_____

_____

_____

_____

_____

_____

Title   *Author*   *grade level*

_____

Why should someone else read this book?

_____

_____

_____

_____

_____

_____

_____

_____

_____

_____

_____

_____

_____

*Student:*_____

Date   *Comments*

_____

_____

_____

_____

_____

Date   *Comments*

_____

_____

_____

_____

_____

Date   *Comments*

_____

_____

_____

_____

_____

Date   *Comments*

_____

_____

_____

_____

_____

Date   *Comments*

_____

_____

_____

_____

_____

I Am a . . .

MONKEY	BANANA	BAR OF SOAP
SNOWFLAKE	DANDELION	HORSE
PENCIL	RING	ICE CUBE
SLED	GOLDFISH	TREE
BUBBLE	CLOUD	KITE
CHAIR	TEDDY BEAR	EAGLE
PAIL	SWEATER	PUPPY
BASEBALL	PICKLE	CAKE
RAINDROP	PEACH	PIANO
DRUM	TRUMPET	ROCK
CABIN	SHOVEL	BOOK
BOX	MUFFIN	COOKIE

Some Things I Know

And I Want to Know

Ideas! Ideas! Ideas! Ideas!

Books I Have Read

Author   Title   Date
_____

Comments:
_____
_____
_____
_____
_____
_____
_____
_____

Author   Title   Date
_____

Comments:
_____
_____
_____
_____
_____
_____
_____
_____

Author   Title   Date
_____

Comments:
_____
_____
_____
_____
_____
_____
_____
_____

Animal Stories

On the left side of this page, list all the animals you can think of. On the right side, list many kinds of places.

Animals	*Places*
ZEBRA	Hockey rink

| LION | Grocery store |

(you do the rest!)

Draw a line from each animal to a place where you would like it to live. Be sure each animal is connected to a place. Now choose one animal and the place you chose for it. Write your story. In your story, put your animal in the place to which you connected it. (That is called the *setting*.)

What will *happen* in your story? (That's called the *plot*.) Maybe you'll need to add another *character* to your story (an animal or a person). Be sure something surprising or exciting happens in your story. When you have finished, cover your ears and read your story aloud softly to yourself. See how it sounds. Listening to it can tell you if you need to make any changes. The *action* in your story will be what *happens*.

There is room on the next page to finish your story. **You may choose your title after you have finished; the story may tell you what the title should be.**

Many people have cats for pets, or dogs, or goldfish. But *you* want an unusual pet, one very few people own, like a *lion* or a *tiger* or a *giraffe* or a *polar bear*. You will have to find some really good reasons to persuade your mom or dad even to *think* about it.

First, write down what you want. (Be polite, and be sure to say *please*.) You might say something like,

Dear Mom,
   I've thought about this for a long time, and I'd really like to have a giraffe. I know it's an unusual pet, but here are some reasons why I think we should get one:
   1. It could be a slide for all the kids in our neighborhood to play on.
   2. It could be a ladder, so you could wash the second-floor windows of our house.
   3. It could give you rides and save on gas for the car.

Give *three good reasons* why you should be allowed to have the unusual pet you want. The reasons must be related to the qualities of the animal you choose. And don't whine or beg—give strong *reasons*. Here's your place to write!

_____

_____

_____

_____

_____

_____

_____

_____

_____

_____

_____

_____

_____

_____

At the end, tell your parent thank-you for reading your letter. When your letter is finished, show it to your mom or dad. Good luck! (P.S. One boy got exactly the pet he wanted when he showed his letter to his parents!)

Good Things to Eat!

Warm caramel rolls; melty chocolate cookies just off the cookie sheets; hot buttered popcorn; chocolate ice cream sundaes—all delicious things to eat! Why do you like them? How do they taste? How do they look? Who makes them best? *Compare* your favorite food to something. (The chocolate chips in my cookies look like dark little mountains.) Comparing something to something else can help others to see it in their imaginations.

What is *one* of your favorite things to eat? Write all about it.

_____

_____

_____

_____

_____

_____

_____

_____

_____

_____

_____

_____

_____

_____

_____

_____

_____

_____

_____

_____

_____

_____

_____

_____

_____

_____

Editing Checklist

This is for you to use as you edit another writer's paper. Mark _____with a check mark if done correctly.

Title:_____ by_____

_____ 1. Each sentence begins with a capital letter.

_____ 2. Each sentence ends with correct punctuation.

_____ 3. Each sentence is a complete sentence.

_____ 4. Descriptive language has been used.

_____ 5. Spelling mistakes have been marked and corrected

_____ 6. All writing is related to the topic.

_____ 7. This writing makes sense.

_____ 8. This paper is interesting to read.

What do you like best about this paper?

_____

_____

_____

_____

_____

Edited by_____

Student-Created Story Starters
These are better than what most adults give them!

My Kind of Day

Yesterday was a warm, springy April day. I strolled down the street on my way home from school; it definitely had not been the best day of my life.

First of all, my mom's lunch and mine got mixed up. I ended up with all the low-fat, no cholesterol, lots-of-fiber, low-in-salt, and oil-healthy foods. I tried some no-fat, no-salt potato chips. They tasted like cardboard.

Then I was late for two of my classes (I'm in seventh grade) and ended up in detention. Real fun. As I walked home from school, I thought deeply. Why was I so plain, so awkward? Nothing exciting ever happens to me! I'm just plain, plain. I live in a normal-size white house. My room has pink wallpaper, my bed has a red quilt.

We have a plain, ugly, brown station wagon. I have no pets, no bike, no trees to climb, no friends to play games with.

A week ago, Alyssa Johnson got a new puppy. Tony Wilson went to the amusement park on Friday. Jane's birthday was the next day, and in three weeks Kelly is going to Hawaii. Guess what *I'm* doing in three weeks . . . *nothing*. Maybe I'll watch "Days of Our Lives," or "I Love Lucy" on our normal, plain, old, fuzzy television set.

At 9 P.M. I brushed my crooked, brace-needing teeth and put on my pajamas. Then I went to bed.

All of a sudden I sat up. Something exciting will happen tomorrow, I whispered to myself. I felt it, clear to the tips of my toes. I set my alarm for 6:45 and promptly fell asleep.

Molly was playing on the swing set when a strange creature came up to her. She couldn't tell what it was. She petted it to see if it was friendly, and it purred like a cat. She looked closer. *That's funny,* she thought. *It looks like a dog!* She stepped back to see what it would do next, and . . .

It was a hot, sunny day. I was out walking my puppy, Buffy, when we spotted a pothole. Buffy looked down and began barking like mad. I knelt down to see a pile of dirt at the bottom. I looked sternly at Buffy and told her to stop barking. She just kept right on. "Woof! Woof! Woof!" I looked down the hole once more, and I couldn't believe my eyes! There was . . .

It was Tom's first day at the new school. Everyone was very nice to him. Then, just as he was leaving, his new friend, Pete, asked, "Are you walking home by yourself?"

"Of course. I don't have anyone to walk with," answered Tom.

"Well, then, you'd better watch out for Billy the Bully," said Pete.

"OK," said Tom. "Thanks."

I was walking around the carnival when I saw this dark-looking tent. A sign out-side it said MADEMOISELLE'S FORTUNE TELLING. COME IN AND LEARN YOUR FUTURE. I walked in. . . . .

It was one of those foggy, rainy nights. I was driving down a winding country road. The trees on both sides of the road looked like tall, dark, straight-standing soldiers, and there was no sound to be heard but the sound of my car's tires rolling over the road. Suddenly I saw a figure in front of my car.

The first day of kindergarten had ended, and the sixth-graders were lining the new kids up to help them get on the right buses. "Hey, Short Stuff, get on Bus 53!" one of them directed me. As I entered the bus, I looked from face to face, unable to find anyone I knew.

The door closed and the bus pulled away, turning in the opposite direction from my house.

Why me?

I often ask that question: Why me? It seems that if bad luck is looking for some-one to spread itself on, it picks me. Now, don't get me wrong. I don't want pity, but it would be nice if bad luck would pick someone else to hang onto for a change.

It all began that Monday. My usual bad luck had begun again at breakfast. My little brother Richie reached for the syrup and I (lucky person that I am) acciden-tally hit his hand and the syrup bottle fell over, landing in my lap. Just my luck—it was the only clean outfit I could wear. Not only that, but syrup got all over my hair and face (don't even *ask* me how *that* happened) and there was no time to shower before school. My mother, being the sympathetic person that she is, sat there laughing at me. Okay, so I did look pretty funny with syrup running down my face . . . but really! She IS my mother!

"I'm a little suspicious about this guy, Vince. I know I've seen him before."

"It's probably nothing, Sammy. I mean, this guy is probably just another one of those trillionaire game show hosts. Let's just go in and watch the show."

He sat there, his wrinkled old hands on the steering wheel, gazing into the dis-tance. Gently, he moved the steering wheel slightly back and forth, back and forth. He leaned against the jet-black leather seat and rested his head on the headrest, his white hair ruffling in the slight breeze that moved across the top of the brand-new convertible.

Suddenly a young girl came hurrying toward the car. "That's MY car!" she said. "What are you doing in my car?"

Read the following information. Read it again carefully so you are sure you understand it. Discuss it with a partner. Then use the lines at the bottom of this page to write the information *in your own words.*

Black Bears

In late summer, black bears spend up to 20 hours a day eating in order to put on enough weight to carry them through a five months' nap in a hollow log, small cave or in the open in "nests" made of leaves and branches. During their dormant period, they don't eat, drink, urinate or defecate. Normal waste products — which would kill other animals if they weren't eliminated — are broken down into harmless chemicals. The little water that a bear needs is produced when the stores of fat are burned. Black bear cubs are born in the middle of the mother's dormant period, but it's not known how alert the mother is during the birth. The blind, hairless cubs nurse by sensing the heat of the mother's body.—from the *Star Tribune,* 12/27/92

Now, write on these lines what you have read and learned.

_____

_____

_____

_____

_____

_____

_____

_____

_____

_____

_____

_____

Write your observations (what you think) about this information.

_____

_____

_____

_____

_____

_____

_____

_____

_____

_____

_____

_____

Gathering Information

Read the following information. Read it again carefully so you are sure you understand it. Discuss it with a partner. Then use the lines at the bottom of this page to write the information *in your own words*.

Amphibious Ice Cube

To shield themselves against the cold, some frogs hibernate at the bottom of ponds or dig deep into the soil. Others, however, spend winter on the forest floor with little or no insulation. Scientists have discovered that these frogs can freeze solid and survive. Common frogs—such as the wood frog, spring peeper, gray tree frog and striped chorus frog—as well as some insects and at least one mammal may be able to stay frozen for days or weeks without suffering irreparable cell damage. Although the process is not completely understood, it is believed that these animals are able to protect vital organs while allowing the rest of their bodies to freeze. Here's how it happens:

1. Ice that forms on the frog's skin triggers a chemical reaction in the liver that produces glucose, or blood sugar. The heart pumps glucose to the major organs.
2. In humans, such high levels of blood sugar could cause diabetic coma and death, but in the wood frog glucose prevents major organs from freezing, although scientists aren't sure how. (The glucose also may help to dramatically slow the frog's metabolism.)
3. While the glucose prevents ice from forming in the organs, ice fills the cavities in the body. A frog might stay with as much as 65% of its total body water frozen until it thaws in warm weather.—from the *Star Tribune*, 12/27/92

Write on these lines what you have read and learned.

_____

_____

_____

_____

_____

_____

_____

_____

Write your observations (what you think) about this information.

_____

_____

_____

_____

_____

_____

_____

Create a new student to join your class.
Tell all you can about the new friend (character):

- Physical description (tall, curly hair, brown eyes, glasses, etc.)
- Likes and dislikes
- Where he or she lives
- Hobbies, special talents
- What he or she likes to wear?
- Family
- Favorite things to do
- Favorite food

What are some interesting things someone might learn about him or her after knowing this student for awhile?

Imagine This!

Imagine this! You are a big, yellow, fluffy farm cat who walks on quiet feet. You are very hungry, and you have been watching a mouse who sits just inside a hole in the barn where you like to prowl. That mouse would taste delicious!

Write about what you see and think. Remember, you're the CAT!

_____

_____

_____

_____

Now you are the MOUSE, looking out at the cat. What do YOU see and think? What do you do?

_____

_____

_____

_____

Imagine this! You arrive at school and find an announcement on your desk: the principal has the chicken pox, and you have been chosen to be the principal for three days.

How will you run your school? What new, terrific ideas do you have for your school that might make learning more exciting? What could teachers do to help students become better writers? Think hard and seriously before you begin writing. You may BE a principal or a teacher one day!

_____

_____

_____

_____

_____

_____

_____

_____

_____

_____

_____

_____

_____

_____

Teamwork

Some things can be done best by working with others. We call that *teamwork*. An example of teamwork is playing a volleyball game. It would be hard to play all by yourself! Write about something you enjoy doing with a team. Tell what is important about teamwork. Describe your feelings about being part of a team.

Working Alone

Some things can be done best by working alone. Write about something you like to do by yourself. How does it make you feel to accomplish something without help from anyone else?

_____

_____

_____

_____

_____

_____

_____

_____

_____

_____

_____

_____

_____

_____

_____

_____

_____

_____

_____

_____

_____

_____

_____

_____

_____

_____

_____

_____

_____

_____

_____

_____

Dreaming

It is important to have dreams—dreams of things we would like to do some day. What is something you would like to do? Write about your dream. Tell what it might be like and why you want to do it. Think of the people who dreamed, many years ago, that one day people would *fly*! Now we *do*! Your dreams are important, too.

_____

_____

_____

_____

_____

_____

_____

_____

_____

_____

_____

_____

_____

_____

_____

_____

_____

_____

_____

_____

_____

_____

_____

_____

_____

_____

_____

_____

_____

Description

Below are simple sentences just waiting to be turned into lively descriptions. This can be accomplished with the use of strong verbs and colorful adjectives.

Example
The boy walked home from school.

As you might write it, adding good description:

Leaving school and studies behind, David dashed down the sidewalk toward home, where his little black puppy would be waiting for him, jumping and yipping with delight at his return.

Here are four sentences for you to improve by using colorful adjectives and strong verbs.

1. The tree fell to the ground.

_____

_____

_____

_____

2. The girl put the money in her pocket.

_____

_____

_____

_____

3. The ball broke the window.

_____

_____

_____

_____

4. The baby climbed into the high chair.

_____

_____

_____

_____

More Description

Choose two sentences from the previous page. Using good description, turn each sentence into a full paragraph.

_____

_____

_____

_____

_____

_____

_____

_____

_____

_____

_____

_____

_____

_____

_____

_____

_____

_____

_____

_____

_____

_____

_____

_____

_____

_____

_____

"We have to get our stuff on and head out to the mountains!"

"What's for breakfast Sue?"

"Grab a roll and get your stuff on and let's go! Mom, we need some money to get lift tickets."

"Okay, here's fifty dollars."

"Hey Buddy, these mountains are huge. Now where's the snowboard hill?"

"Over there Sue."

"Okay Buddy, are you ready?"

"Yep, let's go!"

"Whoa! This is fun!"

"Yea, it is."

"Hey Buddy, let's go off that jmp over there."

"Hey Sue watch my 360."

"Oh yea, watch my 720! Hey, that was fun, let's go down again."

"Yea, let's."

"Hey Buddy, let's bring our boards up to our room and go to the arcade."

"O.K."

"Hi kid's, time for lunch. Let's go to the lodge restaurant for lunch. How does that sound?"

"That sound's fine."

"Well, what do you want for lunch?"

"I'll have some spaghetti and a sprite. What do you want Buddy?"

"I'll have a cheeseburger and a orange pop. Thanks Mom and Dad."

"Your welcome Buddy."

"Hey Dad, this afternoon do you think we could see a movie?"

"Sure, which one do you want to see?"

"How about *Home Alone* ?"

"Sure."

"I'll drive you in after lunch." At the movies... "You two get in the car and I'll be there in a few minutes. Here we are. See you later."

"Ha, ha, ha, this movie is really funny isn't it Buddy!"

"Ha, ha, ha, yes it is Sue."

"Hey I wonder where dad is? Let's call him. Mom said he is on his way."

"Hi dad!"

"How was the movie you two?"

"It was the funniest movie we have ever seen!"

"Well you need to eat dinner when you get to your rooms and go to bed a little early. You have the semi-finals at 10:00 in the morning."

"Hey dad, can we just stop at McDonalds and get something to eat for dinner?"

"Well, why not!"

"We'll have a 20 piece McNuggets and two small fries."

"Quiet you two! I'll have a 20 piece McNuggets and two small fries and two medium Cokes. You can stay up until 9:30. Got that?"

"Yea we got it. Let's watch HBO, *Back to the Future II* is on. Well it's 9:30 we better get to sleep. Wake up Buddy, we have to be out there in one hour!"

Here is what you need to do:
- Brainstorm—get ideas down on paper.
- Look at purpose: Why are you writing?
- Write first draft—mistakes are O.K. You can proofread and revise later.
- Again, why are you writing? Is your purpose clear in what you have written?
- To whom are you writing? Is this the appropriate person/audience, the one who can act on your wishes? Will it be clear to this person what you want?
- Did you give three strong reasons? (Leave out **weak reasons**; they won't help.)
- Think! Does what you wrote make sense? (Read aloud what you write—listen to it.)

Now, get started:
On a separate sheet of paper, jot down three to five ideas about which you would like to write a persuasive letter. From those, select one and use this paper to complete your persuasive letter planning.

What is your idea?

I think

_____

_____

_____

_____

_____

Why? Give **three good reasons** why your idea is a good one. ("Just because I want it" isn't good enough. Discuss with your Teacher and classmates what might be good reasons.)

_____

_____

_____

_____

_____

- Now, on a clean paper, write a first draft of your letter using the information you have just written.
- Read your letter to a partner. Does it persuade your partner? Would it persuade you?
- Make any changes you need to make your letter stronger, more persuasive.

Review: Writing steps

1. Choose a topic.
2. Get your ideas together on paper.
3. Write a first draft.
4. Share it with other students/revise.
5. Proofread carefully.
6. Publish it. This means to write a final draft.
7. *Do* something with it. Show your parents, neighbors, grandparents. Should it be sent to a legislator? The mayor? It can only "go to work" if you *do* something with it.

When you write persuasively

If you are writing about something that has upset you, first get rid of any "mad" you are feeling. Be cool! If you write in anger, the response will probably be angry, too.

Start writing. Stay on your chosen topic. Be brief.

- If you can, compliment the person to whom you are writing. (You may, for example, comment favorably on a food product or on a company's past good service.)
- Explain the problem clearly, briefly. Tell how it affects you (and others).
- Give three good reasons why the recipient should respond as you ask. Threatening is often counterproductive; but sometimes it helps to say that you plan to share your information with others. Three reasons are just enough—five or six can be too many and may confuse your letter's recipient.
- A bit of humor sometimes helps.
- Indicate that you will be expecting an answer.
- Say *thank-you* to the recipient for considering what you have written.

Some benefits of persuasive writing

Something that is on paper can be read over and over again, giving the reader time to think and react; a telephone call, on the other hand, is over once the caller hangs up, and the answering party may forget important parts of what has been said.

Also, a written piece can be shared with others exactly as it has been written; they may be able to help make changes desired by the writer.

It is an excellent means by which one person can make a difference.

It allows the writer to attempt to influence what happens, rather than to just **react** to what happens.

Evaluation of Book

Student Author:_____

Title:_____

Readers: Please read each book carefully, keeping the following questions in mind. Then check yes/no answers and add comments if you wish.

1. Is there a clear introduction? Does the writer "grab" your attention at the beginning of the book? _____yes _____no
Comments:

_____

_____

2. Did the writer develop and continue a storyline? _____yes _____no
Comments:

_____

_____

3. Were characters named and described? _____yes _____no
Comments:

_____

_____

4. Does the story have a satisfactory conclusion? _____yes _____no
Comments:

_____

_____

5. Are illustrations appropriate/helpful to the story? _____yes _____no
Comments:

_____

_____

6. How do you rate spelling, punctuation, mechanics of this book?
_____fair _____good _____excellent

7. Does the entire book present an appearance of having been well done? (Is the cover appropriate? Is the book neat, attractive?) _____yes _____no

Comments:

_____

_____

Overall rating of book: _____good _____very good _____outstanding
Comments:

_____

_____

Read and discuss this letter written to a real bank. (As you can tell, the names have been disguised.) Why was it effective? What techniques did the writer use successfully to obtain satisfaction?

Mr. Philippe A. Phrog
Mudd Puddle Bank
Chicago, IL

Dear Mr. Phrog:

After two and one half years of using an interest-earning account at Hippity Skippity Bank, I heard several Mudd Puddle Bank commercials touting the pluses of its free checking accounts.

Because I had begun to save money through a credit union account at work, I was placing fewer dollars in my checking account and believed a minimum-balance, free checking account would serve me well.

Now, two months later, I know I was wrong. What I saved in using a free checking account was more than offset by the lack of customer service and frustration I experienced at Mudd Puddle Bank—especially during this holiday season.

Not having received an overdraft notice since my college years, I was shocked to get one the week before Christmas. I quickly checked my balance, and indeed the bank was correct: I had made an error.

The following day I immediately deposited $660 to offset my error of less than $100—and the exorbitant overdraft charges of $60. That evening, I received another overdraft notice—evidently Mudd Puddle Bank had not recorded my deposit before that notice was sent.

Three days later, I tried to make a withdrawal using my cash card. The machine refused my card and instructed me to contact the bank.

I immediately went to the bank, asked for my balance and told the teller about the machine's message. She told me my balance was over $550, and that the message must have been a fluke. I wrote a check there for cash, and she gave it to me.

Again, three days later, I tried to use my cash card. Not only did the machine refuse, but it took my card.

Upset, I called the bank and was put in touch with someone in credit who told me that my cash card privileges had been rescinded for six months—without even a warning—because I had had an overdraft the week before.

Not only do I find this policy ludicrous, but in an age when customer service is on the lips of every manager and employee from the largest department store to the smallest convenience shop, your bank would do well to follow suit.

Unless my cash card privileges are reinstated and the overcharges dropped, I will close my account, and certainly won't hesitate to tell my friends and business associates of the service they should expect if they become customers of Mudd Puddle Bank.

Sincerely,
Ms. Twylla Twaddle

This letter resulted in a personal apology from the manager of checking and loan services, a new cash card, rescinding of the $60 charges, and a line of low-interest credit being provided, should her account ever be overdrawn—and a bank deposit of $10, provided by the bank, made to the account.

Parents:
How to encourage children in the use of written language

1. Talk to them, read to them! From the time they are born, fill them with language—with good pictures, books, stories, songs, nursery rhymes, and poetry. They take in far more of this than anyone can ever know. Continue

201

to read together as a family even after your children can read. Let them see you reading and writing—they will want to do what you do.

2. Take them to the library; teach them how to make good use of the library and its resources. Take books home to read and share. Talk about the authors and illustrators, perhaps helping your children to choose some favorites. Write a family letter to an author. (Send c/o the publisher.) Guide them in learning to choose appropriate books.

3. Encourage them to own and care for their own books. Show them some of your old and current favorites. Read with them some of the books you read as a child. Speak with them of your family's books as a family *library*. Help them to start their own personal libraries.

4. Tell them stories—old stories about when you were small often become favorites." Family stories" can become the ones they want to hear over and over. Write down some of these stories together. Let your children illustrate them. Find a special place to display them.

5. Write notes to one another. Help your children write notes to family members. Place a message board (chalkboards are great!) where they can reach it to make their own contributions. Tuck notes into their lunches, pockets, under their pillows. They may want to do the same for you. Be sure paper, pencils, and color crayons are available. Encourage children to use their writings and drawings as gifts for family and friends; they do *not* need to buy gifts with money. Their own creations can be of even more special value.

6. Create a writing place for them. Supply pencils, paper, crayons, tablets, a blank book, a journal, stationery, a children's dictionary, liquid eraser, perhaps an old typewriter (young writers really enjoy these—it may be easier for them to type words than to write them by hand), a clipboard and a box in which to keep writings.

7. Write letters together to friends and family. Encourage those recipients to write back.

8. If your child wishes to keep a journal or diary, respect his or her privacy (ask before reading it). You might share a journal, one of you writing, then the other, passing it back and forth.

9. You might want to keep a *window journal* by a window that gives a good view of your yard. There, anyone in the family can jot down throughout the year things that can be seen through the window: birds, snowflakes, a beautiful sunset, people walking by, etc. Small children may *draw* what they see.

10. Show your children ways in which you use writing: in your work, in your daily living. Explain to them how writing is important to you.

11. Praise your child's writing efforts. Just as we encourage small children as they begin learning to talk, we must encourage them in their writing. Writing combines many complicated skills. Don't draw attention to what you perceive as mistakes in writing, and do not insist on correct spelling; improved writing will come in time. Demanding correct spelling and punctuation of beginning writers may destroy a child's joy and interest in writing.

12. When your family travels, keep a travel diary. Let your child help do the writing some days. When the trip is over, take the diary out and enjoy it again from time to time.

13. Be aware that your child's teacher is also helping your child learn to write competently and to value written language. Be supportive of the teacher's efforts.